Personal and Professional Development

For Counsellors, Psychotherapists and Mental Health Practitioners

Personal and Professional Development
For Counsellors, Psychotherapists and Mental Health Practitioners

John McLeod and
Julia McLeod

McGraw Hill Education

Open University Press

Open University Press
McGraw-Hill Education
McGraw-Hill House
Shoppenhangers Road
Maidenhead
Berkshire
England
SL6 2QL

email: enquiries@openup.co.uk
world wide web: www.openup.co.uk

and Two Penn Plaza, New York, NY 10121-2289, USA

First published 2014

A catalogue record of this book is available from the British Library

ISBN-13: 978-0-33-524733-2 (pb)
ISBN-10: 0-33-524733-4 (pb)
eISBN: 978-0-33-524734-9

Library of Congress Cataloging-in-Publication Data
CIP data applied for

Typesetting and e-book compilations by
RefineCatch Limited, Bungay, Suffolk

Fictitious names of companies, products, people, characters and/or data that may be used herein (in case studies or in examples) are not intended to represent any real individual, company, product or event.

Praise for this book

"John and Julia McLeod have written a superb text that not only presents a strong and coherent case for the importance of personal development for therapists, but also provides a range of activities to stimulate the reader's own reflective development process. A scholarly examination of the developmental path of the practitioner which is firmly grounded in research, this book is a rich personal development resource for students, practitioners and lecturers."

Mark Widdowson, Lecturer in Counselling and Psychotherapy,
University of Salford, UK

"This is a great resource textbook for trainee practitioners, trainers, supervisors in counselling, psychotherapy and mental health – and for anyone interested in personal and professional development in the helping professions. The breadth and depth of John and Julia McLeod's encyclopaedic knowledge is evident in this book. Wise sages indeed, they offer 'voices of wisdom and reason' for those entering the helping professions. Their guidance will help still the inner angst that is an inevitable part of practitioner training and working as a helper. The book offers an excellent resource for counselling, psychotherapy and mental health trainers, with rich resources to inform student and tutor work. I highly recommend this valuable addition to the resource and knowledge base."

Lynne Gabriel, Associate Professor, York St John University, UK

"A fantastic book! This is a comprehensive, engaging and valuable resource that integrates theory and research in an accessible and relevant way. This book approaches a complex and often poorly articulated facet of professional training both practically and effectively. The personal learning tasks bring an added dimension to this book, inviting the reader on a journey of self-discovery and challenge.

This book has relevance for a broad range of psychotherapeutic orientations and mental health roles and is an essential read for practitioners at all stages of their professional journey."

Steff Revell, Lecturer, Counselling and Psychotherapy,
University of Cumbria, UK

"This book offers an invaluable resource for counselling trainers and students alike. It succinctly maps out the terrain of personal and professional development and the importance of these concepts for practice. As a counselling trainer, I found the exercises and learning tasks contained in the book an excellent source of ideas for encouraging student reflection. As a practitioner, it reminded me of the importance of attending to my own 'stuff', of the continuing process of learning to be more in touch with my flawed humanity such that I can be more available to my clients."

Brian Rodgers, Lecturer in Counselling,
The University of Queensland, Australia

Dedication

For Kate, Emma and Hannah

Contents

Acknowledgements

We would like to document our appreciation to the many colleagues, mentors, trainers, supervisors and therapists who have shaped our understanding of the process of personal and professional development. We would also like to thank our students, who have acted as an essential source of learning and inspiration over many years, and the editorial and production team at Open University Press, particularly Monika Lee, Richard Townrow, Sarah Fleming and Nicky Whiteley.

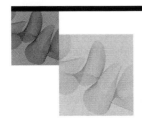

Introduction

Being a therapist involves learning about yourself. Listening to people talk about the troubles in their lives, working with them to make changes and move in a more satisfactory direction – this kind of work inevitably leads to thinking about what these issues mean for you, as a person. If you don't want to learn about yourself, being a therapist is not the right job for you.

Therapists are in the business of helping people to deal with 'problems in *living*', such as recurring experiences of fear, anger, despair or other painful emotions, difficulties in getting along with others, or inability to overcome the effects of traumatic events. Almost all forms of effective help for these problems rely, to a greater or lesser extent, on the establishment of a safe and supportive relationship with another person. It is clear that long-term counselling and psychotherapy involves the development of a close relationship between therapist and client. However, there is evidence that the impact of even minimal contact interventions such as antidepressant medication, or supported use of self-help materials, is also highly influenced by the degree to which the person receiving help trusts the help-giver, and believes that the help-giver is genuinely interested in his or her well-being. The inescapable truth, for anyone working in the field of counselling, psychotherapy, mental health, and allied fields such as social work, medicine and nursing, is that who they are, their quality of being a person, is a major factor in their capacity to make a difference to the lives of people with psychological, relational and mental health issues. The implication of this fact is that practitioners in these fields need to be willing to look at who they are and how they come across to others, with the aim of maximizing the potential use of the positive and life-enhancing aspects of their personality, and minimizing the damage that might be caused by any destructive tendencies that they might possess.

Over the years, different terms have been used to characterize this dimension of the role of being a counsellor, psychotherapist or mental health practitioner. It is an aspect of the work that emphasizes the importance of *self-awareness* and a commitment to personal learning and *personal growth*. It is concerned with the capacity to engage in the constructive *use of self* in relationships with clients. Within the present book, these ideas are subsumed under the broader concept of *personal development*. There are two main advantages to thinking about this topic in terms of 'personal development'. First, the idea of the 'personal' highlights the extent to which each practitioner will have his or her own, individual agenda for learning – the issues that need to be faced by one therapist may be quite different from the issues that are most relevant for his or her colleagues. The idea of the 'personal' invites consideration of a wide range of factors, encompassing thinking, feeling, values, spirituality, embodiment, and much else. A second, and highly relevant aspect of the concept of the person is that it carries with it an implication of being-with-others. Although it is possible to regard the 'self' as a self-contained entity, persons always exist in relation to other persons. Similarly, the concept of 'development' suggests a process of continual becoming: development never ends, and there is never a point of final arrival when this kind of effort can cease.

One of our aims in writing this book is to promote the idea that personal development is an ordinary, everyday aspect of being a therapist. We believe that the best therapists are people who are already committed to their development as persons, and then realize that this is an area in which they can be of service to others. The pattern of deciding that being a therapist is a nice kind of job to have, and then being required by a training establishment to take part in personal development activities, perhaps reluctantly, seems to us to be a less satisfactory pattern. Some of the ordinary, everyday ways in which we attend to our own personal development include:

- talking about things that trouble us;
- keeping a diary;
- reading or watching TV programmes about different cultures and lifestyles;
- attending workshops and trying out new therapeutic techniques;
- reviewing where our lives are going.

Each of these activities involves a willingness to explore, in the sense of moving beyond our current horizons, accompanied by a willingness to reflect, in the sense of making meaningful connections between current experiences and recurring, underlying life themes. These central developmental processes – exploration and meaning-making – turn up again and again throughout the pages of this book.

The type of personal development that is being discussed here is, of course, satisfying and valuable at a personal level. But at the same time it feeds into professional competence. For example, one of us saw a therapist for several months as a means of coming to terms with a long-term health condition. The therapy was useful at that level. At the same time, a great deal of personal learning took place that made a contribution to being a better therapist. For example, there was learning about the experience of being dependent on another person, and the necessity to pay attention to physical signs of stress. These learnings made it possible to have a deeper appreciation of some of the things that were happening to the author's own clients.

Within the field of counselling, psychotherapy and mental health practice, it is not possible to make a clear distinction between *personal* development, which primarily focuses on who one is and how one relates to others,
and *professional* development, which is primarily focused on knowledge
and skills relevant to one's work role. We prefer to view personal and
professional development as occupying a continuum. We believe that all
meaningful learning activities undertaken by therapists incorporate both
personal and professional elements. For example, being a client in therapy
is mainly about who you are, how you have come to be like that, what
choices are available in the future, and so on. Yet, at the same time, a
client who is also a therapist is quietly observing how his or her therapist
operates, in terms of what is helpful and what is not. By contrast, attending
a training day on how to use a new client monitoring form is mainly about
acquiring work-related knowledge and competence. Yet, at the same time,
a therapist attending such a workshop might be thinking: How would I
answer these questions? How would I feel if I was a client and being asked
to fill out this questionnaire? How does collecting this kind of data fit with
my personal beliefs and values? An advantage of thinking about personal
and professional development as existing along a continuum is that it
makes it easier to accept the different ways that these terms are used and
defined in different work contexts. In some organizations, the term
'personal development' (as in 'personal development planning') is used to
describe all developmental activity undertaken by practitioners. In other
settings, all of it is called 'professional' development. Elsewhere, the term
'personal and professional' development is used. These nuances are
important, within particular work contexts. A 'continuum' perspective acts
as a reminder that it is never possible to have one end of the spectrum
without invoking the other pole.

This book is organized in two parts. The first part is mainly concerned
with describing and discussing different aspects of the concept of personal
development. In our experience as trainers, we have found that many
students are confused about what they are meant to be doing within the
'personal development' areas of their course. The first chapter therefore
carefully examines the nature of personal development, from a range of
perspectives. Chapter 2 discusses the pros and cons of various domains
or arenas within which personal development can take place, such as
personal therapy, or participation in a learning group. Chapter 3 looks
at theoretical and research perspectives on personal development.
Attention then turns, in Chapter 4, to the topic of professional development, which is discussed within a single chapter. Finally, Chapter 5 offers
an overview of what has gone before, in the form of a review of criteria for
evaluating personal and professional development: how do we know that
development is on track, and has attained a satisfactory level? Part 2 of
the book comprises a collection of personal learning tasks. This material

provides a set of concrete examples of the kind of areas and topics that typically emerge for therapists during their personal and professional development journey. These learning tasks also represent a resource for students, practitioners and trainers, in relation to areas that might be explored in group discussion, experiential workshops or journal writing. It is very unlikely that all of the tasks will be relevant for any individual reader or learner – it is best to be guided by one's own gut feeling about which tasks seem to demand one's attention. Some of the material in this book was previously published in *The Counsellor's Workbook* (Open University Press, 2010).

The book is primarily intended for participants on training programmes in counselling, psychotherapy, clinical and counselling psychology, mental health nursing, psychiatry, life coaching, social work, occupational therapy, low-intensity support work and related professions. Rather than roll out this long list of occupational titles in every paragraph, we use the generic term 'therapist', or the global descriptor 'counsellor, psychotherapist and mental health practitioner', as appropriate. Our experience has been that tutors and trainers who run programmes within these areas tend to believe that personal development is crucially important, but all too often fail to provide students with much of an explanation of why it is important or how it operates in practice. This book is an attempt to remedy these deficits.

Part 1

Making sense of personal and professional development

Introduction

The chapters in this section of the book explore the meaning of therapist personal and professional development, and the practical ways in which development can be facilitated. The issue of therapist personal and professional development is complex, so we have broken it down into different areas. Our intention has been to provide a straightforward account of what is involved in personal and professional development, that will serve as an introduction to this topic. However, each chapter includes extensive references to theory and research, and indications for further reading, so that readers who wish to explore specific issues in more depth can find their way into the relevant literature. Pathways of therapist personal and professional development are inevitably dependent on a myriad of individual choices. As a result this is an area of inquiry in which large-scale studies are of limited value. As far as possible, in relation to further reading, we have tried to provide references to therapist stories of personal and professional development that capture the personal meaning of this aspect of the therapist's role.

What is personal development? Why is it important?

Introduction

. . . psychotherapy is the manifestation of creative human qualities in a facilitating setting . . .

(Lomas 1981: 3)

. . . the actual techniques employed by the therapists are of lesser importance than the unique character and personality of the therapists themselves. Therapists select techniques and theories because of who they are as persons: therapy strategies are manifestations of the therapist's personality. The therapist as a person is the instrument of primary influence in the therapy enterprise. A corollary of this principle is that the more a therapist accepts and values themselves, the more effective they will be in helping clients to come to know and appreciate themselves.

(McConnaughy 1987: 304)

. . . in the end, each therapist develops his or her own style, and the 'theoretical orientation' falls into the background.

> What remains salient is a unique personality combining artistry and skill. In this respect, a fine therapist closely resembles a painter, novelist or composer.
>
> (Strupp 1978: 31)

> . . . . therapy is very much a personal affair. It is not wise to try to make clones of people by making them Freudians or whatever. Student therapists have to find their own way of being with people that will help them. One can expose them to all sorts of marvellous [theorists], and it will do them a lot of good, but that is not the business. The business is to do with finding their own way, using their own intuition, learning to be themselves in the presence of someone who is asking for help, who is probably putting all kinds of pressures on them.
>
> (Lomas 1999: 25)

> I have learned that when I am fully present with the patient or family, I can move therapeutically with much greater ease. I can simultaneously reach the depths to which I need to go, and at the same time honor the fragility, the power and the sacredness in the life of the other.
>
> (Satir 1987: 23)

These statements, from leading figures in the field of psychotherapy, powerfully convey the belief that the person of the therapist plays an active and central role in the process of therapy. These writers formulated their ideas at a time when there was relatively little research into the impact of the person of the therapist on the outcomes of therapeutic work. More recently, research studies by Kraus *et al.* (2011), Okiishi *et al.* (2003), Saxon and Barkham (2012), and others, have reported major differences in effectiveness between therapists. The most effective therapists are able to facilitate change in almost all of the clients that they see. By contrast, the least effective practitioners produce negative outcomes in the majority of their clients. These differences are not attributable to age, gender, experience or training, but are the result of the personal qualities of the therapist. Understanding what makes a good therapist, and how positive therapist characteristics can be promoted through training and ongoing development and support, represents a key issue for the contemporary professional and research community. It also represents a key issue for clients. The best advice for anyone seeking therapy is that what matters is *who* you see, rather than the therapy approach that they use.

There are many ways that the personal qualities and personal knowledge of a counsellor, psychotherapist or mental health practitioner can have an influence on work with clients or service users. The present chapter explores different aspects of that process. The discussion begins by anchoring the significance of personal development in the needs of clients, and the nature of therapeutic work. The following section of the chapter offers a framework for making sense of the main areas within which therapist personal development takes place. This leads into a review of the practical, tangible ways that therapists can make use of personal knowledge in their interactions with clients. The intention, throughout the chapter, is to portray therapist personal development as both multifaceted and practical. There are many different points of entry into the field of personal development, and particular developmental topics may be more, or less, significant for each practitioner at different stages in his or her career. The vision of personal development offered in this chapter is informed by a desire to do better therapy: personal development activities are valuable because they make a difference to the capacity of a therapist to be responsive and resourceful with their clients.

Box 1.1: *Defining personal development*

At the present time, there does not exist an agreed definition of what is meant by 'therapist personal development', or allied terms such as 'professional development', 'self-awareness' and 'personal growth'. Valuable discussion of the meaning of these concepts can be found in Bager-Charleson (2012), Donati and Watts (2005), Hansen (2009), Irving and Williams (1999), Johns (2012a, 2012b) and other sources. The reason for this ambiguity is that personal development is not a single thing. Instead, it refers to a fairly broad category of activities and possibilities. One of the primary aims of the present book is to map out this territory in a comprehensive manner. At the same time, it is useful to be able to anchor that exploration within some sort of core sense of what therapist personal development is all about. The definition that has informed our own work is: therapist personal development consists of an enduring, career-long, commitment to engage in cycles of collaborative reflection on both life experience and practice, leading to new ways of understanding and active experimentation with new ways of being with others, for the purpose of being able to be as useful as possible to the clients, patients or service users with whom one works.

The key ideas here are (a) it is never over; (b) it is something that needs the active involvement of other people; (c) it is not merely concerned with insight and awareness, but with being able to do things differently; (d) it is not necessarily about coming to terms with personal problems – in the long run, it is more important for therapists to be able to make effective use of their personal gifts and strengths; and (e) the ultimate test is not about how happy or fulfilled you feel, but whether you are able to help other people.

The nature of therapeutic work

We live in a culture in which there are many competing ideas about the causes of emotional and behavioural problems, and a similarly wide range of alternative strategies for helping people whose lives are affected by such problems. For example, depression in adults can be understood in terms of biochemical imbalance, early childhood loss, social inequality, negative thoughts, dysfunctional regulation of emotions, poor diet, lack of exercise, lack of sunlight and many other factors. This complex set of discourses is a reflection of a pluralistic and democratic social world in which individuals and groups have the freedom to pursue divergent versions of reality and ideas of cure.

However, even though psychotherapeutic practitioners within these different traditions may draw on different sets of ideas and intervention techniques, in the end they all (or almost all) meet and interact with their clients through some form of relationship. Around the margins of the therapy world it is possible to find types of therapy, such as self-help books and websites, that do not involve direct personal contact. Nonetheless, the bulk of therapeutic help that is available, is mediated through a person-to-person relationship. In the context of thinking about therapist personal development, this essential dimension of psychotherapeutic work has three important implications:

- the previous relationship experience of the client or service user, and their current relationship skills, shape how they respond to the therapist;
- the previous relationship experience of the therapist, and their current relationship skills, represent resources that can be used within therapy;
- the therapist is exposed to the emotional pain, and interpersonal patters, of the client.

The importance of therapist development is grounded in an appreciation of the significance of these factors.

Box 1.2: *The relationship context of pharmacological interventions*

It might be assumed that the effectiveness of pharmacological interventions for emotional and behavioural problems is a matter of prescribing the right drug at the right dose, and that the personal attributes of the doctor, and the quality of the doctor–patient relationship, is not important. This is not the case. In the USA, the National Institute for Mental Health (NIMH) carried out an influential study that compared the effectiveness of cognitive therapy, psychodynamic therapy and antidepressant medication, for clients who were depressed. One of the areas examined in this investigation was the strength of the relationship between the client/patient and therapist. What emerged was that relationship quality was a predictor of success in all three forms of therapy, including drug treatment (Elkin *et al.* 1989). The psychiatrists who had good relationships with their patients were much more successful in reducing depression, compared with those whose patients described the doctor–patient relationship in less positive terms. Why is this? Antidepressant drugs can certainly make a difference to a client's mood and energy levels. But the patient needs to believe that this shift is useful to them, and then needs to initiate changes in his or her behaviour in relation to others on the back of this new emotional equilibrium. The relationship with the doctor functions as a source of support that allows the patient to make these changes. Further discussion of the relational dimension of drug treatment can be found in Ankarberg and Falkenstrom (2008).

People who seek professional help for problems in living and psychological difficulties will almost certainly have a history of difficult relationships. For some clients, these relationship difficulties represent dramatic and obvious aspects of their problem. These are people who have been abused and neglected, or have experienced major losses and attachment ruptures. However, even people who have lived within more benign relational environments will probably have been exposed to ruptures and disappointments in their relationships with significant others. People who report typical symptom patterns, such as being anxious, self-critical, lethargic or depressed, are usually hard to live with, and experience some degree of rejection from others. In addition, if such people already had access to a reliable supportive relationship it would be unlikely that they would be seeking help from a professional stranger. What all this means is that people who turn up in the office of a counsellor, psychotherapist or other mental health practitioner, bring with them a certain amount of wariness and caution around the possibility of being helped through the efforts of another person. In practice, as a consequence, the client actively 'weighs-up' the therapist: is this a person I can trust? People who have been hurt by others tend to possess finely honed interpersonal survival skills. They are alert to any danger signal that their therapist might, despite a warm and friendly demeanour, and despite the row of framed diplomas on their office wall, turn out to be the next person who has let them down.

Box 1.3: *The client's awareness of the therapist*

Writing from a position as a psychoanalyst treating affluent middle-class clients, Maroda (2010: 31) reflected that 'the client may demonstrate an uncanny awareness of the mood and even the life circumstances of the client'. This observation has been verified in many research studies that have explored therapy from the point of view of the client. For example, a client at a community mental health centre noted that:

> . . . she [current therapist] knows what she is doing. Because she's been in that field for quite a long time. You can always tell, like yourself [interviewer], I can tell by the way you act and how long you been doing this and how long you haven't, it's a difference, I can tell, I can feel it. You can tell by the way the person [counselor] conversation is coming. You could tell if they professional, if they jiving with you or they just starting out cause some of them start out nervous, don't know what to say. They can't look at you directly, eye-to-eye contact.
>
> (Ward 2005: 477)

In another study, a lesbian client talked about her first meeting with a new therapist in the following terms:

> . . she was very, very married, very married..you could see all the rings and everything, I don't know she just seemed very sort of married [laughs]. She was just very straight looking, typical, stereotypical married straight woman . . .
>
> (Ryden and Loewenthal 2001: 47)

These examples underscore the extent to which clients observe and assess the characteristics of a therapist that are particularly significant to them. It is inevitable that important aspects of the self or identity of the therapist will be known to the client, and play some kind of part in the process of therapy.

Being able to handle the relational sensitivity and vulnerability of clients represents one of the most crucial areas for therapist personal development. An effective therapist needs to have an accurate sense of how they might come across to a client. Beyond that, a therapist needs to have sufficient relational flexibility to find a way to connect with clients who may have quite different relationship needs and patterns (Lazarus 1993). At the same time as being flexible and responsive, a good therapist also needs to be authentic and grounded. It can be very disconcerting for someone seeking emotional help, to find themselves in a relationship with a practitioner who comes across as false, as playing some kind of professional role. It is hard to trust such a person. This dilemma, between being genuine, while being able to draw on different aspects of one's self, in the service of the client (and to be aware of when this is happening), represents a key personal development challenge for most therapists. It is a lifelong challenge, because there is always the possibility that the next client will require me to draw on a new, or rarely used, aspect of my relational capability.

In addition to being responsive to the relational patterns and needs of the client, the therapist is also present in the relationship with the client, and one way or another will inevitably express his or her style of being with others, and his or her beliefs and experience around how to make sense of and cope with life problems. From the point of view of the client, it is the therapist who makes the running in terms of building a relationship. In a study by Bedi *et al.* (2005), clients were asked to describe moments in the therapy that had contributed to building a good relationship with their therapist. They described many different types of event, ranging from listening and clarifying goals, through to offering a cup of tea, being well-groomed and having a nice consulting room. Almost all of these events and factors were reported as having been initiated by the therapist. The point here is that personal experience of the therapist is a potential resource for the client. Therapists do all kinds of simple and unremarkable things that draw on their general experience of life: shaking hands, making jokes, smiling, leaning toward and away . . . . Therapists use personal examples to demonstrate how a therapy technique might work ('this is how I have used this breathing exercise . . .', 'this is how I decided what was the best time of day to write in my journal . . .'). A vital aspect of therapist personal development is therefore concerned with being aware of the resources and potentialities (both positive and negative) that one brings to the role of therapist.

A further key implication of the fact that therapy takes place in a relationship is the fact that the therapist is exposed to the suffering of the client, and the client's way of relating to others. This exposure can occur on a moment-by-moment basis, or can be more comprehensive and all-encompassing. At a micro-level, there may be occasions within a therapy session when a client expresses something that is hard for the therapist to take. For example, a client may enter a state of despair and hopelessness, or may get angry with the therapist. Some therapists are comfortable with despair, whereas others are not. Similarly, some therapists value the expression of anger, whereas others are afraid of it. At these moments, a therapist who feels under threat may back off or change the subject. The client gets the message – this is a no-go area. Also at a moment-by-moment level, clients may sometimes express long-established survival skills, such as lying, or being manipulative, controlling or seductive. At a deeper level, some clients have undergone massive humiliation or trauma in their lives. For example, a client who is a refugee may have witnessed family members being murdered, and may have been a victim of torture. Listening to a client sharing their experience of such events may lead a therapist to begin to question his or her core beliefs in the essential goodness of people. To be an effective therapist requires being willing to be open to all of these manifestations of a client's troubles, but without being overwhelmed or emotionally damaged by what is being heard. This area represents another significant domain of therapist personal development. To be an effective therapist requires being able to be resourceful and resilient in the presence of horror, developing a capacity to have the courage to hang on in there when a client is exploring topics around which the therapist is personally sensitive, and generally becoming aware of what these triggers might be.

This discussion of the basic nature of therapeutic work has identified three broad areas in which effective therapy practice requires a willingness to develop self-awareness around different types of relationship challenge. The next section looks at some of the specific therapeutic competencies associated with these issues.

Box 1.4: *The personal development of therapists: a current hot topic*

The professional literature in counselling, psychotherapy and mental health does not expand at a constant rate. Instead, it has a tidal quality. At some points, certain topics are 'in', for a variety of reasons, and then at other times these same topics are 'out'. The topic of therapist personal development appears to be coming in from the cold, following several years of relative neglect. This shift is probably because of the impact of research that has shown that therapist qualities, rather than theoretical model, has the greater impact on client outcomes. Many valuable contributions to the literature on therapist personal development have appeared in recent years (Bager-Charleson 2012; Baldwin 2013; Hughes and Youngson 2009; Johns 2012a, 2012b; Pieterse *et al.* 2013; Skovholt 2012).

The relevance of self-awareness for practice

An important development in recent years, within the field of counselling, psychotherapy and mental health, has been the construction of competency frameworks for different areas of therapy practice (see, for example, Centre for Outcomes Research and Effectiveness 2013; European Association of Psychotherapy 2013). These frameworks reflect the need within large healthcare organizations, such as the National Health Service (NHS) in Britain, to be able to define the criteria through which potential employees could be considered as suitable for particular work roles. These frameworks also help education and training providers to identify the skills and topics that should be addressed within training programmes. Many of the competency statements that have been published are rather arid documents that reflect their bureaucratic origins. At the same time, these frameworks are typically compiled by groups of experts within the field, and can be viewed as attempts to be clear about just what it is that a competent therapist should be able to do. Typically, therapist competence is described in terms of two broad domains: specific technical competencies and generic competencies. Specific competencies refer to knowledge and skills associated with a particular therapeutic approach. For example, a competent CBT therapist would be expected to be able to engage in Socratic questioning, carry out an assessment and case formulation and implement homework assignments. A competent psychodynamic therapist would be expected to be able to make transference interpretations, work with fantasy and dream material, and explore the developmental origins of problems. In addition to these specific technical competencies or techniques there are also generic competencies that reflect skills that *all* therapists can be expected to possess, such as being able to form an effective working relationship with the client, being able to elicit and use client feedback, and demonstrating cultural sensitivity and awareness.

These generic competencies invite reflection on the question: what makes it possible for a therapist to be able to do these things, or to do them well? It is possible to see that these competencies draw on a capacity for mature self-awareness and a fund of personal knowledge. They are not competencies that rely on knowledge of theory or technique. Instead, they are grounded in knowledge of self-in-relationship, and a tacit sense of how one relates and responds to others on a moment-by-moment basis (Baldwin 2013; Rowan and Jacobs 2002; Wosket 1999). The possession of such skills arises from a commitment to question one's own reactions to others, and extend or refine one's repertoire of responses. Generic competencies involve the application of a range of personal skills, such as the following.

- *Awareness of feelings and emotional responses to a client.* The emotions (and associated images, memories and fantasies) that are triggered by contact with a client comprise a crucial source of information. It may be that the therapist is 'resonating' to unspoken or hidden emotions of the client. Alternatively, the way the therapist feels in relation to the client may be similar to the way that other people respond to the client, in everyday situations. In either case, the feelings of the therapist provide a potential clue to important aspects of the emotional life of the client, and the types of relationships that they tend to have. On some occasions, the emotional response of the therapist may also provide information about the well-being or responsiveness of the practitioner. For example, if a therapist feels sad with most of their clients, the chances are that this is the therapist's sadness, rather than an indicator of the emotional world of the client.

• *Grounding therapeutic techniques and processes in personal experience.* Whatever therapy strategy or intervention is being used needs to be tailored to the unique experience of each individual client. It is not possible to do this in the absence of some level of personal knowledge of the processes that are being explored. For example, a cognitive–behavioural therapy (CBT) therapist may help a client to develop relaxation skills, or a more 'mindful' approach to life. A person-centred therapist may invite a client to engage in experiential focusing on his or her felt sense of a problem. In these situations, if the therapist has not personally used these techniques for themselves, they will have only an abstract, textbook understanding of what it might be like to be on the receiving end of such an intervention. The same principle applies to any therapeutic concept of method: if the therapist does not have first-hand experience of what is being implemented, then they do not 'know' what they are talking about. In addition, when a therapist has first-hand experience of a therapeutic theory or method then they are more likely to believe in the value of that approach, and be in a position to convey this to the client in a way that helps the client to take the risk of trying out what is being offered.

• *Using examples from one's own life.* The issue of therapist self-disclosure of personal information has received a great deal of attention in recent years (Bloomgarden and Mennuti 2009; Farber 2006; Hanson 2005; Knox and Hill 2003). Historically, influenced by Freud, mental health practitioners adopted a stance that therapist self-disclosure was to be avoided, as a means of emphasizing the difference between the therapy relationship and a friendship relationship. Also, it is clearly not helpful for a client if their therapist talks at length about their own problems. Gradually, this position has shifted. There is a lot of personal information that therapists convey to clients without saying anything. The appearance of the therapist, or objects in the therapy room, can provide clues about age, gender, sexual orientation, social class and much else. Research has shown that well-timed and sensitively communicated personal information has the potential to be helpful for clients, by strengthening the therapeutic relationship, offering an alternative perspective, 'normalizing' an issue, and conveying hope that a difficult situation can eventually be overcome. Also, in some instances the withholding of personal information has been found to be damaging to the therapeutic relationship. Taken as a whole, clinical examples and research suggest that there are no hard and fast rules for effective therapist self-disclosure. Instead, this is an area that requires the therapist to make use of his or her intuition and clinical judgement. There is a direct link between a capacity to engage in facilitative self-disclosure, and prior personal development work that allows a practitioner to identify, and make use of, his or her personal 'existential touchstones' (Mearns and Cooper 2005). The more that a therapist has examined key events and turning points in their own life, the more that they will be in a position to use their personal life history in a way that is responsive to the needs of a particular client, rather than as a means of personal gratification.

Emotional responsiveness, personal knowledge of theory and method, and judicious self-disclosure, represent three areas of concrete therapist decision-making and action within sessions. These are things that therapists do. The extent to which a therapist is able to exhibit generic therapeutic competencies, will depend on his or her degree of personal development in relation to these areas.

A further way in which personal development activity has an impact on competence is through what can be described as the 'alignment' of the therapist to his or her professional role (Goldfried 2001; Spinelli and Marshall 2001). Therapists are more effective if they are using an approach that fits their values and worldview, and are working with clients with whom they have some kind of meaningful connection. They are also more effective if they are energetic, present, and hopeful, rather than disillusioned and burnt out. As mentioned earlier, research has provided evidence that some therapists are more effective than others. To a large extent, these differences arise from the extent to which the therapist has found his or her 'niche'. There are probably some therapists who are in the job for the wrong reasons, and would be better off finding a different line of work. There are other therapists who, for whatever reason, possess a powerfully healing presence that makes them effective with almost any client. Most of us, however, are somewhere in the middle, and tend to be able to do good work with some clients in some circumstances. For example, some therapists are tremendously helpful with people with depression and struggle with clients who have experienced trauma. Other therapists have the opposite patterns. Therapists also differ in their aptitude for long-term or short-term work, individual, couple or group therapy, number of clients seen per week, and so on. One of the important outcomes of therapist personal development, therefore, is to allow the practitioner to arrive at an appreciation of their own particular gifts (and imitations), and to arrive at an informed and accurate understanding of what they can offer to the profession.

This section of the chapter has emphasized the practical significance of therapist personal development. An ongoing commitment to personal development has an impact on effectiveness with clients, in a number of tangible and observable ways. In the following section, some of the underlying themes in therapist personal development are explored.

Themes in therapist personal development

The content of personal development, the specific issues that are explored, is different for each therapist. Nevertheless, it is possible to identify some general themes that arise on a regular basis within therapist experiences of their personal development activities.

Coherence–incoherence of one's personal narrative

Being able to make sense of life stories is central to any kind of psychotherapeutic work. People seek help from professional practitioners because of some kind of crisis or dissatisfaction in their life. Usually, finding a way forward involves becoming able to see things in perspective, by understanding how current troubles arise from a playing out of previous decisions and responses to earlier events and circumstances. Developing a more coherent and 'joined-up' personal narrative represents an essential element of the capacity to reflect on experience – a quality that is considered by many schools of therapy to be a fundamental change process. The implication here is that therapists need to be able to facilitate a movement in the direction of coherence in the life stories of their clients. To be able to do this, it is a good idea to start with one's own story. Many of the personal development activities undertaken by trainees and experienced therapists, such as personal therapy and journal writing, can be seen as arenas in which a life story can be reviewed and 'thickened'. It is important to recognize that, in this endeavour, the uncovering of *incoherence* and contradiction is just as valuable as the construction of coherent causal sequences. Lives are complex, and can be regarded as organized around a quest to resolve conflicting inner tendencies. Many contemporary theorists have emphasized the idea of self-multiplicity (Honos-Webb and Stiles 1998; Mair 1977; Mearns and Thorne 2000; Rowan and Cooper 1998) as a necessary complement to notions of the 'unity' or coherence of self. The bottom line, here, is that it seems reasonable to expect any decent therapist to be able to offer a considered, detailed account of how they have developed as a person. It also seems reasonable to expect that this account or narrative would not consist merely of a catalogue of success, but would reflect some measure of uncertainty, ambiguity and tension.

Connection and difference

Counselling, psychotherapy and modern mental health care have evolved within a historical and cultural context that promotes self-contained individualism. Most mainstream theories of therapy regard the client as a distinct entity or 'case', whose problems can be understood in terms of internal psychological and biological processes. In this context, it is valuable to retain an appreciation of the fact that people are not merely individual units, but are also interconnected with others, with groups, and with the historical development of these groups, in a myriad of different ways. From this perspective, therapy can be perceived as a process of helping the person to be included, to re-join collective life in respect of some facet of their identity of which they have been ashamed or fearful. One of the most powerful aspects of therapy is that it allows people the opportunity to talk about locked-away thoughts, feelings and memories for the first time, or to *really* talk about them for the first time. For therapists, personal development involves the task of building a capacity to be able to connect with others, to be able to recognize that the client's story is a version of one's own story, and at the same time a version of everyone's story. This capacity is supported through personal development activities that involve being open to the experience of others, such as participation in a training or therapy group, or the choice to work in different cultural settings or with different client groups. One of the big challenges in this area of personal development, for some therapists, is that what is at stake is not merely a deepened capacity to respect others based on an acknowledgement that we are all part of a common humanity. What may be harder to acknowledge is the fact that there are also profound differences between people. Everyone is not like me. Not everyone feels the way I do, or sees the world in the same way as I do. There is a sense in which aspects of therapy theory, diagnostic categories, and cross-cultural training and research, have evolved as ways of reminding therapists that these differences exist.

Courage

Some people who seek therapy have had awful lives. Listening to their stories can be a harrowing and dispiriting experience – how can things ever be different for this person, how can they ever move on from where they are now? Sometimes, a client has previously consulted many other therapists, without success. These situations confront a therapist with a massive personal challenge – who am I, to believe that I can make a mean-ingful difference to this person's life? There are times when being a thera-pist, sitting opposite the client in a consulting room, can raise fundamental questions about personal adequacy. Can I allow myself to become involved in the interpersonal world of this client? To what extent will getting close to this person require me to face my own madness? Can I be strong enough to provide a safe space for the work that this client needs to do? Can I be open to feedback from this client, around how I have let him down? Being a therapist does not always evoke such issues. But inevitably, sooner or later, it does. To be able to do the right thing, in these circumstances, takes courage. Professional courage is a topic that is rarely addressed in the literature, or in training. An important thread of therapist personal development consists of facing up to things that one would rather avoid, being willing to do things with clients that make one afraid, and finding the resilience to keep going when things get tough. A related personal develop-ment theme is concerned with knowledge of when to stop, for example developing a realistic awareness of personal limits.

Courage, connection and coherence can be understood as personal development 'themes' because they weave in and out of the work, in similar fashion to musical themes. Each return of the theme presents a pattern that is recognizable but also different in some respect. The progres-sion of the theme does not consist of a linear progression towards a single 'correct' end-point, such as becoming optimally aware of one's own life story, optimally connected to others, or optimally courageous. What seems to happen, instead, is that we need to arrive at a balance point, a compro-mise between coherence/incoherence, connection/difference or courage/avoidance that is appropriate to the situation in which we find ourselves at different stages in our personal life and career.

Box 1.5: *Cycles of development*

For most therapists, 'personal development' is not something that they do every day, like eating. It is more likely to be something that takes place occasionally, in intensive bursts, such as redecorating a house. For some therapists, the decision to enter training emerges as the outcome of a burst of personal development work. Therapy training creates dilemmas around the intensity of focus on personal development activity. Typically, tutors and trainers expect or require students to engage in personal devel-opment work, for example, by being in therapy, keeping a journal or being a member of an experiential learning group. At the same time, students know that they need to be able to function at a high level of professional competence on a day-to-day basis, in terms of writing assignments and seeing clients. As a result, it can be hard for students to 'let go' to a sufficient extent to allow meaningful personal learning to happen. Throughout a career, therapists tend to go through episodes of immersion in personal self-exploration. For some, this can be triggered by life events or times of professional challenge. Some practitioners find it useful to be in weekly personal therapy throughout their careers. Other therapists take time out, maybe once each year, to reflect on who they are in their job, and use this as a basis for deciding about whether to invest in some kind of personal development project or activity. What seems to be important, for effective practice, is to find a relationship with personal development that fits one's own individual learning preferences and lifestyle.

Frequently occurring personal development issues

It is possible to think about therapist personal development in terms of general themes (as in the preceding section), or through the use of broad, abstract concepts such as 'individuation' or 'self-actualization'. These ideas are useful as a means of gaining an overarching vision of what personal development is about. However, at a day-to-day level, therapist personal development consists of a willingness to struggle with down-to-earth, practical issues. Some of the issues that frequently arise for therapists are listed below.

Avoidance of specific areas of experience: probably every therapist has one or more areas that are uncomfortable or unfamiliar for them, that they avoid exploring with clients if at all possible. These sensitive areas may include: endings, conflict, strong emotion, specific emotions (for example anger), sexuality, money and spirituality. There can be many reasons why a person has developed a 'blind spot' around a specific issue, for example early life experience, exposure to cultural norms or training.

One's own needs taking priority: there are many subtle ways in which the manner in which a therapist relates to clients are a reflection of his or her own emotional and interpersonal needs. For example, a therapist who needs to be liked may be reluctant to challenge a client, a therapist with a need for control and order may not allow a client to explore an issue in an unstructured way. At the extreme, therapist gratification of personal needs becomes an ethical issue, for example when a therapist tries to have a sexual relationship with a client, or tries to keep a client in therapy as a means of generating income. But these ethical examples are the tip of the iceberg. The insistence in many training programmes that trainees should develop a comprehensive understanding of their own motives for becoming a therapist arises from an appreciation that effective therapists should be able to monitor and manage their own needs within therapy relationships.

Crippling self-doubt and invidious comparison: it is important for therapists to be able to call on an 'internal supervisor' that acts as a reality check on their interactions with clients. It is also important to retain a balanced and modest sense of the potential of therapy to make a difference to a client. Some therapists can take these attributes too far, and may become almost paralysed in their capacity to respond to a client, due to the functioning of a harsh inner critic.

Sense of superiority: grandiosity and narcissism are at the opposite pole to self-doubt. Clients tend to prefer to work with a therapist who communicates a sense of confidence and competence. Some practitioners get into difficulties because they are *too* confident of their own abilities and gifts. This personal development issue can manifest itself in an unwillingness to listen to feedback from clients or colleagues, or in a misplaced enthusiasm for taking on 'impossible' clients. In some therapists, both self-doubt and grandiosity may be present at the same time, for example if an overt sense of superiority masks an internal fear of being an imposter. There exists an extensive literature on narcissism and sense of superiority as 'occupational hazards' within the counselling, psychotherapy and mental health professions (Brightman 1984; Glickauf-Hughes and Mehlman 1995; Halewood and Tribe 2003; Marmor 1953).

Boundary issues: any form of therapeutic or mental health work occurs within a space that is marked out by different types of boundaries. There is a boundary around the therapy as a whole, in the shape of time limits, confidentiality of information and privacy within a therapy room. There are various kinds of interpersonal boundary: what level of physical touch is possible? How much is the client allowed to know about the personal life of the therapist? People tend to grow up with a particular set of implicit boundary 'rules', which may not always be appropriate in therapeutic situations. An important area of personal development work centres around the task of becoming aware of how one establishes and maintains boundaries, and responds to boundary threats and violations.

Selective acceptance: being a therapist means being able to work with clients from different backgrounds. It is unlikely that anyone is equally accepting of all categories of person. When asked about this, before they enter practice, many trainees suggest that they would find it impossible to work with a client who was a paedophile. Over time, it usually becomes apparent that therapist barriers and judgementalism are triggered by a somewhat longer list of types of person. Selective acceptance can be the result of specific personal experience or general cultural factors. For example, cultural attitudes to body size in societies influenced by contemporary Western ideas, leads many therapists to be disgusted by clients who are overweight. In some instances, non-acceptance of certain types of client behaviour arises from religious beliefs, as in the case of the difficulties that some Christian counsellors have with gay clients or women who choose to terminate a pregnancy.

Depersonalization: on the whole, clients appreciate it when a therapist is authentic or genuine, and is present in the relationship. Clients do not like it if a therapist is remote and 'overprofessional' and treats them like a 'case'. The concept of *depersonalization* refers to a failure on the part of a therapist to respond to a client (or in extreme instances, to any client) as a person. There are many important issues that can be bound up in this kind of response, such as fear of other people, fear of one's own response to other people, the capacity to care, the capacity to be open to experience, the ability to create a safe-enough environment, or suffering from overwork and emotional burnout.

Being a rescuer: therapy works best when the therapists functions as a facilitator or consultant, who is responsive to the goals and direction of the client. Therapy tends to get stuck, or go round in circles, if the therapist behaves as if they can sort out the client's problems on the client's behalf. This latter pattern can be described as a 'rescuer' role. If a client starts to explore a painful issue, and their therapist reassures them or offers advice, then it is likely that rescuing is happening. Other manifestations of this issue can take the form of pretence or collusion, where there is a tacit agreement between therapist and client not to mention specific topics. Unfortunately, 'rescuing' is a common or default mode of helping in many families, and as a result, many therapy trainees and practitioners find themselves needing to reflect on their own ways of being with clients, in order to differentiate between the few occasions when rescuing a client may be necessary, in contrast to the many occasions where rescuing is actually undermining the ability of the client to face up to difficult issues or learn how to tolerate emotional discomfort.

These are just some of the concrete personal development challenges that can emerge for both students and more experienced practitioners. They represent recurring themes and topics in personal development groups, personal therapy, supervision, reflective journal writing and peer group discussions. These are issues that can be readily dealt with, once they become apparent, or may reflect deep-rooted personal dilemmas that recur over the course of a whole life. Within different theoretical traditions, these issues can be understood in a variety of ways. However, the starting point for exploring them is almost always a basic appreciation that there is some fairly simple way that things are not quite right in a therapist's response to a client.

Conclusions

What is personal development? Why is it important? Personal development is multifaceted, and can involve reflection and learning around many different aspects of personal identity and the capacity to form relationships with others (Horton 1997). Personal development work supports therapist competence in a number of ways, and as a result can be seen as a necessary dimension of safe and effective professional practice. The following chapters seek to deepen this introductory account. Chapter 2 explores the different arenas within which therapist personal development can be facilitated. Chapter 3 reviews research that has been carried out into therapist personal development, and discusses the ways in which relevant theory can be used to inform the process of personal development.

Methods for facilitating personal development

Introduction

The purpose of this chapter is to explore the various ways in which personal development can be facilitated and enhanced. The chapter focuses on *intentional* pathways of personal development – activities that are purposefully chosen for their personal development potential. It is important to keep in mind that, in principle *any* activity may contribute to personal development: the capacity for learning and development is intrinsic to the experience of being human. This chapter begins by considering the role of a set of approaches to personal development that are incorporated, to a greater or lesser extent, in all training programmes, as well as forming part of lifelong learning for many practitioners: groupwork, personal therapy, supervision and journal writing. Attention then turns to a broader set of personal development contexts that represent a valuable arena for therapist personal development, but have received less attention within the professional literature.

Personal development groups

It would be hard for anyone to complete their training as a counsellor, psychotherapist or mental health practitioner without taking part in some kind of personal development group. A wide range of terms are used to describe these groups: personal development, personal and professional development, T-groups, encounter, awareness, therapy, experiential. They tend to consist of a set of around eight trainees meeting with a facilitator for a series of 90 minute meetings. However, many alternative formats can be found: larger or fewer numbers of participants, co-facilitators, community groups comprising all the members of a training programme, peer-facilitated groups and marathon groups that meet over a weekend or even for several days. Sometimes groups are video recorded and participants are required to analyse their interactions. The rationale for the group will depend on the theoretical orientation of the training programme within which it is embedded. Sometimes trainees are taught about group dynamics theory, whereas in other cases they are just left to get on with it.

Why are personal development groups so widely used? The use of the group as a medium for therapeutic learning appears to date from the 1940s. Early forms of groupwork were pioneered by Jacob Moreno with psychodrama, by Kurt Lewin through the invention of 'T-groups' and by Wilfred Bion in his psychoanalytic groups. In the 1960s, Carl Rogers and others were involved in the development of encounter groups. From the 1970s, cognitive–behavioural therapists used structured psycho-educational groups as a means of delivering CBT interventions, and feminist therapists worked with 'consciousness-raising' groups. All of the main theoretical orientations in counselling, psychotherapy and mental health practice are represented in distinctive approaches to the theory and practice of working with groups. Further information about these approaches can be found in a range of widely available group therapy textbooks (Brabender *et al.* 2004; Corey 2010; DeLucia-Waack *et al.* 2004; Jacobs *et al.* 2006; Paleg and Jongsma 2005; Yalom 2005a). Underlying concepts of group dynamics are discussed in Forsyth (2013) and Poole and Hollingshead (2004). A fascinating insight into the experience of being in a group, can be found in the novel *The Schopenhauer Cure*, written by the celebrated group therapist Irvin Yalom (2005b).

There are many advantages to the use of the small group, as a medium for learning and development:

- group members can support each other;
- members can learn through observing the actions of others within the group;
- the facilitator can directly observe how a person interacts with others;
- members can experiment with new ways of relating to others, within the actual group.

In addition to these factors, there can be occasions when a group presents a highly challenging environment. This can be particularly useful for trainees. For example, it can be hard to respond in an empathic manner to an individual client, but it is much harder to respond empathically to seven other members of a personal development group at the same time. Participation in a group therefore functions as a kind of 'testing ground' for trainees – if they can cope with the group, they are likely to be able to cope with clients. Although seldom explicitly acknowledged, the challenging nature of participation in a personal development group also creates the possibility of observing whether a trainee is sufficiently emotionally grounded and stable to survive the rigours of real-life practice.

When reflecting on the experience of being a member of a learning group, it can be helpful to be able to make sense of these experiences in the context of an appreciation of how groups operate, and the distinctive issues and learning opportunities that are highlighted by the process of the group. The area of group dynamics has been a central focus for social psychology and sociology for more than a century, and there exists a wealth of theory and research on this topic. An introduction to some of the main concepts that are used in theories of group dynamics is provided below.

The needs of individual members

In any group, there is a task to be fulfilled. The nature of the task will be different for different groups. For example, management groups must make decisions, ward-based nursing teams must organize and deliver patient care, learning groups must create an environment for the acquisition of new skills and knowledge. But in all these groups the achievement of the group's goals, the fulfilment of its primary task, will be strongly influenced by the quality of the relationships that exist between group members. This is because people are not robots or machines, but have needs that they try to satisfy through contact with colleagues and clients. There appear to be three broad areas of interpersonal needs that are relevant to the way that people act in groups:

- needs for inclusion/belonging/acceptance;
- the need to feel in control of the situation, for power, influence, to experience a sense of order;
- needs for liking/affection/intimacy/expressing feelings.

The interplay between these aspects of group life is powerfully captured in a classic paper by Bennis and Shepard (1956), who argue that, in any group, the salience of these needs changes over time. At the beginning of the life of a group, people are particularly concerned about whether they will be included and accepted by others. This phase may raise personal issues around the person's sense of belonging. The group may then shift to a concern with the question of how it is going to get things done. Needs for order and control, or individual freedom from external constraint, may come to the fore. Also, this stage in the life of the group can raise issues around the perceived need for a strong leader (dependency needs). Finally, the group may reach a stage where there is the possibility for authentic connection and intimacy between group members. At this point, fears and inhibitions associated with interpersonal closeness may be exhibited. In the context of personal development, what all this means is that over the life of a personal development group, each member is faced with a series of moments when they are vividly and dramatically confronted with an awareness of their own emotional response and basic interpersonal needs, while at the same time being in the position of being able to observe that other group members are exhibiting different emotions and different needs. Handled well, this situation provides immense possibilities for learning.

The group as a system

Any human group can be seen as a complex system of relationships, task and roles. Three of the most fundamental aspects of group 'systems' are their norms, their composition and their boundaries. The *norms* of a group represent the shared (and usually unconscious or taken-for-granted) assumptions that group members have about what is OK in the group and what is not OK. Some of the questions which are useful to ask about the norms of a learning group include:

- is it alright to disagree?
- is it alright to express feelings? Which feelings?

The *composition* of a group can critically affect the way it functions. From a role perspective, a group can be seen to consist of a number of 'role-specialists' (for example individuals who consistently behave in particular ways, such as being task-oriented, supportive, creative, critical, humorous, etc.). The *boundary* of a group is like an invisible, but psychologically very real, barrier or fence around a group. When you are 'in' the group you know you have crossed that boundary. It is very difficult for a group of people to see themselves as a unit, or a group, in the absence of a secure boundary. Significant boundary questions include:

- how does someone cross the boundary to enter the group? What are the membership rituals?
- can new ideas or information appropriately cross the boundary?
- is the boundary strong enough to withstand pressure from external sources?
- are there any internal boundaries (for example subgroups, cliques)?
- who looks after the boundaries? How do they do this?

These processes – adhering to norms, playing a role, living within boundaries – represent basic dimensions of human relatedness. Participation in an intensive small-group experience provides many opportunities for members to reflect on and gain an understanding of these processes in ways that can inform their work as therapists.

Leadership

Effective leadership is essential for any group to perform well. However, it is necessary to recognize that the most effective leadership is not something that is only provided by the one individual who is designated as 'the facilitator', but is a quality of a group to which all its members contribute. For example, there cannot be a 'leader' without 'followers'. Each person in a work group will have some ideas or qualities which they can offer – there are a wide range of roles that need to be fulfilled in a group, each of which makes its own unique contribution to the direction taken by the group as a whole. Being an effective therapist requires that a practitioner should be aware of the possibilities and also the limits of his or her own power to make a difference. Involvement in a learning group can allow a therapist to be aware of his or her 'potency'.

Change

One of the most fundamental aspects of any social group is that it *changes* over time. Personnel, priorities, norms, tasks, level of effectiveness, all change over the lifetime of a group, for a multitude of reasons. This is why many write about small groups talk in terms of group *dynamics* or group *processes*. It is important to be aware of change processes in order to be able to understand and cope with situations where the group is either *stuck* or seemingly engaged in a process of chaotic, rapid change. Some useful questions to consider here are:

- how does the group deal with the arrival or departure of members?
- how is time structured (for example does the group proceed through phases of information-gathering, evaluation and action; is there an agenda?)

- how does the group take care of *endings*? Is unfinished business always dealt with? Does the group celebrate its successes?

In some ways, these changes can be seen to unfold as discrete stages or phases in the life of a group. In other ways, however, change in a group can occur over short periods of time, and may take on a cyclical quality, with the group passing fairly rapidly through a sequence of distinct states of functioning. Again, reflection on how one engages with these processes can represent a valuable trigger to personal awareness and development.

These themes – personal needs in relation to others, responding to change, adapting to the social norms – are central to the experience of being a person. As a result, being a member of an intensive small group can represent a situation in which a person can learn a great deal about how they are, and how they relate to others. A small learning group can be viewed as a microcosm of other social groups that a person has experienced during their life. In such a group, people reproduce patterns of being-in-relationship that reflect the ways that they felt and acted in earlier groups in their life, such as their family of origin, or friendship groups at school.

On the basis of the ideas outlined in the preceding paragraphs, it is easy to see why the small experiential learning group is widely regarded as an essential method for promoting personal development. In reality, the potential impact of the small group experience can be attenuated by a number of hindering factors. Right from the start of the small group 'movement' in the 1960s, it was clear that such groups worked best if they took place in a space that was outside of everyday life. If a temporary 'cultural island' (Back 1972, 1973) could be created, group members would feel more free to be honest with each other and experiment with new behaviours. Although most leaders of training programmes do their best to construct a safe, boundaried space for personal development groups to take place, there is no avoiding the fact that group members will inevitably interact outside the group in many different ways – as friends, colleagues, rivals. Moreover, the group is embedded within an evaluative context. Even if interaction in the group is not formally assessed, participants tend to assume that the way they are in the group will have an impact on the way that they are perceived by staff.

Another factor that has a bearing on the use of experiential groups in therapist personal development is that, in recent decades, society as a whole has moved in the direction of individualism, with the result that participants either do not see the point of groupwork, lack prior experience in groups or are highly fearful and defensive. The trend toward individualism has also meant that relatively few tutors or faculty members have had specific training in working with groups. A further issue is that although participation in an experiential group may help a trainee to be more open, there tends to be little opportunity to process and assimilate this new information at a personal level. For example, in a group, someone may realize that they keep other people at a distance by deflecting praise or affirmation. This kind of learning can be enormously significant. But there is unlikely to be the time or space in the group to make sense of this pattern of behaviour in terms of its origins in early childhood, and so on. That kind of processing needs to be done somewhere else.

The outcome of these hindering factors is that the personal development 'yield' of time spent in a reflective learning group, can be patchy. Some people report that they get a lot out of this sort of experience, either through bonding and experience of intimacy, and/or through the experience of finding creative ways to resolve conflict and impasses within the group. Other people, however, report that time spent in such groups has been, for them, time that is wasted.

Box 2.1: *The power of the large group experience*

Within both the psychoanalytic and humanistic/person-centred approaches, there has been a tradition of using large group experiences as a vehicle for personal development. These large groups may be convened as stand-alone events, or may comprise all the members of a training programme. In this context, a 'large group' can be considered as a meeting of between 20 and 200 persons. Some large groups (for example community meetings) may last for two or three hours, whereas other events may continue for several days. Usually, large groups are run by a team of facilitators. There are several group learning processes that are heightened by the large group context. For most people, talking in a large group is quite a scary experience. Participation in the group therefore opens up areas of learning around managing fear and anxiety, and the possibility of an enhanced sense of self-worth through overcoming these fears. Because there are large numbers of people involved, the kinds of themes that emerge tend to go beyond personal and interpersonal issues. Instead, the large group can become a context for exploring fundamental existential themes (what does it mean to care? what does it mean to make a choice? what responsibility do I have for other people?) and social processes (how do we reconcile the differences between us? who has power and how is it exerted?). Further information on the kinds of learning processes that can occur in large groups can be found in Hill (2002) and Wood (1984).

Suggested further reading

Some of the most interesting perspectives on group dynamics are derived from psychoanalytic theory, particularly the ideas of the British psychoanalyst Wilfred Bion.

Bion, W. (1961) *Experiences in Groups*. London: Tavistock.
Rioch, M. (1970) The work of Wilfred Bion on groups, *Psychiatry*, 33, 56–66.
Whitman, R. and Stock, D. (1958) The group focal conflict, *Psychiatry*, 21, 269–76.

Issues associated with the use of small groups to facilitate therapist personal development are discussed in:

Aveline, M.O. (1986) Personal themes from training groups for health care professionals, *British Journal of Medical Psychology*, 59, 325–35.
Gordon, T. (1951) Group-centered leadership and administration. In C.R. Rogers (ed.) *Client-centered Therapy*. London: Constable.
Lago, C. and Macmillan, M. (eds) (2000) *Experiences in Relatedness: Groupwork and the Person-Centred Approach*. Hay-on-Wye: PCCS Books.
Rose, C. (2008) *The Personal Development Group: The Students' Guide*. London: Karnac.

Personal therapy

The term 'personal therapy' is used within the counselling and psychotherapy literature to describe therapy that is received by (rather than delivered by) a counsellor or psychotherapist. Personal therapy may be the same as any other therapy – the person decides on his or her own initiative to see a therapist, at the time of their choosing. Alternatively, personal therapy may be a requirement on some training programmes, so that the trainee may need to attend therapy whether they feel the need for it at that point in their life. This requirement may include attendance for a specified number of sessions, selection of a therapist from a list of approved practitioners or participation in group as well as individual therapy. In a few training programmes, the therapist submits a report to a training committee on the suitability of the candidate (Curtis and Qaiser 2005).

There has been a substantial amount of research into personal therapy. The evidence from this research shows that at least 80% of therapists, within all therapy approaches, have made use of personal therapy at some stage in their career. The majority engage in therapy both during training and as necessary through the course of their working lives. Some therapists see other therapists within their theoretical approach, whereas others opt to use personal therapy to gain first-hand experience of a variety of approaches. The overwhelming consensus across many studies is that practitioners report that personal therapy has helped them to be better therapists. Reviews of this evidence base can be found in Bike *et al.* (2009), Geller (2011) and Orlinsky *et al.* (2011).

For therapists who enter therapy, there are two main ways in which personal development can be enhanced. First, progress can be achieved in relation to understanding and resolving personal issues around such areas as anxiety, depression and marital difficulties. Second, being a client affords a unique perspective on the process of therapy. Personal therapy therefore provides an opportunity to learn about the helpful and unhelpful processes that can occur within the therapy hour.

There are a number of issues and dilemmas associated with the use of personal therapy. A requirement to be in therapy during training may represent an unhelpful source of stress for some students. There can be a tension between the need to be organized, 'professional' and in control when working with clients, or operating as a very junior member of a pressurized therapy agency, and the need to open up and 'let go' during personal therapy. This tension can lead in different directions. Many therapists believe that trainees who come to them in order to accumulate therapy hours are just going through the motions and not really using therapy in an optimal way. On the other hand, some students become very deeply involved in a personal change process and as a result find it hard to manage the demands of the training programme, or even sometimes the demands of their own family life. There can be moral and ethical dilemmas arising from mandated personal therapy for trainees. For example, if a trainee has completed a successful course of therapy immediately prior to entering training, it may be harmful to re-open the same issues – a period of consolidation is required. In some instances, the requirement to choose a therapist from a specified list may resemble a form of financial exploitation. More broadly, some people may find it more helpful to use other methods of personal development, rather than therapy. For these individuals, it may be that what they learn from personal therapy is that their developmental needs are best fulfilled somewhere else.

Another dilemma in personal therapy is that at some point in the future the therapist may become a colleague. This factor is exacerbated when the person in therapy and their therapist are members of a relatively circumscribed professional community, such as gestalt therapists or feminist therapists in a small city. This dynamic creates a situation that is quite different from 'ordinary' therapy. For example, most therapy proceeds on the basis that it is extremely unlikely that the therapist and client will have an ongoing relationship after therapy is ended. By contrast, in some personal therapy scenarios it is highly *likely* that a future relationship will occur. This kind of consideration can add depth to both the therapy that is received and to the ongoing professional relationship, if it is explicitly addressed during the therapy. On the other hand, there can be risks to both parties when such issues are not explored to a sufficient degree. Another version of this type of dilemma arises for senior therapists. Many experienced therapists travel long distances for their personal therapy, to avoid using junior colleagues within their own local network. In some professional communities, there may be two or three very senior therapists who specialize in providing personal therapy to slightly-less-senior colleagues.

In Chapter 3, it is suggested that therapist autobiographical accounts of their personal therapy and other personal development activities represent a valuable source of learning and insight. These narratives provide a wealth of examples of how therapists try out different therapists for their personal therapy in an effort to resolve the issues that have been highlighted in this section. One of the themes that emerges from these narratives is that few trainees find the right therapist first time round. However, their knowledge of the possibilities of therapy makes them discerning consumers, and eventually they find what they need. What is missing from this body of literature are the narratives of the 15 per cent of therapists who appear to have never made use of personal therapy. It is not known whether these colleagues are finding more appropriate ways (for them) of facilitating their personal development, whether they are avoiding personal development or whether they are 'naturals' who somehow just do not need it.

Box 2.2: *The everyday life context of personal therapy*

Using survey questionnaires, Norcross and Prochaska (1986a, 1986b; Prochaska and Norcross 1983; Prochaska *et al.* 1986) collected information on the strategies used by both therapists and lay people in dealing with psychological problems. These papers are reported in the form of a series of complex statistical analyses, that are somewhat hard to follow. Nevertheless, some clear conclusions emerged from these studies: (a) therapists make use of a wide range of strategies to deal with their problems; (b) almost all of the psychological problems reported by therapists relate to situations in their everyday life – stress arising from their work was rarely identified as a source of difficulty; (c) even when therapists made use of personal therapy, this had been preceded by a lengthy period of time when they had used other strategies to address their problem; (d) therapists made use of a wider range of strategies than were used by lay people; (e) therapists made extensive use of change strategies that were not consistent with their core theoretical model. These studies were conducted 30 years ago – it would be very interesting to discover if similar patterns were found today. The findings reported by Norcross and Prochaska provide a valuable context for makings sense of the meaning of personal therapy for therapists. Although personal therapy is undoubtedly valuable, it appears that it rarely functions in isolation. Instead, therapists are people who are resourceful and creative in making use of a whole spectrum of change processes in their everyday lives. It may be that those therapists who flourish are those who achieve an appropriate balance between personal therapy and other coping strategies.

Suggested further reading

Geller, J.D., Norcross, J.C. and Orlinsky, D.E. (eds) (2005) *The Psychotherapist's Own Psychotherapy: Patient and Clinician Perspectives*. New York: Oxford University Press.

Journal writing

Keeping a personal reflective diary or journal is a widely used method of therapist personal development. Participants in some training programmes are required to keep personal learning journals, which may be submitted to the tutor in their entirety or form the basis for edited or summary accounts of personal learning. In some situations, trainees may be asked to hand in weekly learning logs. Beyond these formalized approaches to the use of journaling, there are many trainees and practitioners who use journals on their own initiative.

There exists a broad range of techniques that can be employed to facilitate the effective use of journals. Further information on these methods can be found in an ever-expanding literature on this topic, listed on pages 156–7. There are a number of writing techniques that are widely favoured.

- *Techniques for releasing unconscious processes*: anyone who keeps a journal knows that it is common for internal self-monitoring or self-censoring processes to occur – the writer pauses for a moment to wonder whether an idea is 'acceptable' or 'appropriate', and loses the thread of the topic that is being explored. By contrast, if these self-sabotaging (or self-protective) processes can be set aside, there is the possibility that new and creative material will emerge. In psycho-analytic terms, the aim is to by-pass defence mechanisms and gain some kind of direct access to the unconscious. There are several ways in which this can be achieved: forcing oneself to write for several minutes without pausing; writing very early in the morning; writing with the non-dominant hand; using dream content as a starting point for writing.

- *Dialogical writing*: many psychological and psychotherapy theories suggest that the 'self' is not a unitary construct, but consists of different parts or sub-selves. For example, transactional analysis theory is built around a three-part structure of self – the parent, adult and child ego states. It is also possible to identify idiosyncratic configurations or parts of the self, that are unique to one's own personal experience. Journal writing offers a highly effective means of developing a greater awareness of these elements of self, how they interact with each other, and how they have an impact on relationships and behaviour. One of the ways that this can be done is to construct a dialogue between different parts, as if they were in conversation with each other. Sometimes it can be helpful to use images and diagrams to represent the linkages between these elements.

- *Systematic reflection on critical events or incidents*: it is possible to use a journal to support rational analysis of one's therapeutic practice, for example by working through a series of prompts. One methodology that has been adopted by many organizations, to assist collective learning, and which can be readily applied to reflection on therapy practice, is the 'after action review'. This consists of a set of key questions: *What did I/we set out to do? What happened? What went well? What went badly? What have I/we learned? What will I/we do differently?*

Many other journal-writing strategies and techniques can be found in the sources listed in chapter 6. There is no one 'right' way to keep a journal – what is important is to experiment with different possibilities in order to arrive at a style of journal keeping that fits one's own needs at a particular point in time, and that is consistent with one's preferred approach to learning. There are wide differences between people in the extent to which they find journal writing helpful. Some therapists report that they gain a huge amount from writing, whereas for others it never develops beyond being a meaningless ritual or chore.

How and why is writing helpful? How can it contribute to personal development? There are several ways in which journal writing is helpful for people. Writing functions to externalize what would otherwise be internal experience. It is hard to get a handle on memories and images that rattle around in one's head. By contrast, when these memories and images are out there on the page it is possible to look at them in a more reflective way. In addition, the act of writing, through the use of structured sentences and statements that follow some kind of sequence, has the effect of bringing a degree of logical or temporal order to one's thoughts. From a different perspective, the act of holding in, or holding on to, difficult or painful memories, is in itself a source of physiological stress (Pennebaker 1997, 2004).

The act of writing can therefore be associated with a gradual release of bodily tension, which in turn makes it possible to reflect on that topic or problem in a more expansive way. Writing can also be a source of creativity – the writer may be surprised by images, ideas and metaphors that are generated, and as a result may be more able to think about an issue in new ways. Writing things down makes a historical record, which allows the writer to track back through journals to look at how they have changed (or has not been able to change) over time. Finally, writing offers the possibility of connection with others. What is written in a journal may function as a rehearsal for what is then actually said to another person. The material in a journal may lead the writer to seek out, or remember, the words of other writers, and this way become better able to see how his or her experience reflects a collective sense of what it means to be human.

Suggested further reading

Nicholls, S. (2009) Beyond expressive writing: evolving models of developmental creative writing, *Journal of Health Psychology*, 14, 171–80.

Supervision, consultation and peer support

There is a general acceptance within all branches of the counselling, psychotherapy and mental health professions that it is necessary for practitioners to organize regular opportunities to reflect on their practice with the assistance of colleagues. This activity can take the form of individual or group supervision, consultation or membership of a peer supervision group. The focus of supervision and other, similar arrangements tends to be oriented toward what needs to be done to provide the best possible service for the client. So, for example, supervision can be used to address how the client's problem can be understood, how various interventions might be used, ethical dilemmas associated with the case and so on. The personal development and self-awareness of the therapist represents an important thread within the overall fabric of supervision. From within the person-centred tradition, Lambers (2006, 2013) argues that the congruence or authenticity of the therapist, and his or her capacity to be present to the client and allow moments of relational depth, are key areas for exploration in supervision. These are all areas that draw on the therapist's capacity to use 'self' in the therapy relationship, and getting better at using the qualities requires the supervisee to reflect on who they are, and which parts of their sense of self or personal history are evoked in their work with a client. Carroll (2009, 2010; Carroll and Gilbert 2011) have constructed an integrative model of supervision as learning-through-reflection. The aim of supervision is to create a reflective space in which the supervisee can find it possible to engage in 'transformational' learning, that encompasses all aspects of their emotional and personal response to their clients, and contributes to building a richly described sense of professional identity (Crocket 2004).

Supervision is not primarily concerned with the personal development of the therapist. However, supervision can make a valuable contribution to personal development if a supervision contract acknowledges that this is an acceptable area for exploration in supervision, and both supervisor and supervisee routinely reflect on the 'personal' dimension of work with clients.

Box 2.3: *The impact of the client on the therapist*

There are some clients who function as catalysts for the personal development of their therapists. Barry Duncan was a young intern, working in a residential unit for disturbed adolescents. The policy of the unit was to make extensive use of psychotropic medication to control patients. Duncan worked closely with a female client, Tamara, and began to realize that the medication that she was being prescribed were hindering her recovery. He eventually took a stand, challenged the director of the unit about the over-reliance on drugs, and lost his job. In an interview conducted several years later, Duncan (2005) described this as a 'turning point' in his life and his career – the moment when he realized the importance of courage, and became willing (like his client) to stand up for what was right.

Leigh McCulloch was already an experienced therapist when she began to work with a new client whose problems were rooted in a sense of 'not mattering' to others. In a highly dramatic and intense session, McCulloch invited her client to test this hypothesis, by looking directly into her face: 'if you look into my face, how does it seem to you that I am feeling toward you?'. This moment, and the process of change that followed for the client, were hugely significant for Leigh McCulloch as a person: . . . this has all been such a huge gift for me. Growing up, I never knew this level of human contact with others. Now I have that not only with my patients, but in my personal life. (McCulloch 2005: 184).

Other examples of therapist personal growth triggered by working with specific clients, or groups of clients, can be found in Dryden (1987), Goldfried (2001), Kahn and Harkavy-Friedman (1997), Kahn and Fromm (2000), Katz and Johnson (2006), Kottler and Carlson (2005), Prengel and Somerstein (2013) and Trotter-Mathison *et al.* (2010).

Workshops

A *workshop* can be defined as a stand-alone learning event, the duration of which can range from half a day to two or three days. Workshops play a particularly valuable role in meeting the continuing personal and professional development needs of therapists, because they are relatively accessible, in terms of cost and time, and allow practitioners to try out many different types of therapy method and personal development experience. By contrast, signing up for long-term training or an ongoing group, requires a major commitment, and closes down options around learning in areas not covered by that specific training programme or group. Workshops can also serve a valuable function in relation to therapist well-being, by providing time out from routine practice, and making it possible to network with colleagues. The limitation of workshops is that they tend to be pitched at a relatively introductory level, and offer little opportunity to practice or consolidate new skills, or explore new self-insights in-depth.

Broadening cultural horizons

One of the most significant and powerful ways of facilitating personal development is to seek out new types of cultural encounter. This kind of activity can involve choosing to work with clients from diverse cultural backgrounds, studying or receiving training in specific religious and cultural traditions and practices, friendship and travel. The life stories of leading figures in the field of counselling and psychotherapy, such as Carl Rogers and Jeffrey Kottler, demonstrate the profound influence on their identity that arose from time spent in China (Rogers) and Nepal (Kottler). Also relevant are accounts of therapists from other cultural backgrounds, who have then gone on to live and work in the USA (see, for example, Comas-Dias 2010; Mirsalimi 2010). An autoethnographic study by Charlés (2007) provides an exploration of ways in which he came to question some of his own personal values and attitudes, as the result of being an American working in the Philippines. Similar themes can be found in a report by Lemma (1999), on the experience of being a British psychologist in Bangladesh. The experience of being a cultural 'outsider' opens up many possibilities for learning about who one is, as a person, and how one relates to others.

> ## Box 2.4: *The interpersonal dynamic of training*
>
> The experience of therapy training can often function as a trigger for important personal development. In interviews with trainees in psychodynamic training, Davies (2008) found that participants talked about a range of sources of very significant stress within the training process, such as a sense of being judged as a person, and the fear that things might go badly wrong with their clients. Davies (2008) suggests that this intense stress creates a situation where the trainee conforms to the ideas and teachings of his teachers, as a strategy for survival. Rizq argues that the goal of training should be that the trainee is able to move beyond experiencing the trainer as a god-like authority figure, and arrive at a point of being able to *use* the tutor as 'someone through whom the student will be able to translate academic learning into real-life professional clinical practice' (2009: 368). A key factor here is that this kind of emotionally charged relationship with a tutor or trainer is not something that only occurs in a personal development group or in personal therapy, but permeates all aspects of training, such as seminars and case discussion groups. Both Rizq (2009) and Carlsson *et al.* (2011) propose that a vital stage in this transition is the experience on the part of the trainee that their ability as a therapist is recognized by their tutor. The findings of these studies make it possible to identify some of the personal development tasks and challenges that arise in training: revisiting strategies for coping with stress, learning about how one conforms or rebels in the presence of authority, accepting the affirmation of others that one is 'good enough'.

Work experience

There are many aspects of the experience of work that can contribute to personal development. The shift to a new job, or a new role within the same organization, inevitably presents challenges and opportunities for personal growth and development. Autobiographical accounts of the career trajectories of therapists, for example in collections edited by Dryden and Spurling (1989) and Goldfried (2001) or the autobiography of Marzillier (2010), consistently show that effective therapists use new work experiences as a trigger for personal and professional development. This process can involve seeking out new areas of work, in order to extend and complete one's understanding, or discovering that the need to respond to the demands of a new client group leads to a personal crisis of confidence and competence. Many therapists actively arrange internships, secondments, sabbaticals and visits in order to expose themselves to this source of learning. There is also evidence that the experience of work difficulties or a sense of incompetence in a work role can function as a stimulus to personal and professional development (Davis *et al.* 1987; Schroder and Davis 2004; Theriault and Gazzola 2006).

Life events

Significant events in the life of a therapist may lead to personal development. There are many types of life event that can happen to people: marriage, divorce, parenthood, bereavement, illness, accidents, disability, financial loss, being a victim of crime. These life events are hard for the person directly experiencing them, and also for those who are close to the primary person. For example, for a parent, the illness of a child can be more stressful than an illness to self. Research into the characteristics of experienced and highly respected therapists, by Jennings and Skovholt (1999) and others, has found that these practitioners report multiple occasions over the course of their lives when their experience of a major life event has resulted, in the long run, in enabling them to learn and grow as people as well as in their therapeutic role.

Box: 2.5: *Trauma in the life of a therapist*

Kaethe Weingarten has been a key figure in the area of narrative and family therapy for several years. Much of her work is concerned with supporting people who have experienced trauma, or are living through a period of trauma such as the terminal illness of a family member. In Weingarten (2010) she described some of the connections during the course of her career between trauma in her own life and similar difficulties in the lives of her clients. For example, Weingarten (2010) recounts how her initial training had not provided her with any strategies for working with clients who had experienced trauma. However, at that time, her mother was dying. She was able to draw on her experience with her mother, to develop a method of 'radical listening' that could be useful for trauma clients. Later in her career, when her daughter was seriously ill, she needed to work out how to hold a conversation with a particularly demanding client, around her own need to reduce the intensity and frequency of their meetings, in a way that would not leave the client feeling abandoned. This paper by Weingarten (2010) offers a glimpse into the kind of process that few therapists ever write about: the reciprocal interplay between coming to terms with a personal life event, and continuing to be responsive to clients. Other examples of therapists' accounts of ways in which significant life events have shaped their personal and professional development can be found in a special issue of the journal *Professional Psychology* (Callahan and Ditloff 2007).

Spiritual practice

An increasing proportion of counsellors, psychotherapists and mental health practitioners regard spiritual involvement as an essential element of their commitment to personal and professional development. The literature on the relationship between spiritual/religious traditions, and therapy, encompasses discussion of the therapeutic relevance of all known forms of spirituality. In terms of actual spiritual practice, many therapists make use of methods such as prayer, retreats, meditation, yoga, mindfulness, tai chi, shamanic ritual, and sweat lodges. Some therapists use wilderness experiences as a form of spiritual practice.

Art-making

Participation in art-making represents a personal development resource for many therapists, through such activities as music-making, painting, sculpture, poetry, drama and dance. The fact that art therapy and expressive therapies represent distinct approaches to therapy can obscure the reality that an involvement in art tends to be an important aspect of the lives of therapists from all schools and traditions. Art offers a reflective space in relation to the core questions of human existence, and acts as a reminder that facilitating change usually involves at least some moments of unpredictable and almost magical personal creativity. In addition, most forms of art are based around physical or bodily knowing, rather than verbal knowing – this can serve as a counterbalance to the over-reliance in most therapy approaches on the use of language.

Involvement in research

Carrying out research, or being involved in research as a participant, can offer opportunities to reflect on one's approach to therapy, and become open to new possibilities. Examples of some of the ways that this can happen can be found in Etherington (2004), Soldz and McCullough (2000) and Waters (2011). For the most part, the methods of personal development outlined in earlier sections of this chapter are grounded in *personal* knowing, and in various ways rely on reflection on personal experience. By contrast, although there is always some degree of personal knowing associated with doing research, the research process also offers a distinctive type of *de-centred* knowing. Most of the time, research is not primarily concerned with what the researcher thinks and feels, but instead trains its focus on how other people think, feel and act. Moreover, the meaning of whatever knowledge is generated by a research study only becomes clear when connections are made with the findings of prior studies (the 'literature'). An interest in research, therefore, can help therapists to see their own personal experience in a broader context.

Conclusions

The array of personal development methods that have been discussed in this chapter is not, and cannot be, comprehensive. There are therapists who find meaning and growth in cooking, gardening, politics, caring for family members, and many other activities. It would be valuable for everyone if more of these stories could be told, and made available, as sources of inspiration. In addition, little has ever been written about the balance between being a therapist, and these supplementary activities. No doubt there are people who are mainly artists, musicians, clergy or members of other occupational groups, for whom being a therapist is a supplementary source of personal development. Again, these stories are not readily accessible within the existing literature.

Taking this set of personal development methods as a whole, there are some tentative conclusions that can be offered. An obvious conclusion is that many possibilities exist. It therefore seems sensible to try out different personal development methods, at different times, to discover what works best for you. Another conclusion is that there are clear parallels between methods of personal development, and methods of therapy: groups, writing, meditation, therapy, art-making – these are all strategies that are widely used within contemporary counselling, psychotherapy and mental health care. There is plentiful evidence that clients are helped by these approaches, and also that they tend to have preferences around which methods they regard as most credible or relevant to their specific problems. If practitioners regard it as important to be attuned to attunement to client preferences then it makes sense to use personal development time to gain first-hand experience of a reasonably wide range of what is potentially on offer.

Theoretical and research perspectives

Introduction

Personal development is fundamentally a lived experience, a process of building up layers of awareness and personal knowing. It is also very much an individual activity, grounded in the particular learning needs of each practitioner. It is hard to imagine that therapist personal development could ever become driven by 'evidence-based' guidelines. At the same time it can be helpful to make use of ideas and examples that reach beyond the domain of individual experience, as a way of enabling reflection and meaning-making. The present chapter offers some ways of thinking about therapist personal development, drawn from theory and research. What follows does not claim to reflect a comprehensive and systematic review of the theoretical and research literature on this topic. Instead, we focus on some of the theoretical and research perspectives that have influenced us in our own development and have informed our work as trainers and supervisors.

Theoretical perspectives on learning and development

The field of theory and research into human learning and development comprises a massive literature. One of the important themes within this literature, in recent years, has been a general recognition that learning is not a passive process through which information and skills are channelled from teacher to student in a mechanical fashion, but that learners are actively involved in trying to make sense of their world, and attain practical mastery. This image of the learning process is often described as *constructivist*. The key idea is that the world contains a range of possibilities, and that each of us actively constructs our own version of reality, through a combination of personal discovery and collective co-construction. The theories of learning and development that are outlined in the following paragraphs need to be understood from a constructivist stance. It is a mistake to regard these theories as fixed templates of how development 'should' unfold. Rather, they describe some of the pathways of development that can be followed. Each person is located within a particular set of horizons, constructed by factors such as age, gender, culture, health and personal circumstances. As a result, each person negotiates his or her unique trajectory through and across these pathways.

The concept of 'development'

It is important to be aware of what we are talking about when we use the term 'development'. There is more to development than mere learning. The concept of development implies an irreversible shift from one level of understanding and functioning, to another level. For example, most people in contemporary societies undergo a developmental shift from 'adolescence' to 'adulthood'. During the period of adolescence, which may span several years, a person will learn a lot. For example they will learn about friendship and sex (as well as other things). But at some point the person enters a new stage of life, and needs to begin to learn about work and responsibility (and much else). In retrospect, it is possible to see that the person has followed a pathway that has led through childhood and adolescence, and that various events on this journey have shaped the way they approach the developmental task of being an adult. But there is something intrinsically new and unknown, for the person, in the transition that then occurs. All cultures incorporate rituals that facilitate such transitions, and provide pathways that the person can choose to follow.

Development therefore consists of shifts in the direction of more integrated and functional ways of being. Compared with an adolescent, we would expect an adult to be able to take a wider perspective on life, drawing on a broader horizon of understanding, and to be able to function effectively in a wider range of situations.

What does this mean for therapist personal development? It is helpful to think about this question from two angles. First, each therapist passes through a series of stages of *professional* development, such as novice or trainee, then qualified practitioner, then supervisor or trainer. Each of these 'normative' stages or transition points in the life course of a therapy career is associated with personal challenges and personal learning, and supported by culturally available rituals and training pathways. However, in parallel with these professional transitions, there are also *personal* shifts. For example, McCulloch (2005) describes how she arrived at a point, in her work as a therapist, when she realized that she did not understand what true 'intimacy' meant. This realization opened the door to a lengthy trajectory of personal learning around this topic. These personal shifts can be exciting and energizing, but also scary and destabilizing. Unlike the fairly well-defined pathways and transitions associated with professional development, there does not seem to be any particular sequence in which therapist development unfolds. It is all very personal. It is possible to identify the various domains within which therapist personal learning and awareness should occur (see, for example, Pieterse *et al.* 2013), but it is not possible to predict which issues will emerge as most salient for which therapist, or when this emergence will take place.

Theories of human development

A useful starting point for thinking about development is the model of stages of psychosocial development associated with the work of Erik Erikson (1950). This model considers development as occurring across the entire lifespan, in terms of eight general stages (Table 3.1). Erikson argued that each stage represented the point in life when a particular psychosocial issue or challenge would be most likely to be salient, and have the best chance of being resolved. However, all of these issues were relevant, to a greater or lesser extent, at all stages of life. In particular, the degree to which an issue had been successfully resolved earlier in the lifespan, would influence the capacity of the person to cope with the primary issue

TABLE 3.1 Erikson's model of psychosocial stages

Psychosocial issue/stage of development	Age
Trust–mistrust	Birth to 18 months
Autonomy–shame	18 months to 3 years
Initiative–guilt	3–5 years
Industry–inferiority	6–12 years
Identity–role confusion	12–18 years
Intimacy–isolation	18–35 years
Generativity–self-absorption	35–60 years
Integrity–despair	60 to death

associated with the age group to which the person belonged. For example, in modern society the teenage years are very much associated with the struggle to develop a social role and identity ('who am I?'). The extent to which a person can develop a secure sense of identity will inevitably be influenced by their capacity to trust others – an issue that is the main theme of the first months of life.

The Erikson model can be used as a framework for making sense of therapist personal development. Being able to respond effectively to the challenges associated with the role of therapist may depend on practitioner 'unfinished business' from earlier, or current, development stages. For example, the capacity to form a therapeutic bond with a client draws on the ability to trust. The capacity to establish boundaries draws on a sense of autonomy. The capacity to be actively involved in the world of the client depends on therapist acceptance of his or her capacity to take the initiative. During their active working careers, most counselling, psychotherapy and mental health practitioners proceed through Erikson's *intimacy–isolation* or *generativity–self-absorption* stages of development. There are striking parallels between these stages, and widely reported challenges experienced by therapists within their work roles. The intensity of work with clients can lead therapists to neglect family and friendship relationships, resulting in interpersonal isolation (Henry 1966, 1977). The level of emotional demand associated with working with people in crisis can, over time, result in therapist burnout that is reflected in self-absorption and a struggle for occupational survival, rather than in making a contribution commensurate with senior status within the profession.

The Erikson model provides a valuable starting point for thinking about developmental themes, and tasks may be reflected in therapist personal development. Other developmental therapists have built on Erikson's ideas in ways that offer additional insights. One of the most important developmental therapists is Dan McAdams (1985, 1993, 2001, 2004, 2006, 2009) who has paid particular attention to the ways in which developmental themes are expressed in the types of stories that people tell about themselves, and in the ways in which these stories are constructed. McAdams offers us a framework for standing back from our own stories, and reflecting on the type of story that we consistently tell, and how that story is constructed (McAdams *et al.* 1996). He argues that being able to live a satisfying life, and making effective connections with different people in different situations, depends on the possession of a secure sense of identity. For McAdams, personal identity is a narrative construction – it is the story we tell ourself and others about who we are. That story needs to be sufficiently rich and complex to reflect the multiple relationships and possibilities in our life. At the same time a life-story needs to be sufficiently coherent to convey a sense of purpose and consistent set of values. McAdams suggests that life-stories are broadly organized around 'chapters' or 'lifetime periods'. Within each chapter, there are a number of self-defining or autobiographical memories of specific events, that encapsulate our core beliefs, goals and relationship patterns. McAdams (1993) has used the term 'nuclear episodes' to describe these events, because there is a sense in which they reflect the 'nucleus' of who we really are. For example, the self-defining narratives of some people portray the person as a hero who goes out and gets what they want or need ('agency' stories). For other people, by contrast, their self-defining narratives convey an importance of being with others and working together ('communion' narratives). Life-stories are also organized around sequential patterns. *Contamination* narratives describe situations where life was good then something bad happened. By contrast, *redemption* narratives describe the opposite pattern – something positive emerging from negative experiences.

The work of McAdams represents a valuable resource for therapists, in relation to our personal development, because most of the methods that are used to facilitate therapist development, such as personal therapy or keeping a reflective journal, are based in a process of telling one's story. Many of the learning tasks in Part 2 of the present book are designed to facilitate access to nuclear episodes or self-defining autobiographical memories, and to reflect on what these episodes mean in terms of one's sense of identity as a therapist. Other learning tasks invite reflection on longer segments of one's life-story, such as chapters and sequences. An appreciation of the way that life-stories are structured can be helpful as a therapist. For example, therapy can be regarded as a process that involves a shift from a contamination narrative ('I was fine until I got depressed') to a redemption story ('it was coming to terms with depression that allowed me to get in touch with my assertiveness'). Therapist personal development can be seen as a redemption narrative; a therapist who described his or her life as a contamination narrative would not inspire hope. Therapy is also a process that involves helping people to achieve an appropriate (for them) balance between themes of agency and communion. Hansen (2009) makes use of the narrative developmental perspective of McAdams in suggesting that therapist personal development is essentially a process of 'self-storying' – when we engage in personal development activities we are gradually building a more vivid, accessible, differentiated and coherent life-story, which functions as a resource in our work with clients.

Suggested further reading

McAdams, D.P. (2001) The psychology of life stories, *Review of General Psychology*, 5, 100–22.

Sugarman, L. (2001) *Life Span Development: Frameworks, Accounts and Strategies*, 2nd edn. London: Sage.

Theories of therapist professional development

There have been several attempts to identify stages in the professional development of therapists. Some of these models, such as the work of Goldberg (1988), describe therapist development in terms of a journey or quest that is characterized by recurring themes. Other theorists have suggested that there are discrete stages in therapist development. For example, in their own research, Ronnestad and Skovholt (2013) found that therapists pass through the following phases over the course of their career: novice student, advanced student, novice professional, experienced professional, senior professional. In their book, Ronnestad and Skovholt (2013) review and discuss several other models of therapist professional development. On the whole, these models have tended to highlight specifically professional or job-related aspects of development, and have regarded more personal dimensions of development as secondary. An important conclusion across various studies and models is the observation that therapists undergo a personal and professional significant shift in the period immediately following primary training, reflecting a search for an approach to practice that is explicitly aligned to personal values (see, for example, Carlsson and Schubert 2009). This shift offers an example of the way in which personal development issues may be triggered by professional challenges and transition points.

Suggested further reading

Ronnestad, M.H. and Skovholt, T.M. (2013) *The Developing Practitioner. Growth and Stagnation of Therapists and Counselors*. New York: Routledge.

Box 3.1: *The concept of transformational learning*

Personal development can sometimes be experienced as a process of building something – gradually adding awareness, insight and new ways of relating, bit by bit. However, there are moments when personal development may be experienced as an act of transformation, a process of being torn apart and rebuilt along different lines. The concept of *transformative learning* was introduced, within the field of adult learning by Mezirow (1991) and in therapy by White (2004). The idea of 'quantum change' has been used within the psychotherapy literature to describe occasions when clients change in an all-encompassing and fundamental way (Miller 2004). Notions of 'peak experience' and 'epiphany' refer to a similar territory within human experiencing. It is certainly the case some people describe therapy training as having been transformative within their lives (see, for example, Alred *et al.* 2004; Chang 2011), although other therapists describe transformative experiences triggered by involvement with clients (Kottler and Carlson 2005). There are also people who have undergone a transformative episode prior to entering training. It is a big mistake to assume that transformative 'Hollywood' moments represent the only type of development that is worth having, or even that it is the most important type of development. It depends on the person.

Models of experiential learning

The idea of *experiential* learning refers to a process of learning that is based on reflecting on action and experience. Experiential learning can be contrasted with conventional classroom or textbook-based learning, which is concerned with acquiring information that is divorced or abstracted from its real-life context. Because it is grounded in everyday activity, experiential knowing inevitably needs to take account of the emotions and values of the learner. The topic of experiential learning has been of great interest to tutors and trainers in fields such as medicine, nursing, social work, counselling and psychotherapy, that require students to gain much of their learning in the context of a practice placement. Within the extensive literature on experiential learning, the models devised by Kolb and Lewin are particularly relevant to the area of therapist personal development.

David Kolb was an educational researcher who proposed that it was necessary to view experiential learning as a cyclical process consisting of four main phases (Figure 3.1; Kolb and Fry 1975). In their everyday activity, the person has an experience that seems significant to them in some way. In order to make sense of what has happened, the person reflects on what has happened. To deepen and extend their understanding

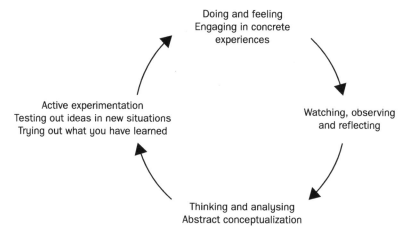

Doing and feeling
Engaging in concrete
experiences

Active experimentation
Testing out ideas in new situations
Trying out what you have learned

Watching, observing
and reflecting

Thinking and analysing
Abstract conceptualization

FIGURE 3.1 Kolb's cycle of experiential learning.

of the event, the person refers to relevant theory and research, and creates some kind of 'working model' or hypothesis regarding the experience (abstract conceptualization). This model or hypothesis is then used as a guide to action the next time the person is in the same situation (active experimentation). These actions then generate a new experience, which forms the basis for a further cycle of learning. This framework for understanding experiential learning may seem familiar to many counsellors and psychotherapists, because it is essentially the same as the 'three-stage' models (exploration > insight > action) of the counselling process developed by leading figures such as Carkhuff (1969a, 1969b), Egan (2004) and Hill (2004).

The Kolb model has some important implications for therapist personal development. What it tells us is that none of the separate points in the cycle (having an experience; reflecting on that experience; making sense of the experience in terms of concepts; experimenting with new behaviour) is sufficient in itself – what is necessary is to be able to move through the cycle. For example, a practitioner may attend personal therapy for months or years, but if they do not figure out how to use this source of learning to enable them to act in different ways, they are not really developing. Similarly, a practitioner who acquires intellectual insight cannot be regarded as 'knowing' about his or her field of interest, unless that abstract knowledge is linked to action and first-hand experience.

Another useful way of thinking about experiential learning is associated with the work of the social psychologist Kurt Lewin, who made major contributions in the areas of action learning and action research (Marrow 1969). Lewin pointed out that, in respect of being able to respond to events in the social world, a person will almost always possess some kind of common-sense understanding or set of coping strategies. In order to learn a new way of responding, the person needs to be able to let go of his or her existing ideas and strategies, in order to allow a new way of responding to be constricted. He described this process as a cycle of 'unfreezing' followed by 're-freezing'. What this means is that genuine personal learning involves a period of time during which the person is *less* competent, leading into a gradual growth of competence at a new and higher level. This idea is also reflected in many 'transition curve' models, which hypothesize that when a person is faced with a difficult new situation (such as moving to a new country), they may need to pass through a period of personal crisis and re-appraisal, before emerging stronger. The key message here is that experiential learning is not necessarily a cumulative and linear process in which understanding or awareness develops piece by piece. Instead, experiential learning is likely to include phases where the person feels as though they are getting nowhere, or even moving backwards.

The Kolb and Lewin models of experiential learning highlight the cyclical nature of personal development. They remind us that development is not a matter of doing the same thing over and over again, but requires different types of activity at different times. They also serve as a reminder that personal development can be fun, exciting and satisfying at some points in the cycle, but hard work and frustrating at other points. These models emphasize the importance of *feedback* from others. In practice, the impetus to shift from one stage of development (or comfort zone) to the next, comes from a willingness to be open to the impact that one has on other people. These models also emphasize the necessity to engage in risk and experimentation – true development requires a willingness to do something new and potentially scary.

The concept of learning style

An intellectual and practical spin-off from research into experiential learning has been a body of work into the topic of *learning style*. Observation of how people learn in real-life situations, makes it clear that different people have different preferred ways of learning. One of the most influential models of learning style, developed by Honey and Mumford (1982), is based on the Kolb model. Honey and Mumford suggest that people tend to be most comfortable in one of the Kolb phases of learning, and may actively avoid other stages. For example, one therapist might devote his or her personal development time to taking part in all sorts of different experiential workshops – Gestalt therapy one weekend, a spiritual retreat the next. Meanwhile, a colleague may dedicate their personal development time to keeping a detailed personal journal. However, it seems certain that there are other important dimensions of learning style that go beyond the categories specified in the Kolb model. People differ in the extent to which they can make use of various channels of communication, such as verbal, imagery-based and musical/rhythmic. People differ in the degree to which they learn best on their own or in groups. Within group-based learning some people do better in highly structured and directed groups, whereas others learn more when the group is organized around more democratic lines.

Effective personal development probably consists of a judicious mix of what works for you (that is, activities centred around a preferred learning style), alongside activities that have been chosen on the basis that they draw on less-used or dormant personal learning capabilities. It is also helpful for counsellors, psychotherapists and mental health practitioners to be able to identify their own learning style, and to possess an understanding and appreciation of the preferred learning styles of other people. At least some clients and service users will not be able to relate to the preferred learning style of their therapist. For example, a therapist who personally prefers a predominantly reflective way of learning, such as person-centred therapy, may struggle to engage with clients who prefer a more action-oriented form of learning. A client who makes sense of life largely through images, will struggle to get on the same wavelength as a therapist who is highly verbal.

Box 3.2: *'Big picture' theories of personal development*

The approach taken in this book has been to view therapist personal development as an everyday, pragmatic kind of activity – being committed to learning about yourself is a necessary and inevitable part of the package when you sign up as a therapist. However, it can also be useful to think about personal development as a grander, more heroic enterprise. The person-centred and humanistic concept of *self-actualization* represents a framework for understanding personal development that has meaning for many counsellors, psychotherapists and mental health practitioners. The Jungian concept of *individuation* can serve a similar function. The idea of self-actualization or actualizing tendency refers to a general human need to move in the direction of fulfilling one's potential. The notion of individuation has a similar meaning, but introduces additional elements, such as reconciling conflicting parts of the self, and gaining awareness of unconscious aspects of experience (Dirkx 2000; Fordham 1985). Exploring these narratives, and the literatures that they have generated, can open up a deeper sense of the possibilities of personal development.

Learning and development in a social context: communities of practice

Research and theory around learning and development has largely focused on the process and outcomes of formal, structured learning and teaching opportunities facilitated by professional teachers and trainers. An alternative approach has been developed by two social anthropologists, Jean Lave and Etienne Wenger, who have explored the organization and functioning of informal learning networks that occur in everyday life (Lave and Wenger 1991). Their research has looked in-depth at groups of people who are committed to an area of work, or practice, and have evolved ways of developing and sharing knowledge that is relevant to their goals. Examples of groups they have studied are self-employed tailors in a developing country, people working in a meat processing plant and workers in an insurance claims office (Lave and Wenger 1991; Wenger 1998). What they found was that a community of practice consists of a complex set of informal meetings and conversations between people. At the heart of the community are people with long-standing, expert knowledge, whereas at the periphery are those who are just beginning to participate in the community and who spend time just observing and asking questions. Gradually, those peripheral participants gradually get drawn into more complex and demanding aspects of the work. However, exchange of information is not hierarchical. Instead, there is a high degree of openness and cooperation between members of the community. Because this form of learning takes place outside the classroom, there are no formal entrance or attendance criteria, or examinations. Knowledge and learning are oriented around getting the job done. In recent years, many large organizations have recognized the value of communities of practice, and have tried to find ways to promote and support this kind of informal networking among employees. Research by Gabbay and Le May (2011) into the functioning of primary health care practices in the NHS in Britain, found that the most effective practices operate as communities of practice.

Research into communities of practice is relevant for an understanding of therapist personal development, because it shows that learning and development within groups of people with a shared purpose and occupational identity (such as groups of counsellors, psychotherapists and mental health practitioners) depends not only on the commitment and motivation of individual members, but is also strongly influenced by the presence (or absence) of a vibrant learning community. Sometimes these learning communities grow up around training programmes and therapy centres, and sometimes they consist of networks of practitioners who work with a specific client group, or use a particular therapy approach. What they offer are opportunities to learn from others, share experience, and consult others around difficult issues. The concept of a community of practice also provides a potentially valuable perspective on the pathways through which people become therapists and mental health practitioners in the first place. We live in a complex and fragmented culture and society in which the task of coping with fractured relationships and 'inappropriate' emotions is a challenge faced by a significant proportion of the population. There exists a very wide and loosely defined 'community of practice' organized around strategies for dealing with this type of problem in living: self-help books and websites, magazine articles, public talks, TV programmes, slimming clubs, and so on. In terms of the Lave and Wenger model, these activities represent the real periphery of the interlocking sets of communities of practice that make up the counselling, psychotherapy and mental health professions. Typically, this periphery is where people who eventually become therapists, start to become interested in psychotherapeutic practices.

Box 3.3: *How therapist development is shaped by cultural context*

One of the triggers for therapist reflection, learning and development, that is discussed elsewhere in this chapter, is the experience of working with clients who have undergone traumatic events in their lives. This kind of situation is always hard for therapists. A study by O'Neill (2010) highlights some of the ways in which the impact of trauma work depends on the type of community within which one is living. O'Neill (2010) studied therapeutic helpers who worked in small, remote, tight-knit, rural communities in the far north of Canada. These therapists described very strong ties with the community, that made it hard for them to find any respite from the issues presented by their clients:

> . . . in my life I feel I have to try to support this community. I can never walk away, not emotionally, not spiritually. Even if I could physically leave, I would still be tied . . . still be connected. There would be a sense of obligation or duty. (p. 137)
> . . . being so bound up within the community as a whole and the individuals in it means that you are so much more vulnerable to the pain that goes with it; the pain of deaths and injuries and emotional trauma. You can't see these people that you care about and see that they are suffering and not care too. (p. 137)
> . . . you don't have a place you can refer someone to. (p. 137)

O'Neill (2010) describes these practitioners as being 'caught up' in crises that occurred: 'this type of work has the potential to take over a person's life' (p. 140). As a result, despite the existence of strong support networks, many of these therapists were profoundly affected by this aspect of their work.

Understanding personal development through different theoretical lenses

At the present time, the field of counselling and psychotherapy is in a state of transition. To a large extent, therapy theory and research is still dominated by specific traditions or 'schools' of thought, such as psychodynamic, cognitive–behavioural, person-centred, family systems and so on. However, at the same time an ever-increasing proportion of practitioners describe themselves as eclectic, integrative or pluralistic in theoretical orientation. This situation has acted as a barrier to the emergence of a theoretical foundation for making sense of therapist personal development. This is because each specific theoretical tradition is associated with a distinct personal development agenda, whereas the personal development implications of post-schoolism forms of practice have not yet been worked out.

The following list provides an indication of the meaning and aims of personal development activity as understood within some mainstream theoretical traditions:

- *Psychodynamic/psychoanalytic.* The development of insight, particularly in respect of early attachment experiences and progressions through developmental stages. Cultivating awareness of how one responds to others (counter-transference).

- *Cognitive–behavioural.* Becoming able to draw on personal experiences of core CBT concepts and techniques, such as negative automatic thoughts, cognitive schema, use of relaxation and mindfulness skills, etc.

- *Person-centred.* The development of the 'core conditions' of acceptance, empathy and congruence. Becoming able to engage with others at a level of relational depth. Development of a capacity for accessing and using an inner, experiential 'felt sense'. Gaining an understanding of personal experiences of conditions of worth and locus of evaluation.

- *Systemic/family therapy*. Developing an understanding of how child-hood experiences in the family of origin shape current patterns of personal relationship. Making sense of intergenerational sources of personal identity. Engaging in a process of self-differentiation.
- *Feminist therapy*. Developing an awareness of personal development around gender identity. Gaining an understanding of historical and cultural factors that shaped personal choices.

The personal development themes listed above are incomplete – the intention is not to provide a comprehensive account of how personal development is understood within each tradition, but to highlight the contrasting emphases across traditions. For the most part, these ideas are implicit within the literature associated with each approach, rather than being explicitly stated. The person-centred approach is unusual in being clear about the type of 'person' that personal development is aiming to produce (Rogers 1961).

It is not possible to identify distinctive personal development goals associated with integrative and eclectic approaches to therapy. For the most part, these approaches consist of various types of combination of mainstream 'unitary' theories, and as a result encourage personal development in the areas specified by these core models.

The personal development agenda of a pluralistic framework for practice (Cooper and McLeod 2011) is somewhat different. A pluralistic position invites consideration of all of the personal development themes outlined above. However, it also suggests that such explorations might occur in the context of lifelong learning, rather than all of it being addressed at the same time during primary training. The personal development agenda of primary training in pluralistic therapy consists of three main areas of focus:

- developing a capacity for collaboration cooperation and dialogue, and understanding the factors in one's personal life history that enable or inhibit this capacity;
- understanding who you are in relation to the culture within which you live – a specific task here is to become aware of how cultural resources have contributed to one's own personal learning and development;
- identifying one's own 'starting point' or 'menu' in respect of ideas, skills, qualities and personal experiences that are available to be used to help clients to achieve their goals for therapy.

The personal and professional development learning tasks outlined in Part 2 of this book are informed by a pluralistic stance. Many of these tasks are inspired by mainstream therapy models, such as psychodynamic or CBT. However, the intention has been to present them in such a way that they make sense to students and practitioners from all traditions of counselling, psychotherapy and mental health practice.

Research into the qualities and attributes of effective therapists

A valuable place to look, in respect of how personal development issues have an impact on the process of therapy, is within research into the characteristics of effective and ineffective therapists. What are the qualities and attributes that are associated with success and failure as a therapist, and what do effective therapists do to develop these qualities? In recent years, these questions have been approached from two directions. One line of inquiry has explored the attributes of effective therapists. A complementary line of inquiry has examined the characteristics of ineffective therapists.

It is possible to identify effective therapists either through peer nomination (for example inviting practitioners within a region to list the therapists to whom they would refer members of their family) or through outcome statistics obtained from scales completed by clients at every session. There is no evidence that being an effective therapist is associated with length and type of training, intelligence, attitudes, personality or presence/absence of mental health issues. Rather, effective or 'master' therapists appear to be people who have highly developed interpersonal skills, coupled with an 'intense commitment to learn' (Jennings and Skovholt 1999; Ronnestad and Skovholt 2013; Skovholt and Jennings 2004). These two qualities merge in a willingness and ability to seek and use feedback from clients, and to use personal life events (such as personal illness, marital difficulties) as a source of learning that ultimately informs therapeutic awareness.

It has been harder to pin down the attributes in ineffective therapists, for the obvious reason that practitioners are reluctant to take part in research on this topic. However, it is possible to begin to assemble a pattern, based on evidence from some research studies, alongside anecdotal evidence and case descriptions of examples of abusive therapy. In interpreting this body of evidence, it needs to be kept in mind that individuals who clearly lack empathy, or who are overtly manipulative and destructive, are usually filtered out at selection or during training. In addition, there are therapists who may possess only moderate levels of interpersonal skills or commitment to learn, or who find certain client groups to be hard for them to work with. These therapists can be regarded as perhaps being a disappointment to some or most of their clients, but tend not to do harm. Ineffective therapists, therefore, are those who appear to function in a facilitative manner, but in practice cause damage to many of their clients.

While acknowledging the limitations of the evidence base in this area, it is nevertheless possible to highlight two main danger signals in respect of therapist attributes. Harmful practitioners are people who are using their role as therapist to compensate for their own problems, and/or have a narcissistic or grandiose sense of their own superiority. The most compelling evidence for the destructiveness of therapists who are using their role as a source of gratification and compensation, comes from studies of practitioners who engage in sexual relationships with their clients. The most compelling evidence for the destructive potential of therapist narcissism comes from studies of cases where clients report that their therapist has been abusive (for example Bates 2006).

In making sense of research into the characteristics of effective and ineffective therapists, it is useful to take account of research into the early childhood experiences of people who choose to enter training in counselling, psychotherapy and other mental health professions. A survey conducted by Burton and Topham (1997) found that therapists reported high levels of childhood experience of sexual abuse, neglect, parental mental health problems or parental marital conflict. Similar results have been found in other studies. What this means is that a significant proportion of therapists have personal experience of the types of problems being exhibited by their clients. The 'wounded healer' model (Guggenbuhl-Craig 1971; Nouwen 1979; Zerubavel and Wright 2012) suggests that these early 'wounds' are the source of the sensitivity, compassion and motivation that might enable someone to be an effective 'healer'. However, being a wounded healer only works in the interests of the client if the wounds have been sufficiently healed to the extent that they can function as a positive resource (Cain 2002; Gilbert and Stickley 2012; Gilroy *et al.* 2001; Martin 2011; Rippere and Williams 1985). If the wounds have not been healed to a sufficient extent, then the therapist may be in a position of using clients as a source of support (that is, the client healing the therapist).

The findings of these studies begin to suggest some of the areas that are particularly important in relation to therapist personal development. Specifically, they point to the necessity for therapists to have an awareness of the early experiences that underpinned and led to their choice of therapy as a career, and to make sure that, as far as possible, they are using these experiences in the service of their clients. For example, it may be possible to trace therapist narcissism back to the experience of being the child who was the 'peacemaker' in the family. This quality is a source of trouble within the therapist role, and is perhaps something that colleagues and supervisors might well be urged to confront when they observe it in practitioners. Narcissistic and grandiose therapists are those who believe that they know the answers; by contrast, effective therapists are those who possess a measure of professional self-doubt and an 'intense commitment to learn'.

> ### Box 3.4: *Personal recovery in therapists working in the field of eating disorders*
>
> A balanced and informative analysis of some of the issues associated with the 'wounded healer' model can be found in a study by Costin and Johnson (2002) of therapists who have had eating disorders, who have chosen to work with clients with eating disorders. In one of the therapy centres discussed in this paper, 85% of the staff were people who had 'recovered' from an eating disorder. The directors of these centres believed that staff who were able to draw on this type of personal experience were more likely to be more hopeful, empathic and motivated, and less shame-inducing and grandiose. The risks of employing such staff were regarded as slight, but included counter-transference vulnerability, sense of mission and risk of personal relapse. Overall, the directors of these centres strongly believed that therapists with eating disorder personal histories had a great deal to offer, as long as the person could demonstrate that they had been 'recovered' for more than two years.

Suggested further reading

Theory and research around the qualities and attributes of effective therapists is discussed in more detail in:

McLeod, J. (2013) *An Introduction to Counselling*, 5th edn. Maidenhead: Open University Press (Chapter 24).

Research into the impact of different therapist personal development activities

Various research studies have attempted to examine the impact of therapist development activities, such as personal therapy or participation in a personal development group, on therapist effectiveness with clients, and on specific therapy skills such as empathy. On the whole, these studies have produced somewhat inconclusive results, probably for two main reasons. First, therapist personal development activities do not take place in isolation. For example, if a student is involved in a personal development group it is likely that they may be receiving personal therapy, keeping a learning journal, attending experiential workshops, engaged in self-help reading and talking things through with colleagues. It is therefore very difficult to design a study that focuses on the impact of just one of these activities – in reality, they tend to be inextricably interconnected. A second reason why there have been inconclusive findings in this area is that the relationship between personal development work and therapist effectiveness may not be linear, but may in fact be complex and reciprocal. For example, it might be reasonable to hypothesize that therapists who have had more personal therapy may be more effective than those who have had less personal therapy. This would suggest a linear relationship between these factors. But it may be that therapists who regard themselves as less effective seek more personal therapy as a means of compensating and catching up. This would suggest a reciprocal relationship between these factors. It could also be that there are differences among therapists in the extent to which they benefit from different activities. Maybe the effectiveness of some therapists is massively helped by personal therapy, whereas for others it is helped by participation in spiritual practice. This would suggest that the relationship between personal therapy and effectiveness was complex, and mediated by other factors. It may well be that at some point in the future, someone will be imaginative enough to come up with a research design that will address these issues. At present, though, the important question of the extent to which personal development activity enhances effectiveness, cannot be answered with any confidence.

An overview of some of the main research themes and methodologies within the area of therapist development, is provided below.

Personal development groups

Several studies have been published of participant experiences of personal development groups offered in the context of therapy training (Ieva *et al.* 2009; Lennie 2007; Payne 1999, 2010; Robson and Robson 2008; Sammons and Speight 2008; Spencer 2006; Wheeler *et al.* 1998). Although each of these studies offers valuable insights, it is difficult to generalize on the basis of this body of evidence: researchers have asked different questions and have examined different types of training experience. One theme that emerges across several studies is a general sense of dissatisfaction on the part of both staff and group members. A further theme that is apparent in several studies is the extent to which participants are concerned about whether there is sufficient emotional safety and confidentiality within the group (see, for example, Robson and Robson 2008). In a questionnaire survey of participants who had completed a predominantly group-based introductory counselling skills course, MacKenzie and Hamilton (2007) found that trainees described substantial positive gains in relationship satisfaction and self-awareness. Rowell and Benshoff (2008) conducted a comparative study, looking at differences in cultural awareness in students who had participated in a cultural awareness personal growth group, and those who had received cultural awareness training through classroom instruction. This study found significantly enhanced levels of awareness in the students who had been in groups.

Of considerable relevance to an understanding of what happens in personal development groups, is the major study of encounter group process and outcome conducted by Lieberman *et al.* (1973) in the USA. In that investigation it was found that positive outcomes were associated with groups in which emotional stimulation was accompanied by meaning-making – where only one of the factors was present, outcomes were significantly diminished. The other headline finding from Lieberman *et al.* (1973) was that in some groups, around 10% of participants could be described, by the end, as 'emotional casualties' who had been damaged by the experience. The research approach used by Lieberman and colleagues could readily be applied in the study of personal development groups for therapy trainees and students, but this has not happened.

Personal therapy

There have been a large number of studies that have explored the characteristics and proportion of practitioners who make use of personal therapy, and the impact of therapy on their well-being and therapeutic effectiveness (Bike *et al.* 2009; Curtis *et al.* 2004; Orlinsky *et al.* 2011). These studies have shown that at least 80% of therapists have engaged in personal therapy at some point in their careers, and that most of these practitioners report that this experience has been extremely valuable for them. There have been no studies that have been able to examine directly the effect of practitioner personal therapy on actual client outcomes – this would be an extremely difficult study to carry out. Edwards (2013) has reviewed research into the specific issues associated with mandated personal therapy undertaken by students during training.

Keeping a reflective journal

There do not appear to have been any studies that have explored the experiences of trainees or experienced therapists who use journal writing to facilitate their personal development. However, there have been many studies that have investigated the process and outcome of therapeutic writing in different client groups (Bolton *et al.* 2004; Lepore and Smyth 2002). In general, these studies have found that therapeutic writing is a valuable therapeutic tool for clients. It seems reasonable to assume that it would therefore also represent a valuable developmental tool for therapists.

Narrative accounts of therapist personal development

As mentioned above, it is hard to tease out the usefulness or otherwise of specific personal development methods, such as personal development groups or personal therapy, because the people who participate in these activities are almost always engaged in other developmental activities at the same time. It is therefore useful to look at autobiographical accounts of personal and professional development written by therapists. These accounts include descriptions of the experience of personal therapy (Anonymous 2011; Comas-Dias 2010; Curtis 2011; Dryden 2005; Freeman 2011; Hill 2005; Kirsch 2005; Masson 1991; Pinsof 2005) as well as broader accounts of professional development as a whole (Dryden and Spurling 1989; Haldeman 2010; Marzillier 2010; Soldz and McCullough 2000). Almost all of these accounts describe 'false starts' made by therapists, for example trying out one or two personal therapists before finding the right one, and making use of different types of training experience. This kind of process can be valuable, enabling a practitioner to learn about what does not work (at least, what does not work for them), and to become more sensitive to any vulnerability and ambivalence in their own clients. These narratives of therapist development provide a crucial resource for the profession, in demonstrating the complexity of therapist professional development and the extent to which positive learning depends on active choices made by practitioners, based on their own personal values and preferences. Also relevant here are the stories of those undergoing training as therapists (Buchanan and Hughes 2001; Folkes-Skinner *et al.* 2010; Harding-Davies *et al.* 2004; Johns 1998).

These are the main areas of research into therapist personal development – examples of specific studies are provided in various places throughout this book.

Box 3.5: *Being and becoming a therapist has an impact on personal relationships*

A recurring theme in studies of the experience of training as a counsellor, psychotherapist or mental health practitioner is the impact of training on the way that the trainee relates to his or her spouse and family members (Kannan and Levitt 2009; Pack 2010; Rath 2008; Truell 2001). For example, in a study by Rath (2008) women who were training to be rape crisis counsellors described significant shifts in their relationships with their partners:

> . . . when we were discussing partners and I said 'my husband sulks'. And she [another course member] said 'well after he's sulked for a while do you then give in?' And I said 'yes'. And she said 'well you know what you are teaching

> him, what you're teaching is if he sulks on you you'll sort of
> do what he wants'. I went 'oh God, yes'. Twenty years and
> it's just dawned on me. (p. 26)
>
> One participant, whose marriage ended during the training, observed
> that:
>
>> . . . . what I find now is that having analysed a lot of things I
>> can't fool myself anymore. I'm almost sad that I can't. I
>> analysed a lot of things about my relationship with my
>> husband instead of just saying aren't I lucky and isn't this
>> nice. And haven't I got a nice secure marriage and focusing
>> on all the positive things about him. I looked at the negative
>> things about the relationship and about him, and having
>> looked at them I had to act on them I couldn't pretend they
>> weren't there anymore. (pp. 25–6)
>
> These examples illustrate some of the very direct ways that the effects of
> therapy training ripples out into family life. The trainee is learning new
> ways of making sense of emotions and relationships, and engaging in new
> types of conversations. This leads the person in training to have a different
> sense of self, and to initiate different ways of talking with other people in
> everyday life situations. In turn, these changes elicit reactions from
> others. Similar themes were found by Garrity (2011), in a study of sexual
> abuse counsellors who had completed their training before starting to
> work with this client group.

The research agenda

The topic of therapist personal development has not been the focus for
any type of rigorous and systematic programme of research. As a result,
the evidence base in this area is fragmented and incomplete, has not been
subjected to critical review, and does not provide reliable guidance for practice. It is highly probable that a large number of studies have been
conducted by Masters and Doctoral students, but never published. It
seems obvious that research into therapist personal development is one of
the lines of inquiry that will form an essential element in solving the puzzle
of what it is that makes some therapists more effective than others in relation to client outcomes. The existing research into therapist personal
development supplies a starting point and basis for further work, and there
are many research questions of practical and theoretical relevance that
are waiting to be investigated.

Conclusions

The aim of this chapter has been to offer some wider perspectives on therapist personal development, informed by theory and research. It is clear that there are many theoretical perspectives that are potentially relevant, and many research studies that provide snapshots of how therapist development unfolds. However, there are no grounds for complacency. There is much more that is not known about therapist personal development, than is known. There are many people from marginalized or disempowered social groups who experience great difficulty, and much hurt, in their journey through therapist training. Conversely, it would be hard to say that anyone really understands what constitutes an optimal training environment for therapists, in terms of promoting personal development. There is no literature on non-optimal pathways of development, such as the experiences of people who fail to become therapists, who quit the profession or are thrown out. There are differences between men and women in the kinds of developmental pathways that are open. These are just some of the important areas that await further investigation and discussion.

CHAPTER 4

Professional development: maintaining and enhancing practical competence and career progression

Introduction

In the introduction to this book it was argued that personal development and professional development can be regarded as existing on a continuum. Counsellors, psychotherapists and mental health practitioners are always engaged in a process of learning and reflection. Some of these learning activities are more oriented to the person of the therapist, whereas other activities are more oriented to specific job-related skills and knowledge. However, this is not an either/or situation. For someone who is committed to doing the best they can as a therapist, all learning has both a personal and professional dimension. The intertwined nature of personal and professional development is reflected in the varied, and sometimes confusing, ways that these terms are used in different organizational contexts. In some settings, the term 'personal development' is used to describe attendance on training courses and professional updating seminars. In other settings, 'professional development' may refer to all areas of development of staff members, including the use of personal therapy.

This chapter concentrates on the 'professional' end of the personal–professional development continuum and professional development is defined as 'learning activities that are primarily aimed at promoting specific job-relevant skills and knowledge'. It is possible to identify a number of key domains of therapist professional development:

- learning about specific therapeutic techniques and interventions;
- updating and awareness training around general issues, such as cultural difference, disability, research evidence, applying ethical guidelines;
- consolidating and deepening a sense of professional identity;
- involvement in specific projects, such as carrying out a research study or initiating a therapy service for a new client population;
- career planning;
- maintaining practitioner well-being.

Meaningful learning development within each of these domains can be pursued using a variety of methods. For example, learning about a new therapy technique can be accomplished through private study, making use of the skills of a mentor or supervisor, attendance at an in-house training workshop or completion of an accredited external qualification. It would be tedious and repetitive to attempt to itemize all of the potential methods that could be applied in relation to each domain of professional development. Instead, the following section offers an overview of the most widely used methods.

Box 4.1: *Professional development: it is never too soon to start*

There can be a tendency for students on training programmes to assume that professional development is not something that they need to think about at that stage in their lives. After all, they are immersed in a demanding, all-encompassing period of training, and therefore developing at a maximum capacity. They probably do not have therapy jobs, so the idea of engaging in job-related development does not make much sense. However, ignoring the topic of professional development is a mistake. One of the core messages of the present chapter is that productive professional development involves documenting and reflecting on all of the different types of learning activity in which one participates and having some kind of plan or forward horizon of where one is aiming to get to. It is not helpful to regard training and learning as something that only occurs during a Diploma, Masters or Doctoral programme. It is better to regard being a therapist as requiring a commitment to lifelong learning. Initial training provides an arena for acquiring the habits of lifelong learning, such as keeping a professional development portfolio or log and devising a professional development plan. In addition, being able to refer to a carefully documented log of professional development activities, that reflects considered and realistic career objectives is the kind of thing that is likely to create a good impression with potential employers.

Methods for facilitating professional development

There exists a very wide range of activities that can be considered as contributing to therapist professional development. It is probable that most therapists are in fact engaged in more professional development than they ever list in their curriculum vitaes or job appraisals. It is important to keep in mind that what does or does not 'count' as professional development will depend in some circumstances on the policies of the professional associations to which a therapist belongs and maybe also the requirements of his or her employer. For example, some professional associations will only recognize professional development courses that they have accredited. Attendance at other courses, no matter how relevant, may not count in terms of an annual number of professional development hours that need to be recorded.

Professional development activities cover a wide range of formats and structures, in relation to the number of people involved, time commitment, cost, formal accreditation and learning style. In principle, therefore, it should be possible for the majority of practitioners to access the kind of activity that is most meaningful for them. Some of the main professional development methods include the following.

- *Reflection on routine practice*. It is a standard requirement for therapists of all types to make use of regular clinical supervision. In addition, may practitioners have access to opportunities to reflect on their practice through peer groups, learning sets, consultation with experienced colleagues, and case discussion groups. To some extent, these forms of reflection on practice have the intention of ensuring the quality of service received by clients. However, they also provide opportunities for practitioners to reflect on their professional work, learn about different ways of approaching client issues, and identify areas where they might need to engage in further training.

- *Personal therapy*. The value of personal therapy as a means of facilitating person development in therapists was reviewed in Chapter 2. All of the studies of personal therapy have highlighted the relevance of therapy for the professional development of therapists. The experience of being a client enables a practitioner to have close, first-hand exposure to the work of a senior colleague, and to gain an understanding of what works and does not work for them (and by implication for their own clients). Many practitioners report that the experience of personal therapy played a central role in shaping their own therapeutic style and professional identity.

- *Participation in peer learning*. There are many examples of professional development initiatives in which groups of practitioners organize themselves into peer learning groups. These peer groups can consist of people who have trained together, colleagues within an agency, colleagues within a city or region, or practitioners who share an interest in a particular client group. These groups may function on the basis of sharing knowledge and skill (for example if someone attends an external training workshop they report back to the others on what they have learned). Alternatively, members of the group may consult each other on difficult clients or may decide to read and discuss certain texts. Some organizations allow time for 'journal clubs', where colleagues discuss the findings of recent or classic research papers. Schaub-de Jong *et al.* (2009) discuss some of the issues involved in helping students in initial training to become aware of the potential of peer learning.

- *Private, independent study*. There exists a massive literature on counselling, psychotherapy and mental health topics, consisting of books, articles, reports and websites. For many therapists, reading comprises the largest single portion of the time that they allocate to professional development. Reading can consist of general updating, or can be focused on deepening an understanding of a specific skill or theory. The development in recent years of training manuals that specify in detail what is involved in using a particular model of therapy represents a form of reading and private study that is potentially directly relevant to clinical practice (Addis and Krasnow 2000; Addis *et al.* 1999; Duncan *et al.* 2004; Najavits *et al.* 2000). By contrast, some therapists make a point of reading fiction in order to extend their understanding of the human condition. Burns and Dallos (2008) interviewed family therapists about the ways in which they made use of insights from novels, drama and poetry to inform their practice. Beyond reading, the study of video recordings of 'master therapists' at work, opens up a further avenue for private, independent study. For example, the American Psychological Association (APA) has published an extensive series of therapy videos. There are also many therapy videos available on YouTube.

- *Participation in seminars, workshops, conferences and training courses*. There are innumerable organized learning events that are available to therapists, ranging from one-day workshops through to masters degrees.

- *Involvement in professional associations*. Practitioners can learn a great deal, and consolidate their sense of professional identity, by serving on committees and working parties of the professional association with which they are accredited.

- *Work-related projects*. A highly flexible and cost-effective way of promoting professional development can be to engage in new kinds of work role and activity. For example, a therapist who has no experience in running groups may become a co-facilitator for a therapy group that is led by an experienced colleague. There may be particular projects and initiatives that arise in the workplace that provide opportunities for professional development. For example, a counselling agency that seeks to introduce a new client evaluation and feedback system may give one of its counselling staff time away from clinical work to learn about the options that are available and introduce a pilot project. Work-related professional development can also involve secondment to a different organization, or *pro bono* voluntary work outside of paid hours.

- *Writing and research*. Carrying out research as a principal investigator or member of a research team can be a satisfying means of acquiring new skills and knowledge. Writing books, chapters and articles on either clinical topics or research findings can serve a similar function.

This section has outlined a wide range of methods that can be used to support ongoing professional development. Each of these strategies can be valuable at different times, for the same individual. In a study by Neimeyer *et al.* (2012a), over 1000 therapists in the USA completed a survey questionnaire about their perception of the extent to which different continuing professional development (CPD) activities contributed to their career development and effectiveness. On the whole, they rated informal activities, such as self-directed learning and peer consultation, more helpful than formal activities such as attendance on accredited courses. But all of the professional development activities included in the question-naire were rated as very helpful by at least 10% of the sample.

Box 4.2: *Practitioner perspectives on professional development*

There have been few studies that have invited therapists to talk, in an open-ended way, about what professional development means to them. A study conducted in Australia by Cleary *et al.* (2011) was based on in-depth interviews with 50 mental health nurses, around their experiences and plans concerning CPD. One of the surprising findings to emerge from this study was that the majority of the participants regarded access to good-quality CPD as an essential factor in their decision to continue to work in a particular unit, rather than seeking a new job elsewhere. Support for CPD was regarded as an indicator of the general quality of a working envi-ronment. Beyond this factor, these practitioners were most interested in engaging in clinically relevant CPD that would allow them to diversify their practice.

Maximizing the benefit from professional development activities: using a reflective portfolio

There are many benefits from participating in professional development – acquiring new skills and knowledge, professional renewal, networking, etc. However, continuing professional development also represents a way of demonstrating to employers, training providers and professional associations that an individual is seriously committed to his or her work. Using a portfolio to collect and display evidence of professional development activities, is a good way of ensuring that one's CPD achievements are accessible to others. Most counselling organizations, training programmes and professional bodies have their own ideas and requirements around the documentation of CPD. These requirements may change so it is a good idea for practitioners to develop their own approach to storing this kind of information. Harley *et al.* (2004) offer some sensible guidelines for setting up a professional development portfolio. Their advice is: 'save everything', on the basis that it is never possible to predict what information will be needed in the future. A professional development portfolio can also function as the basis for annual appraisals and reviews and career planning.

Box 4.3: *How much professional development is enough?*

It is hard to know whether one's level of personal investment in professional development activity is sufficient. The pace of change within contemporary society is ever-increasing: there are always new discoveries and techniques. A study by Neimeyer and colleagues (2012b) investigated this issue through a poll in which experts in different branches of therapy and psychology were asked to estimate the 'half-life' of knowledge within their specialism. The concept of 'half-life' can never be considered as yielding an objective measure, but nevertheless does provide some sense of the intensity of knowledge 'churn'. It seems reasonable to assume that if a practitioner starts off with a certain stock of knowledge by the time half of it is out-of-date, then that person will not be functioning at an acceptable level of professional competence. Some of the half-life estimates that were obtained included: psychopharmacology (5 years), serious mental illness (9 years), counselling (10 years) and psychoanalysis (16 years). In addition, these experts took the view that the half-life of all areas of therapeutic knowledge (other than psychoanalysis) was decreasing decade-by-decade. These figures offer some kind of indication of professional development requirements in different areas. In respect of psychopharmacology, it would seem wise to commit to regular updates on at least an annual basis, to remain in touch with current developments.

Strategies for coping with the stress of the therapist role

All forms of work can be stressful, at times. In this respect, being a counsellor, psychotherapist or mental health practitioner is no different from any other job. However, alongside the general sources of stress that are associated with twenty-first century working life there are some specific stress processes that are more likely to occur in therapists than in other workers (Dryden 1994; Wise *et al.* 2012). The challenge of being able to cope with stress is particularly important for anyone in a psychotherapeutic role, because of two factors. First, most therapists work on their own with clients – if they are having a bad day, there is no one else who can readily step in and take over. Second, a therapy session is a high-intensity event that takes place at a set time. There is a sense in which therapists need to be highly 'present' and responsive – it is hard to coast. Of course, many clients will understand and appreciate that their therapist has a life outside the therapy room and may occasionally seem tired or preoccupied. But, in the end, clients are there to be on the receiving end of care and attention and have a limited tolerance for therapist jadedness. And some, very needy, clients, may have an extremely low tolerance.

There are two source of stress that occur in all occupational settings: *general stress* and *post-traumatic stress disorder* (PTSD). General stress is ubiquitous, and usually consists of an accumulation of minor 'hassles' that are manageable in themselves, but just become too much when added together (Farber and Heifetz 1981; Hellman and Morrison 1987; Lawson 2007). The main sources of general stress include work pressure (too many clients to see, too much paperwork); poor working environment (the data entry system keeps breaking down, there is insufficient sound insulation in the counselling rooms); conflict and tension in relationships with co-workers or managers; low job satisfaction (poor pay, short-term contracts, no chance of promotion); and issues around work–life balance (a suicidal client needs an emergency session on the same day one of your children is taken ill and cannot go to school). These are the kinds of occurrences that most resourceful people can take in their stride when things are going well. It is when these occurrences pile up, or when a person is depleted through illness, or lacks support or is undergoing a personal life event such as a family bereavement, that general stress leads to difficulties in concentrating, headache and back pain, irritability, self-soothing through eating or alcohol use and sickness absence. Sustained general stress has been shown to be associated with more serious health outcomes. There is evidence that a wide range of strategies can be helpful in coping with general stress, including counselling, coaching and life planning, meditation and yoga, physical exercise and changes to diet. These strategies can be implemented on an individual basis or promoted at an organizational level.

A further source of stress that can happen to anyone is PTSD, which refers to highly threatening events (or a series of events) that lie outside the normal everyday experience of a person and as a result are very hard to assimilate into his or her view of the world. Everyday examples of PTSD include being in a traffic accident, being the victim of a criminal assault, or suddenly falling ill (for example having a stroke). Examples of traumatic events that can happen to therapists include being attacked by a client, being stalked or a client dying by suicide. Although rare, these events are not unknown. For instance, practitioners working with clients with severe mental health difficulties may be exposed to the possibility of client suicide on a daily basis. The impact of PTSD takes the form of intrusive thoughts and memories about the event, along with avoidance of any reminders of what happened. Most people are able to work through such symptoms with the support of friends and family. However, it can sometimes be the case that a person begins to turn to alcohol or drugs to obliterate unwelcome thoughts, or becomes physically exhausted through not being able to sleep. This pattern can then lead to substance misuse problems, depression, and relationship breakdown. In general, therapy and mental health agencies where there is a risk of traumatization of staff tend to develop procedures for minimizing the consequences of such occurrences. For example, if there are protocols in place for how to respond to a suicidal client, it is less likely that an individual therapist will be left with a burden of sole responsibility if one of his or her clients take their own life. Therapists in private practice, or in agencies where traumatic events are infrequent (and which may feel that there is no need for a protocol) are more exposed to this type of stress, if and when it occurs.

There are three forms of stress that are particularly associated with the role of being a therapist: *vicarious traumatization, burnout* and *isolation*.

Vicarious, or secondary, traumatization, refers to the potential impact on a therapist of working with a client who has been a victim/survivor of extreme trauma, such as sexual abuse, torture or genocide (Morrissette 2004; Pearlman and McIan 1995; Sexton 1999). Essentially, the process of therapy with such clients involves opening up a space where the person can tell their story of what happened to them, in detail. In addition, the process of therapy is likely to encourage the client to express emotions associated with these traumatic events. All this can be very, very hard for a therapist to hear. The therapist is exposed to accounts of events that may be beyond their imagining. The therapist may find themselves in the grip of strong emotions, such as rage, disgust and deep despair. A few minutes after the end of a session, a therapist may find themselves walking down an ordinary street, or talking to ordinary people who have no idea that such horror could exist in the world. This impact may be heightened by the fact that this kind of work is often carried out by therapy agencies and clinics who specialize in that particular client group. As a result, a therapist may have several clients who are refugees from genocide, and hear that same kind of awful story several times in the same day. To some extent, the process and impact of vicarious traumatization is similar to PTSD. But there are also important differences. For example, a therapist who has been physically attacked by a patient would have no hesitation in telling their family about what had happened. By contrast, a therapist who works with abuse survivors is very unlikely to want to share any details with their family. Vicarious or secondary traumatization is therefore a somewhat hidden phenomenon. Again, this is a stress issue that can be addressed through a combination of individual and organizational strategies.

The concept of *burnout* emerged from research by the psychologist Christina Maslach, into the specific stress patterns associated with 'human services' roles (Leiter and Maslach 2005; Maslach and Leiter 1997). What Maslach found was that many human services practitioners were passionately committed to their work and had a tendency to give as much of themselves as they could to their clients. Some of these practitioners also saw themselves as special people who never needed to ask for help or support for themselves. These passionate practitioners could be highly effective in the early part of their careers. Over time, however, they became emotionally depleted and exhausted (their inner fire 'burned out'). Maslach identified three main characteristics of practitioner burnout: *depersonalization* (seeing the client as a statistic or 'case' rather than as a person), *emotional exhaustion*; and disillusionment or *lack of personal accomplishment* ('its all a waste of time . . . I have being doing this job for ten years and nothing has changed . . .'). Therapists who suffer from burnout find it harder and harder to meet their own high standards. As a consequence, they make themselves ill, or sacrifice their personal and family relationships (Barnett *et al.* 2007; Farber 1983; Farber and Heifetz 1982). It can be hard to offer supportive feedback to colleagues who are burning out, because they resent and deflect any messages that they interpret as critical of their motives. Individual or group therapy can be a helpful and effective method of moving on from burnout, by providing a situation in which the person can reflect on their own grandiosity, the reasons for their tendency to deny themselves pleasure or the functioning of their harsh inner critic. It is, of course, extremely helpful to begin this work during training, rather than waiting for a mid-career crisis to develop.

The presence of *isolation* in the lives of counsellors, psychotherapists and mental health practitioners is not a direct source of stress, but functions as a factor that exacerbates the impact of the sources that have been discussed already. Studies of therapists who have retired, or who are at the later stages of their careers, have found that many of them describe themselves as socially isolated (Goldberg 1988; Guy 1987; Henry 1977;

Henry *et al.* 1971). The work of being a full-time therapist brings a person into a close relationship with his or her clients or patients. This may gradually lead to withdrawal from other relationships – there is only a certain amount of emotional or relational 'load' that one person can take. This situation can be exacerbated by the fact that confidentiality concerns may make a therapist unwilling to talk about his or her work to their partner or friends. A further factor may be that ordinary, everyday social conversation may seem trivial and superficial, in contrast to the issues that clients talk about. Taken together, these aspects of the role of therapist may mean that a practitioner lacks social support when things go wrong in his or her personal or professional life. Isolation may be a particular issue for therapists in private practice.

Professional development activities for therapists, around stress management and the promotion of well-being, generally address areas such as:

- understanding the nature of therapist stress;
- identifying risks and danger signals;
- reviewing coping mechanisms and if necessary developing more appropriate strategies;
- making adjustments to lifestyle and work role;
- using stress episodes as a basis for growth and development.

The final item in this list is particularly important. It is highly likely that anyone who is committed to their work will have times when they become depleted. By using critical reflection and feedback from others, these episodes can become opportunities for moving to a different level of understanding and functioning.

The approach to therapist professional development outlined in this chapter offers an effective framework for addressing the issue of work-related stress. By keeping a reflective portfolio or log of professional development activity, and submitting this document to external scrutiny on a regular basis (from one's therapist, supervisor, peer group or manager), it is readily possible to identify when stress is happening, where it is coming from, and what to do about it. For example, alarm bells are likely to ring in the mind of any consultant or colleague who reads a portfolio of a therapist who is seeing a lot of clients with complex problems, has no time for self-renewing personal and professional activities and has no supervision or consultation with a colleague who has specific expertise with that client group. It is particularly important to resist the temptation to attribute any stress-related difficulties being experienced by a therapist solely to 'personal' inadequacies. Yes, the tendency to be a rescuer (from childhood) may contribute to a therapist becoming stressed. But it is almost certainly also an issue for the organization within which that therapist is working. For example, it may make a big difference to a therapist's ability to cope with stress if his or her manager reviews workload patterns to enable sufficient recovery and preparation time between highly demanding clients or arranges teambuilding events to enhance the level of peer support across a group of co-workers.

Box 4.4: *The death or suicide of a client: a major source of therapist stress*

The death of a client is an event that can have a profound impact on therapist well-being. The death of a client can be the outcome of a known, long-term illness or it can be sudden and unexpected. Client suicide, and situations of sudden unexplained death that could be suicide, can be particularly stressful. The therapist response to the death of a client represents a topic that has been the focus of a substantial amount of research. For example, in a survey carried out by Hendin *et al.* (2004), into the experiences of therapists who had lost a client to suicide, more that one in three of participants reported high levels of emotional distress. The factors that contributed to stress included a sense of responsibility at not having arranged hospitalization of the client, having made a therapeutic intervention that may have contributed to the client's decision to end their life, negative reactions from colleagues and management, and fear of a complaint or lawsuit from relatives of the client. Some of these practitioners came close to leaving the profession as a result of this episode. Therapists were particularly badly affected by the suicide of clients with whom they felt strong connections. It was as if the grief that was triggered by the loss made the practitioner vulnerable to other aspects of the event. In general, women therapists appeared to be more affected by client suicide than their male colleagues seemed to be. Other studies of the impact on therapists of client suicide and other forms of death include Caffrey (2000), Dwyer *et al.* (2012), O'Brien (2011), Hendin *et al.* (2000), Knox *et al.* (2006), Schaverian (1999), Veilleux (2011) and Webb (2011).

The existence of this research literature provides a valuable resource for therapists who have lost a client, in making it possible to see how colleagues cope with this kind of highly personal and troubling, but also rare, experience. The research also reinforces the notion of the inevitable interconnectedness of personal and professional development in counsellors, psychotherapists and mental health professionals. How a therapist copes with the death of a client is not merely an individual matter, but is shaped in many ways by organizational policies and practices, and the strength of the support network that exists within a group of colleagues.

Box 4.5: *How prevalent is therapist stress?*

It is difficult to determine the extent to which occupational stress is a problem within the counselling, psychotherapy and mental health professions. Almost all of the research into this question makes use of self-report questionnaires to evaluate stress levels. It seems likely that therapists might under-report their distress or impairment, because they know that they 'should' know how to deal with such issues.

A survey carried out by Lawson (2007) yielded findings that are typical of previous research into this topic. Questionnaires were completed by 500 counsellors in the USA, working in a wide range of settings. Most of the respondents in this study had high client loads, with around 10% of their clients being high-risk cases. Depending on the particular way that the question was asked between 5% and 20% of respondents described themselves as being stressed or impaired. When asked about their colleagues, respondents believed that 50% of the people with whom they worked were stressed or impaired. At the same time, the overwhelming majority of study participants reported that they were satisfied in their jobs. When asked what they did to maintain a sense of well-being and sustain their careers, the most frequently mentioned activities were: maintaining a sense of humour, spending time with partner/family, maintaining a balance between professional and personal lives, maintaining self-awareness, exerting control over work responsibilities, reflecting on positive experiences, trying to maintain objectivity about clients, quiet leisure activities, maintaining professional identity, participating in continuing education, engaging in physical activities, and spending time with friends. Some other well-being practices that are generally highlighted as essential within the therapist well-being literature, such as formal exercise, clinical supervision, peer support and personal therapy, were considered as less helpful.

What this study tells us is that therapist stress is certainly a significant issue for at least some practitioners, and that the therapists who are best able to deal with stress have found ways of integrating well-being activities into their everyday lives rather than using more formal support mechanisms. Also, hard-pressed therapists find it important to develop ways of distancing themselves from their work, such as humour and objectivity.

Suggested further reading

Barnett, J.E., Baker, E.K., Elman, N.S. and Schoener, G.R. (2007) In pursuit of wellness: the self-care imperative, *Professional Psychology: Research and Practice*, 38, 603–12.

Rothschild, B. (2006) *Help for the Helper: The Psychophysiology of Compassion Fatigue and Vicarious Trauma*. New York: Norton.

Skovholt, T.M. and Trotter-Mathison, M.J. (2011) *The Resilient Practitioner: Burnout Prevention and Self-Care Strategies for Counselors, Therapists, Teachers, and Health Professionals*, 2nd edn. New York: Routledge.

Wise, E.H., Hersh, M.A. and Gibson, C.M. (2012) Ethics, self-care and well-being for psychologists: reenvisioning the stress-distress continuum, *Professional Psychology: Research and Practice*, 43, 487–94.

Building a career

One of the places where the multiple strands of therapist personal and professional development come together is around the question of career development. Both therapeutic effectiveness and personal job satisfaction are strongly influenced by being in the right job at the right time. Each of us, as practitioners, has our own set of gifts and limitations, personal values, life goals and sense of direction. On the other side of the equation, the world of counselling, psychotherapy and mental health incorporates a huge array of different types of roles and jobs. It is important to make use of personal and professional development activities, such as personal therapy, supervision, peer support and maintaining a portfolio, to carry out regular reviews of potential career pathways, and to work out the small steps that may be required in order to arrive at particular career destinations. A significant aspect of this, over the course of a career, is to think about being a therapist as one among several occupational roles. It is very hard to sustain full-time work as a therapist over the long term. Although little research has been carried out on therapist career trajectories, our own experience has been that most practitioners find ways to balance the demands of clinical work with other work roles. Sometimes these roles can be within the world of therapy, for example being a supervisor, trainer, manager, researcher or author. In other instances, these other roles can be highly diverse, such as being an artist, running a business or being a carer.

> ### Box 4.6: *Gender differences in the career pathways of therapists*
>
> It seems clear that there are quite distinct gender differences in the career choices and pathways of male and female therapists. Over the past 20 or 30 years, this area of professional work has become more female-dominated, with training places and clinical jobs becoming increasingly

likely to be filled by women. However, management and academic roles are, relatively speaking, more likely to be filled by men. Further exploration of the reasons behind these developments can be found in Philipson (1993) and Lewis (2004). An implication of these factors is that it may be useful, when reflecting on career direction, to take time to consider the extent to which personal attitudes to gender identity might play a part in this decision-making process, and whether this influence is desirable in the context of one's personal values.

Conclusions

The topic of therapist professional development encompasses a wide range of issues. It is clearly in the interests of practitioners, their employers and the professional bodies to which they are affiliated for relevant CPD to be accessible to therapists. It is also important to construct collaborative structures within which practitioners can review and reflect on their professional development on a regular basis, and make plans for future developmental activities.

CHAPTER 5

Criteria for assessing the adequacy of personal and professional development

Introduction

The aim of the preceding four chapters has been to offer some ways of making sense of the meaning of personal and professional development for counsellors, psychotherapists and mental health practitioners. What emerged from that exploration was that the notion of 'personal and professional development' is hard to pin down – it encompasses a wide range of processes and activities. It is important to be willing to accept the complexity and subtlety of therapist development. One of the key values that underpins all psychotherapeutic work is then acknowledgement of difference and the freedom of people to make their own choices. At a fundamental level therapy positions itself in opposition to social control. This respect for difference carries over to the field of therapist development. There are lots of different types of psychotherapeutic work, and lots of different types of people have made a contribution within this area of professional activity.

At the same time, the question of adequacy of personal and professional development represents a significant issue. Therapists in training, and in practice, need to decide whether what they are doing is enough or is good enough. Trainers of therapists, and employers, make decisions about readiness or fitness to practice. Professional bodies make decisions about therapist accreditation. On what basis can such decisions be made? The present chapter brings together some of the key themes that have threaded through earlier chapters, with the aim of identifying some criteria that can be used to assess the adequacy of personal and professional development.

Criteria for assessing therapist development

It is hard to imagine that there could ever be a standardized checklist that could be used in an objective manner to determine levels of therapist development. To some extent, therapist development depends on context. The types of issues being faced by a trainee or novice therapist and the level of self-awareness and use of self that might be expected will be different from that of a more experienced practitioner. Therapist development is also shaped by the social, cultural and organizational context within which a therapist is operating. Some practitioners work in organizations that take personal and professional development very seriously, and provide structures and resources that are readily available to employees. Other practitioners work in environments where few such resources are available. To give an extreme example, a therapist working in a large university-affiliated teaching hospital in any European country will have access to a wide range of online research databases and research-knowledgeable colleagues, and will easily be able to keep in touch with the research literature that is relevant to their area of work. By contrast, a therapist working in a Church-based counselling centre in a developing country might struggle to get access to any research papers at all.

It is possible to identify four broad dimensions along which the adequacy of therapist personal and professional development can be evaluated. A general sense of development can be gained by looking at the pattern of *professional activity* of a therapist. A more fine-grained appreciation can be obtained by considering three further dimensions: *interpersonal skills, cognitive processes*, and *awareness of emotions* (Elman *et al.* 2005). Finally, a comprehensive understanding requires consideration of the *trajectory* of development (Ronnestad and Skovholt 2013).

These dimensions can be seen to reflect different aspects of the concept of *professionalism*. Although there exist different ideas about what constitutes a 'profession', what seems clear is that the public views a profession as an organized occupational group, which has specialist knowledge in relation to a specific area of life, and which adheres to high standards of competence and ethical probity. To perform in a professional manner, therefore, means that a practitioner is doing his or her best to serve the community and perform at the highest level. An important implication here is that the question of what comprises a satisfactory level of professional development is ultimately a moral or ethical issue. Any professional has a duty of care toward the users of his or her services, and the underlying purpose of personal and professional development is to create the conditions for ensuring faithfulness to that moral imperative.

Level of basic professional activity

The personal and professional development of a therapist is expressed in the work that they do. If that work is satisfactory there cannot be too much wrong with that practitioner's development. By contrast, flawed or unsafe work suggests that there are unresolved developmental issues. The work of being a therapist incorporates a range of activities:

- seeing clients;
- receiving clinical supervision;
- keeping up-to-date in respect of knowledge and skills.

Using a portfolio, it is possible to collect and present evidence in relation to each of these areas of activity. For example, how many client sessions have been cancelled by the therapist? What proportion of clients have unplanned endings? What information is available on client satisfaction and change? Have client notes been filed? How much supervision time was used? What was discussed in supervision? Has a supervision review or report been carried out? How many items were read over a six-month period? What kind of CPD or training events were attended? Were there any complaints from clients or colleagues? Has the information presented under these headings been independently verified? The pattern of information that emerges, concerning the professional activity of a therapist, indicates whether a therapist is (a) on track and functioning at a level that would be expected from someone with their years of training and experience, and working in that setting; (b) stagnating (Ronnestad and Skovholt 2013) – no sense of an active commitment to learning and improvement, and possibly signs of drift in the direction of burnout; or (c) in crisis and not coping. In addition, an annual or bi-annual audit and review of professional activity is a useful means of identifying potential developmental issues. For example, if a therapist is generally effective in helping clients but has difficulties with a particular subgroup of clients, it may be relevant for him or her to consider further training or independent study, a change of work role, or personal therapy to address counter-transference issues triggered by that type of client.

Reflecting on the adequacy of professional activity does not focus directly on personal and professional development, but is more of a litmus test or diagnostic screening in respect of whether development is on track or is stuck in some way. An understanding of therapist personal and professional development requires attention to the three areas in which any therapist should be continuing to learn and develop across the whole of their career: being able to relate to people, being able to make sense of what happens in therapy, and being able to be emotionally available.

The interpersonal dimension of development

Therapist interpersonal skills and awareness have been highlighted in innumerable research studies as essential aspects of effective therapy. All therapist competence checklists and measures acknowledge the role of interpersonal skills in the delivery of whatever model of therapy is being used. What does this mean in relation to therapist personal and professional development? Basically, in childhood each of us acquires a capacity to establish, maintain and end relationships with other people. This capacity is grounded in early attachment experience, reinforced and modified through interaction with others in the family, at school, in the workplace and so on. It can be assumed that anyone who is accepted for training as a counsellor, psychotherapist or mental health practitioner already has a good capacity for relating to other people. What then happens is that therapy training and working with clients places the therapist's pre-existing interpersonal skills under a lot of strain. A therapist needs to be able to connect with people that they might normally avoid in everyday-life situations. Moreover, a therapist needs to be able to form relationships with people who are spectacularly bad at making relationships, or who have culturally different expectations and values around relationships. As a result, being a therapist involves a constant process of reflecting on relationships with clients (and sometimes, also, relationships with colleagues) in order to become more resourceful, skilful, intentional and flexible in their relational competence.

Therapy training and ongoing personal and professional activity usually provides therapists with plentiful opportunities for developing ways of making sense of relationships, through learning about theories and research. However, at a practical level, getting better at using interpersonal skills is driven by two learning processes: feedback and active experimentation. In other words, the interpersonal dimension of therapist personal and professional development depends on actual interaction with others. In terms of evaluating the adequacy of therapist development in this domain it is important to explore questions such as:

- on what occasions did you invite, or receive, feedback from other people regarding the way they see you, or how you relate to them?

- what did you do with this information? In what ways did your reflection on feedback result in modification to your way of relating to your clients (or other people)?
- on what occasions did you respond to invitations from others to provide them with feedback or initiate a feedback process?

The answers to these questions provide a marker of whether personal and professional development is taking place, in the era of interpersonal skills and awareness. For anyone who is assessing or being consulted on a personal development portfolio compiled by a therapist, an obvious place to look for evidence of collaborative interpersonal skills is in the construction of the portfolio itself: to what extent is the portfolio informed by a genuine process of seeking feedback (not testimonial) from others? To what extent does the portfolio refer to actual or potential modification of interpersonal skills in response to such feedback?

Most of the time, reflecting on the adequacy of personal and professional development in the area of interpersonal skills or engaging in consultative review with a supervisor, therapist or peer group, tends to involve conversations around emerging issues, possible new ways of exploring old issues and so on. However, sometimes these conversations will need to focus on potential danger signals. One cause for concern is if a therapist believes that they have *no* issues or difficulties in the area of relationships and interpersonal skills. Another cause for concern arises if the balance of care seems to have tipped in the wrong direction: the therapist seems to be relating to clients in ways that gratify his or her needs rather than being in the service of the client.

The cognitive dimension of development

In the ordinary course of events, people manage to cope with difficulties using their own resources. People only seek professional help when they get stuck with an issue, or when it seems too complex. At a very basic level, people expect the professional who they consult to possess a better understanding of the problem than they do themselves. This seems a reasonable expectation. On the other side, a professional practitioner is someone who is deeply interested in a particular area of life, and has devoted years to training, study and work in that area. As a result, they will have had plenty of opportunity to think about that set of issues from a variety of perspectives. These factors have led many researchers and trainers to be interested in the question of how 'experts' think about their work, and the cognitive processes that are used by experts to solve problems. One of the defining characteristics of any profession is that an experienced practitioner will 'think like a doctor' or 'think like a lawyer'. A key goal of training is to help students to begin to think in the right way.

A key feature of the work of respected senior members of a profession is that they are able to think about the work in a particularly deep or insightful manner – they have 'wisdom'.

What is involved in 'thinking like a therapist', and how does this skill develop? A comprehensive review of relevant theory and research on this topic, and implications for therapy training and practice, can be found in Ronnestad and Skovholt (2013). In understanding the nature of expert information-processing and problem-solving, it is helpful to draw analogies with the process of cognitive development in chess players. In the beginning, a novice chess player needs to learn the rules of the game and some general strategies (for example it is acceptable to sacrifice a pawn but protect your Queen at all costs). A similar process can be observed in novice therapists, who need to learn to take into account (think about) the basic 'rules' of therapy: establish a relationship, maintain professional boundaries, use interventions specified within your core theoretical model. After a while, and in the light of experience, a competent chess player becomes able to think ahead, in the form of a mental map of possible sequences of moves and counter-moves. In a similar fashion, a competent therapist develops a capacity to identify ways in which the process of therapy can unfold over time. Finally, expert chess players, and therapists, acquire a highly developed capacity for pattern recognition, demonstrated in an intuitive ability to 'see' what is important in a case. This capacity allows expert practitioners to respond flexibly in difficult situations, and to be creative.

The journey from thinking like a novice to thinking like an expert does not automatically follow from years of practice. It is possible for practitioners to continue to think in the same way in year ten of their professional career as they did in year one. Cognitive development arises from an 'intense commitment to learn' (Ronnestad and Skovholt 2013) that is manifested in a number of important ways. Practitioners who are open to learning engage in reflection on their practice. This reflexivity has a critical edge – there is a desire and drive to do better, and to ask difficult questions about any aspect of the work in order to arrive at a more adequate understanding. In addition, concepts, metaphors and images are used as a means of referring to complex patterns.

Theory and research on the development of cognitive capacity from novice through to expert practitioner status suggests that novices and experts approach problems in quite different ways. There is clearly something missing in the personal and professional development pathway of a therapist who is well on in their career but is still thinking in the concrete, rule-bound style of a novice. Conversely, novice therapists who try to walk before they can run, in terms of trying to create elaborate idiosyncratic assemblages of ideas or attempting to function in a highly intuitive manner are also exhibiting a failure of development. Not asking critical questions about their own theoretical model and assumptions represents a further sign of limited cognitive development. Even within tightly defined theoretical models, such as psychoanalysis, CBT or person-centred, there are always debates between groups of therapists who understand core concepts in different ways. Even during early training, therapists with a commitment to learning should be able to articulate a nuanced understanding of the concepts and ideas on which their practice is based.

Box 5.1: *The reasoning processes of expert and novice therapists*

A programme of research led by Tracey Eells has examined the reasoning processes of expert and novice therapists in the context of situations in which they are invited to verbally construct a case formulation in response to information presented in a brief case vignette (see, for example, Eells 2010). Using this simple technique, it was possible to observe that expert therapists generated hypotheses on the basis of carefully considering each piece of information (forward reasoning), whereas novices tended to jump to conclusions, by beginning with a hypothesis and then looking for information that would back it up (backward reasoning). Several other studies have also looked at the ways in which cognitive processing becomes transformed over the course of a career (Fitzpatrick *et al.* 2010; Martin *et al.* 1989; Mayfield *et al.* 1999). Reviewing these studies, Chang (2011: 408) concludes that, in comparison with novice therapists, more experienced practitioners are able to:

- perceive meaningful patterns;
- think more quickly;
- recall relevant information;
- conceptualize problems according to overarching abstract principles;
- know the limits of their expertise, evaluate the difficulty or complexity of problems, and explain their reasoning.

Chang (2011: 408) suggests that this type of cognitive development can have a major impact on practice: 'when counsellors are more cognitively efficient they can be more emotionally available'.

A further essential strand within the cognitive development of therapists consists of an enduring curiosity and willingness to learn in the area of therapy theory. Research into experienced and esteemed therapists (Jennings and Skovholt 1999; Ronnestad and Skovholt 2013) has shown that these highly effective practitioners continue to read about theory, and be interested in new ideas, all the way through their careers. The process of attaining a deeper understanding of theory can take a number of forms. Simon (2003, 2006, 2012) has argued that it is essential for therapists to find a theoretical 'home' that is consistent with their own personal worldview and values. Simon (2006: 337) suggests that the evidence of research indicates that 'a therapist becomes maximally effective if she commits herself to a model whose underlying worldview closely matches her own'. Blow and colleagues (2012) take the view that 'therapist-worldview matching' needs to be supplemented by a capacity to make use of whatever model is best suited to a particular client. Hansen (2006) takes this idea further, in proposing that therapist training and development needs to encourage an appreciation of all theories as potential 'narratives' that may be valuable in helping clients to make sense of patterns in their lives.

A study by Polkinghorne (1992), where experienced therapists were invited to identify the theories and concepts that they used in their practice with clients, supports all of these perspectives. The practitioners in the Polkinghorne (1992) study were aware of which ideas corresponded to their own personal worldview, and which did not. But they were also aware of which concepts and models made most sense to their clients, or provided greatest leverage in relation to specific moment-by-moment change processes being pursued at any one time. It is clear that, at the start of his or her training, a counsellor, psychotherapist or mental health worker will only be able to draw on a relatively limited set of ideas. Over the course of personal and professional development, these ideas expand, both in relation to making sense of the practitioner's own life, and also externally, in relation to making sense of client's lives.

Box 5.2: *The development of therapist creativity*

A significant indicator of therapist personal and professional development is the emergence of a willingness to work with clients in creative ways, and to trust personal intuition. At the beginning of a therapy career, novice practitioners tend to operate 'according to the book', and adhere to the procedures specified by their chosen therapy approach. However, as Bohart (1999) has pointed out, creativity is an inherent part of all human behaviour, arising from the potential to engage in intuitive, tacit knowing. As therapists gain experience and confidence, they become more able to make use of their bodily knowing, capacity to use metaphor, imagery and humour, and ability to grasp complex patterns at an intuitive level. Acts of creativity involve the expression of these attributes within the therapeutic relationship (Anderson *et al.* 1999; Bohart 1999; Carson and Becker 2003; Kottler and Carlson 2009; Raskin 1999).

The emotional dimension of development

No matter what other issues there may be in their lives, one of the main reasons why people seek counselling, psychotherapy or mental health treatment is because they feel bad. Depending on the person, the emotional struggle may be concerned with loss of control of emotions, an inability to feel or express feelings, or secondary reactions to threatening emotion, such as feeling ashamed or guilty about what is being felt. Therapy is a form of 'emotion work' or 'emotional labour', and being a therapist means being able to function with a sufficient level of comfort in the presence of strong emotions, and being willing to accept the value of all emotions. For most therapists, this is a hard task, because most of us have been socialized into feeling OK about certain emotions, and regarding other emotions as threatening, embarrassing or dangerous. The emotion-focused dimension of therapy is made even more challenging because different cultural and subcultural groups have different ways of expressing emotions, and different norms around which emotions are acceptable and which are not. As if all of that was not hard enough, the emotion work that may need to be pursued in therapy is often inhibited by the conditions under which therapy takes place, such as offices that subtly encourage rational conversation and allow little scope for bodily movement.

One of the basic learning experiences that occurs across all therapist personal development activities, is the opportunity to feel, to express emotion, to observe how others behave around their emotions, to develop a language for emotion, and to experiment with new ways of relating to one's own internal and external emotional life. There are also many areas of therapy theory and research that provide a basis for learning about emotion (see, for example, Gendlin 2003; Gratz and Roemer 2004; Greenberg 2002a, 2002b). Also relevant is the literature on emotional literacy (Goleman 2005; Steiner 2003). Over the course of their career, many therapists make deliberate use of emotion-focused personal development activities as a means of becoming more aware of their capacity to feel. Examples of such activities include participating in body therapy, attending mindfulness training and using outdoor adventure activities (such as, abseiling, wilderness journeys) to confront and work through the experience of fear or evoke the experience of joy. Conversely, a major sign of therapist stress is burnout, which manifests itself in a general sense of emotional numbness and disconnectedness.

Box 5.3: *A classic study of therapist emotional development*

A book by Magai and Haviland-Jones (2002) represents a landmark inquiry into therapy personal and professional development and is essential reading for anyone who wishes to acquire a deeper understanding of how different threads of a therapist's life come together in their practice. Magai and Haviland-Jones (2002) carried out a detailed analysis of the patterns of emotional awareness and expressiveness in three leading figures in therapy – Carl Rogers, Fritz Perls and Albert Ellis. In this study, they made careful comparisons across three main sources of evidence: the video recordings of each therapist working in turn with one client (Gloria); biographical information about early childhood experience and emotional socialization; and the way that emotions were understood within their theoretical writings. What emerges very clearly from this analysis is that the differences in therapeutic theory and style between these practitioners can be attributed to fundamental differences in their emotional expressiveness, and their efforts to channel their emotional strengths and blind spots into a viable way of working with clients. Because these therapists were well-known, a great deal of information is available about all of these aspects of their lives. It seems reasonable to assume that similar conclusions would apply to other therapists.

Other dimensions of therapist personal and professional development

It is possible to come up with extensive lists of personal and professional development issues that therapists need to take into account. For example, Bassey and Melluish (2013) and McLeod (2013) place an emphasis on the importance of becoming aware of one's cultural identity and all aspects of cultural diversity. Pieterse *et al.* (2013) have constructed a complex model of dimensions of therapist self-awareness. It is essential to acknowledge that, for any individual practitioner, or group of practitioners working together in an organization, the particular developmental challenge that is most pressing at any one time may take a wide number of forms. However, at a more basic level, all of these challenges arise from a commitment to engage in cycles of development fuelled by an intense willingness to learn in the core domains of relationships, theory and emotions.

Cyclical progression

The concept of 'development' implies an irreversible shift from one level of functioning, to a qualitatively different level. In Chapter 3, some of the implications of this idea were explored, including the notion that development occurs in response to trouble. If someone is functioning in a satisfactory manner, why would they want to change? Development arises from the experience of a crisis of some kind. This is essentially a *cyclical* model: development can never be identified on the basis of observation of what is happening at one point in time. Instead, the concept of development refers to a cyclical process consisting of at least four steps: equilibrium > crisis > period of reflection and learning > attainment of new equilibrium. From this perspective, assessment of the adequacy of personal and professional development requires attention to long-term cycles within a professional career. Ronnestad and Skovholt (2013) suggest that three basic cycles of development can be observed in therapists. First, there is a *positive* cycle, in which a challenge of some kind is acknowledged and worked through, leading to personal and professional growth. These authors also identify two negative cycles of therapist development. In an *inadequate closure* trajectory, the therapist acknowledges that there is a problem, but fails to resolve it or achieve adequate closure around it. This leads to a state of exhaustion, because the problem continues to represent an ongoing source of stress. In a *premature closure* trajectory, the practitioner engages in only very limited reflection on the issue, which does not get to the root of what has gone wrong, and then proceeds to ignore the issue. Over time, this strategy results in a state of personal and professional disengagement, because the practitioner has closed off much (or all) of the potentially creative and growing edge of his or her capacity to help others.

These cyclical patterns are illustrated in the following example:

Angela is a thoughtful, energetic therapist, who has a highly developed capacity to use language and imagery, and is able to help many of her clients to see themselves in a new and more positive, light. Her crisis is associated with poor relationships with colleagues in the agency within which she works, who she sees as not understanding her and envious of her skills and accomplishments. The level of tension with colleagues makes it hard for Angela to feel emotionally safe and grounded when she is in the office, and in her work with clients. She recognizes that there is a problem that needs to be sorted out. What can she do?

- *Premature closure and disengagement*: Angela talks about these issues with her supervisor and therapist, and comes to the conclusion that she does not fit in this particular therapy organization, because she has different values. She finds a job in a different agency, which she believes is more aligned to her philosophy. Within six months, she begins to experience conflict with this new set of colleagues. Eventually, Angela decides to start a new career, as a web designer, while maintaining a small private therapy practice.

- *Inadequate closure and exhaustion*: Angela talks about these issues with her supervisor and therapist, and comes to the conclusion that it is necessary to take the problem back to the staff team in her therapy agency and deal with the issues in the open. The manager of the agency agrees to bring an independent consultant to facilitate a one-day meeting at a retreat centre, where the value concerns raised by Angela can be explored and worked through. This is a very painful event for Angela, who feels misunderstood and unsupported. Over subsequent weeks, she finds it harder and harder to go to work, and becomes physically ill.

- *Positive cycle of development*: Angela talks about these issues with her supervisor and therapist. Her therapist confronts her with the feedback that similar patterns have occurred on a regular basis throughout Angela's life, and that maybe now would be the time to make sense of these issues, and perhaps make some new decisions. It took Angela some time to accept this idea. She negotiated a contract with her therapist for additional sessions over a three-month period, buttressed by a policy of abstaining from disputes with colleagues, attendance at a mindfulness group and consultations with a life coach. Angela emerged from this intense phase of personal development with a new understanding of the connection between her troubles at work and very painful early experiences of exclusion and victimization by members of her family. She was also able to develop a more realistic appreciation of the similarities and differences between her values and philosophy, and the positions taken by colleagues. She became able to cultivate friendships and alliances with some colleagues, and play a leading role as an instigator of constructive organizational renewal.

Further examples of developmental cycles can be found in Ronnestad and Skovholt (2013: 171–5) and in Wise (2008).

Box 5.4: *The development of ethical maturity*

The domain of morality and ethics represents an area in which cognitive, interpersonal and practical aspects of therapist development come together. At the beginning of their careers, most therapists possess an intuitive, unexamined sense of right and wrong, and look towards professional codes of conduct for guidance around ethical 'rules' that they should follow. Over the course of a career, a therapist is required to make complex ethical judgements in situations of uncertainty, and to provide moral leadership. Carroll and Shaw (2012) have argued that it is important to move beyond static discussion of ethical principles and guidelines and think instead in terms of ways of facilitating the development of *ethical maturity*. They define ethical maturity as:

> . . . having the reflective, rational, emotional and intuitive capacity to decide actions are right and wrong or good and better, having the resilience and courage to implement these decisions, being accountable for ethical decisions made (publically or privately), being able to live with the decisions made and integrating the learning into our moral character and future actions (p. 139).

This perspective opens up a powerful agenda for training and research (see, for example, Williams and Levitt 2007).

The organizational context of personal and professional development

It is always important to keep in mind the idea that it is not sufficient to view personal and professional development as merely individual processes. The type of development that is possible depends to a large extent on the organizational and cultural context within which a therapist is operating. For example, many therapists who are trained and practice in Western societies find that is meaningful and significant for them to become more aware of the experiences of diversity in the area of sexuality. Typically 'straight' therapists learn what is involved in working from a 'gay affirmative' therapeutic stance. In Western societies, there exists a wealth of reading materials and training workshops around this topic. By contrast, for therapists training and practising in traditional Muslim societies, this would not be possible, because of prevailing religious values, cultural attitudes and legal restrictions. At a more 'micro' level, different counselling, psychotherapy and mental health clinics, agencies and services each have their own distinctive organizational climate and culture. For example, Cook and colleagues (2009) carried out a study of attitudes to innovation in two therapy services that worked with similar client populations and found major differences in how each organization approached this issue. Within developmental psychology the concept of 'scaffolding' refers to the notion that the process of development occurs within a framework that supports the learner. As the learner gains more confidence and competence the scaffolding may be removed, piece by piece. This concept can provide a valuable metaphor for making sense of the relationship between therapist personal development and the organizational context within which that development takes place: there are many types of 'developmental scaffolding' that can be deployed. The literature and traditions of narrative therapy offer an invaluable perspective on the importance of a collective, rather than individualized, approach to therapist development (White 1995, 2011; White and Hales 1997).

The question of how organizations function to support or hinder staff development is highly complex. Within the same organization there may be positive and negative practices happening at the same time. Nevertheless, we suggest that it is possible to identify three general patterns.

1 *Organizational environments that inhibit learning and development.* There are some therapy organizations in which personal and professional development just does not appear on the agenda. This can happen for a variety of reasons. Some therapy services are wedded to particular models of practice, which are assumed to be true and valid, and which cannot be questioned. There is thus little point in engaging in ongoing learning – once a therapist has been trained in that model, what else do they need to know? Other therapy organizations may be characterized by a climate of fear, blame and bullying. These settings are not safe enough for genuine learning and development to take place – other than in private, and outside the walls of the agency. There are also some services that are so underfunded and overworked that the work has become limited to just seeing as many clients as possible, and keeping the doors open.

2 *Organizations that support development, at an individual level.* The most common pattern within counselling, psychotherapy and mental health organizations, is for personal and professional development to be recognized and valued at the level of individual staff members. These organizations may offer financial support for attendance at professional development events, or time off. There may be a library and subscriptions to professional journals. Managers may meet with staff on an annual basis, to review personal and professional development activity, and agree goals or targets for the following year. Within such organizations, personal and professional development is definitely on the agenda, but it is handled through a focus on individual needs.

3 *Organizations where personal and professional development is integrated into everyday practice.* There are some exceptional organizations in which learning and development forms an integral part of the

fabric of the working day. We do not know of any published examples of therapy organizations that fit this pattern. However, Gabbay and Le May (2011) carried out observational research in general practitioner (GP) clinics in the UK NHS, looking at how doctors used knowledge to arrive at clinical judgements. What they found was that in the best GP practices, doctors and nurses were engaged in a constant exchange of information and peer consultation around the best way to respond to particular patients. Individual members of the team were acknowledged as possessing special knowledge, experience and skills in relation to specific illnesses or scenarios. The team met regularly as a group to exchange ideas and invited outside experts in to brief them on new developments. Although these doctors and nurses also made use of personal development portfolios and appraisals, and attended external courses and workshops, the core of their personal and professional development was grounded in a collective approach.

These descriptions of organizational patterns are undoubtedly oversimplified, but hopefully they offer a sense of what is possible. On the whole, therapy organizations have a tendency to adopt an over-individualized perspective on therapist personal and professional development, due to the generally individualistic nature of therapy theory and practice. Our view is that movement in the direction of a more collectivist approach has a great deal to offer in relation to both practitioner job satisfaction and well-being, and therapeutic effectiveness. Basically, a collective approach reflects a stance that we are all involved in a process of learning and development, and we all have a lot to offer each other.

Box 5.5: *Contrasting professional environments*

The counselling, psychotherapy and mental health professions are largely organized around discrete professional groupings. Although each of these professional communities may be doing broadly similar work they tend to define their uniqueness and identity in terms of specific aspects of personal and professional development that are highly valued. For example, the narrative therapy professional community places a lot of emphasis on political awareness and sensitivity to the use of language. The various branches of the humanistic and experiential therapy movement tend to emphasize personal authenticity. Psychoanalytic groups expect members to be highly sensitive to boundaries. Professional associations for mental health nurses and psychiatrists place great store in technical knowledge, around psychopharmacology and the legal framework within which they operate, and interprofessional working. These areas of emphasis can be useful for practitioners, because they are associated with various types of support and mentoring around these themes. But they are also potentially hindering of personal and professional development, because they can lead to downplaying of other dimensions of personal and professional development that are potentially of equal importance.

Conclusions

This chapter has considered the issue of the adequacy of therapist personal and professional development in terms of six areas: *professional activity, interpersonal skills, cognitive processes, emotional self-awareness, cycles of progress* and *organizational scaffolding*. From a developmental perspective an appraisal of therapist development is not a matter of assessing performance in any one of these areas. Instead, each area indicates a topic of conversation and invitation to engage in dialogue. For example, at the end of a training programme it makes sense to evaluate the cognitive and problem-solving capacity of a student by asking them to submit a case formulation or case study, and to evaluate their interpersonal skills by looking at a video of their work with a client. Whoever is running the training programme needs to decide what level of cognitive or interpersonal skills is considered as satisfactory for a pass. The issue of development, on the other hand, is concerned with direction of travel, rather than current location. In a case study, a trainee may exhibit a rather limited conceptualization of the client. This is not acceptable, from a developmental perspective, if the level of conceptualization has not shifted from the case report that was submitted a year ago, if the student seems unable to respond to the 'scaffolding' offered by a tutor, if the student is unable to recognize what is wrong, has no plans for moving forward, and has not taken on board the feedback offered by their clinical supervisor or peer group members. If the answer to these questions is negative, then the student is stuck, or stagnating, and not engaged in a process of development. One of the practical implications arising from these factors is that it is only possible to gain an understanding of a therapist's trajectory of development by actually talking about it in an open and respectful manner. This, of course, takes time.

Part 2

Learning tasks for personal development

Introduction

The following chapters offer a series or personal learning tasks that relate to a wide range of themes and issues in therapist personal and professional development. These learning tasks reflect a *narrative* approach to personal and professional development based on the idea that effective therapists need to possess a detailed understanding of their own personal history and the way in which their life-story both impacts on clients and is affected by the client's story. No matter what therapeutic theory or model is being used, it is necessary for a practitioner to possess a *personal* understanding of what it means and how it operates; techniques and concepts are conveyed to the client through the person of the practitioner. The key personal and professional development questions that need to be explored during training are:

- who am I as a therapist?
- what do I bring, from my personal experience of life, to the role of therapist?
- what meaning do therapeutic concepts have for me personally, in relation to their capacity to enable me to live a good life?

In order to make pragmatic use of the answers to these questions, in terms of being able to work effectively with clients, it is necessary that the personal understanding that emerges is sufficiently *comprehensive*, in taking account of all relevant aspects of life experience, and sufficiently *coherent*, in offering a life-story that makes overall sense rather than being confusing and contradictory.

A narrative approach to personal and professional development contributes to a process of autobiographical exploration (thickening my story of who I am). The aim is to use systematic reflection to enable meaningful links to be made between current experience and the broader life-story. This kind of learning can take place in many different settings, for example keeping a personal journal, seeing a therapist, consultations with tutors, conversations with friends and family members. It can be particularly useful to carry out such activity in a small group of co-learners. The group is a setting in which the person hears other course members tell their stories, which is helpful in enabling connections to be made between personal experience and broader patterns of shared cultural experience. The small group is also a place in which the person can be called to account, for example if they describe themselves in ways that contradict the ways in which they are experienced by other members of the group. One way that a learning or experiential group operating along narrative lines can function is to choose one learning task each week and use that as the starting point for exploration and discussion. It can also be helpful to use a personal learning journal to reflect in private on the topic that has been selected.

Conceptually, the rationale for the kind of narrative perspective on personal and professional development that is being proposed here, is informed by the theoretical work of Hansen (2006, 2009). On the basis of detailed discussion of the meaning and usage of the concept of self-awareness, in various theories of therapy, Hansen (2009) concludes that it is more helpful for therapists to view the aim of personal development as being the construction of richly detailed 'self-story', rather than the attainment of 'self-awareness':

> . . . [when]self-awareness is the goal of counseling, the helping dyad is structured around finding the correct insights. This severely limits the variety of narratives that can be used. However, if self-storying becomes the goal, multiple storylines can be considered and appraised for their utility in meeting the objectives of the helping encounter. (p. 191)
>
> Substituting self-storying for self-awareness . . . . thaws the frozen narrative dynamic of helping encounters that are based on awareness, thereby freeing up new possibilities for human transformation. (p. 192)

This statement captures the spirit in which the learning tasks in this part of the book are offered. There is no intention of encouraging the discovery of 'correct insights', or even that such entities exist. Instead, these learning tasks constitute an invitation to 'free up new possibilities' in relation to your understanding of your own life and career.

At a more prosaic level, it is perhaps worth noting that the various learning tasks in the following chapters are divided into broad themes that correspond to general stages in a personal and professional development journey: reflecting on personal experience, being a member of a group, constructing a framework for understanding, building a relationship repertoire and developing a professional identity. In reality these stages and areas of exploration are all interconnected: you may find that your responses to some of the learning tasks may touch on a range of themes. An extensive set of learning tasks is provided. There is no expectation that it is necessarily helpful to attempt to work on all of these tasks. Instead, our experience has been that different individuals and groups are drawn to specific tasks that have a particular meaning or resonance for them. We do suggest, however, that you begin with the autobiography task at the start of Chapter 6, which functions as an anchor point for subsequent exploration.

Introduction

This section contains a series of tasks that invite you to write about various aspects of your own life. To be a counsellor or psychotherapist involves being able to draw upon your own experience, as a means of relating to the people you are trying to help. Your own life-story therefore becomes a resource, within which you can find meaning in response to the issues presented by those who visit you for help.

The writing tasks in this chapter serve two purposes in relation to developing therapeutic competence. First, they require you to explore both difficult and hidden, and also joyful, moments in your own life. They are intended to encourage you to look at yourself in terms of certain key questions.

- What are my strengths and gifts in connection with the task of being a therapist?
- What are my areas of vulnerability or uncertainty in relation to the activity of counselling/psychotherapy/mental health practice?
- What is my own personal understanding, arising from my life experience of core therapeutic processes such as initiating and maintaining change, sustaining satisfying relationships with others, and taking account of the ways in which my childhood and cultural environment have shaped my behaviour and identity?

By writing openly, honestly and in detail about your life you can begin to build what narrative therapists call a 'thick description' of your identity as a counsellor: 'thin description allows little space for the complexities and contradictions of life . . . It allows little space for people to articulate their own particular meanings of their actions and the context within which they occurred' (Morgan 2000: 12). By contrast, a *thick* story is one that is 'richly described', in which the intricacy of one's story, and the way it interlocks with the stories of other people, is expressed. A *thick* story encompasses multiple possibilities, in terms of what it says about the person's capacity to act and feel. Second, several exercises in later chapters make reference to the writing tasks in the present chapter. At various places, you will be invited to reflect on what you have written here from a range of theoretical and practical perspectives. It is a good idea, therefore, to spend some time writing in response to at least four or five of the activities in the present chapter, *before* moving on to tackle any of the activities in the chapters that follow.

All of these writing tasks present substantial challenges. It would not be realistic, or possible, to attempt all of them at one sitting. Some of these pieces of writing may be best tackled in short sections, adding new material on different occasions. It is possible that some of the writing tasks open up areas of memory and experience that are painful or unresolved. It may be right for you to wait until the right moment before embarking on these pieces of writing.

In any personal writing of this type, it can be helpful to create your own rituals and space within which you feel free to express yourself. Before you begin, you might wish to think about where and when would be the best time and place for you to do this kind of work.

Writing your autobiography: getting started

The purpose of this activity is to give you an opportunity to sketch the story of your life – your autobiography – in outline form. Being able to develop an understanding of your own development over time, and the ways in which you have responded to different external situations and demands can represent an invaluable resource for a therapist. Biographical self-awareness can help to provide you with a means of understanding your own reactions to clients and of empathizing with the experiences and dilemmas that clients describe in relation to their own lives.

Instructions

Spend some time thinking about your life – its past, present and future. Imagine your life is like a book, with each of the major parts or stages comprising a chapter. Provide titles for each of the chapters, and describe the content of each in a little more detail.

What is the underlying theme of the book? Can you find a title for the story as a whole?

Feel free to add anything else that seems relevant to constructing a framework for your autobiography. For example, there may be photographs, objects or pieces of music that represent significant memories. Remember – the purpose of this task is to facilitate *your* learning – go with what feels right for you.

As you are writing your autobiography reflect on how it feels to write about yourself in this way. Are there some memories that are painful which you would rather avoid? Are there other memories that are joyful and self-affirming?

You may find that, once you have started to write your autobiography, further episodes, scenes and themes come to mind. It may be valuable to add these to what you have written, so that you gradually build a more complete story of your life. It can often be useful to return to what you have written months or years later, and reflect on the ways in which you have 're-written' your personal history.

Suggested further reading

This activity draws on the work of the narrative psychologist Dan McAdams.

McAdams, D.P. (1993) *The Stories We Live By: Personal Myths and the Making of the Self*. New York: William Murrow.

McAdams, D.P. (2000) *The Person: an Integrated Introduction*, 3rd edn. New York: Wiley.

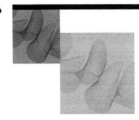

Keeping a personal learning journal

Many counselling and psychotherapy courses require students to keep personal learning diaries or journals as a means of reflecting on experience, and integrating theory and practice. A learning journal also makes it possible to keep track of personal change and development, and to keep hold of new insights (by writing them down) rather than losing them through forgetting. There is evidence that writing can in itself be therapeutic (at some point in the future you may want to suggest to some of your therapy clients that they might want to keep personal journals). Learning how to use a learning journal can be viewed as an opportunity to gain first-hand experience of a powerful therapeutic tool.

Some suggestions for how to keep a learning journal:

1 Choose a medium that is right for you. This could be a notebook, a ring binder that you can add pages to, or a word processor folder.

2 Keep it safe. You will not want other people to see what you have written unless you ask them to. Find a way of maintaining your privacy.

3 Date each entry in the journal and give it a title. This will help you to make sense of what you have written when you read it later.

4 Write quickly, as if you are allowing your 'stream of consciousness' to flow onto the page. Try not to censor what you write. Don't worry about spelling, punctuation or grammar – what you are writing is just for you.

5 Experiment with different ways of writing. Sometimes it is useful to write a list of ideas or images rather than attempting to produce continuous prose. Sometimes it may be helpful to draw pictures, use coloured pens or construct diagrams.

6 Some people find it helpful to get into a routine or ritual where they write their journal at a particular time and place each day.

7 Other people find it helpful to keep notebooks or scraps of paper with them so that they can note down 'flashes' or sudden ideas and insights.

8 A learning journal is not a personal diary. It is focused on your involvement with the roles, tasks and challenges of being or becoming a therapist.

Suggested further reading

Adams, K. (1990) Journal to the Self. New York: Warner Books.

Rainer, T. (1978) *The New Diary*. London: Angus and Robertson.

Rainer, T. (1997) *Your Life as Story: Writing the New Autobiography*. New York: G.P. Putnam.

Thompson, K. (2004) Journal writing as a therapeutic tool. In G. Bolton, S. Howlett, C. Lago and J. Wright (eds) *Writing Cures: An Introductory Handbook of Writing in Counselling and Psychotherapy*. London: Brunner-Routledge.

The story of a helping relationship

If you are to build on your own experience, then it is important to be aware of your own strengths and 'gifts' in therapy situations. The aim of this exercise is to give you an opportunity to begin to reflect on what you already know in relation to counselling – what are the skills and areas of awareness that you already possess?

This task requires writing about an occasion in which you were involved in a helping relationship with someone. The person you were helping could have been a counselling client, or equally well may have been a friend or family member. The helping relationship may be a formal one, in the context of your work, or an informal one, in the context of family or friends. Your task is to write an account of what happened when you helped this person. You should cover such points as:

- what led up to the helping incident, what was the background to you being involved with the person in this way?
- what were your aims, what did you want to accomplish?
- what did you say and do?
- what was going on in your mind at every stage of the process?
- what did you feel about what you were doing?
- what was the outcome – how did it all end?

Your account of this incident should have a beginning, a middle and an end. Keep it descriptive of what actually happened and what you actually did and felt – there is no need to interpret or explain your actions for the purpose of the exercise. It is best if you choose an incident to write about where you felt you were reasonably successful in what you were trying to achieve. Do not include any identifying characteristics of the person being helped. Change their name and any other possible identifying features, just in case anyone else reads what you have written.

The event you select should be a reasonably complex incident, something that lets you express and explore your capacity to help. You can write as much or as little as seems right to you, but aim to reach at least 500 words. Give your story a title.

Later exercises invite you to look at what you have written from a variety of different theoretical perspectives.

Suggested further reading

Combs, A.W. (1986) What makes a good helper? *Person-Centered Review*, 1, 51–61.

Combs, A.W. (1989) *A Theory of Therapy. Guidelines for Counseling Practice*. London: Sage.

The origins and development of your interest in therapy

This learning task gives you an opportunity to explore some of the ways that what it means for you to be a counsellor or psychotherapist has its roots in your life experience.

Instructions

Imagine yourself some time in the future, when you are established in your career as a counsellor or psychotherapist. Imagine that you are in *your* therapy room. It is your *ideal* therapy room, furnished and decorated to create an optimal working environment for you. Look around it – what do you see? What is this room like? Now, imagine that three or four of your closest professional colleagues or friends are coming to visit you in this room. These are people who really know you, who understand and accept you. Who are they? Welcome them. They have come for a special reason, to hear you tell your story of how you became a therapist. Think about becoming a therapist as a journey. Start right at the beginning of that journey. Tell them about your earliest experiences in family and school that somehow seem connected to your choice of becoming a therapist. Describe the people, places, relationships and events that have influenced you in the direction of therapy. Identify the choice points where you made decisions to commit yourself more fully to this type of work. Bring the story up to date. Tell them where you have arrived on your 'therapy journey'.

You may find it useful to close your eyes for a few minutes and imagine telling this story. Then write it down. Try to write in as much detail as you can. Write quickly – don't censor what you put down. You may find that there are other bits of your story that occur to you over the next few days – add these in later. Remember, this is your personal story. There are no right or wrong answers, and no one will see what you have written, unless you invite them to.

Your favourite story

Most of us have a story that, somehow, has a special appeal to us. This learning activity invites you to identify, then write down your favourite story, and then reflect on what you have written in terms of a series of prompt questions.

Identifying your favourite story

- What is your favourite story? This could be a fairy tale, novel, short story, play, film, TV show, etc. It may be a story that you always treasured and returned to at different points in your life, or it could be the first story that came to mind when you started to read these instructions.

- Write the story in your own words. It does not matter whether your version is different from the original – what matters is the story as *you* recall it. Write the story in as much vivid detail as you can, from beginning to end.

- If you have more than one favourite story complete this exercise at another time in relation to one or more further stories.

Exploring the personal meaning of your favourite story

Slowly read through the story you have written, and makes notes in response to the following questions:

- who is your favourite character in the story?
- why do you like this character so much?
- what happens to this character?
- who are the other characters? What kind of relationship does your favourite character have with these other characters?
- what is the setting for the story? Where does it take place?
- what is the main feeling tone of the story?
- How does the story end? How do you feel about the ending? If you could change the ending, what would your preferred ending be like?

- when did you first come across this story? How often, and in what ways, do you refresh your acquaintance with this story?
- why do you like this particular story? Why do you think that you chose it?

Your responses to these questions may suggest further details of the story – add these in to your written version as you go along.

Finally – give yourself some time to reflect on what you have learned about yourself from this process.

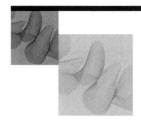

The self-puzzle

Most approaches to therapy emphasize the importance, in one way or another, of the person's sense of *self*. The notion of an individual self, as the core of who a person feels themselves to be, lies at the heart of counselling and psychotherapy.

There are many different ways of understanding or picturing the self. Sigmund Freud, for example, portrayed the self as similar to an iceberg, with the largest part beneath the surface.

In order to engage with a client's sense of self, it is usual to have an appreciation of your own sense of self. This activity introduces a simple method for beginning to explore the way that the self is structured and organized.

The exercise requires access to coloured pens or crayons, and a piece of blank paper (a large piece of paper is best). The task is to draw a map or puzzle, to represent the way you view yourself, following these guidelines.

- In some ways everyone is a puzzle, consisting of many different parts. You are a puzzle with parts that are unique to you. Draw a puzzle with parts that are labelled that best describe you, as you see yourself now. The number of parts, the shape of the parts and the positioning of the parts are all up to you. They should, however, be used to represent yourself as descriptively as possible. There are no right and wrong answers.

- This self-puzzle is your own creation – take as long as you wish to complete it. An alternative way of thinking about this creation is to look at it as a map. Similarly, the map of how you see yourself now will include areas that are labelled.

Be aware of the thoughts and feelings that accompany this task as you construct your puzzle or map. After you have made your drawing, it may be helpful to write some notes about these thoughts and feelings, and also what you have learned about yourself through engaging in this activity.

Once you have completed this exercise, you may find it useful to turn to the *Making sense of self* learning task in Chapter 8, which includes some guidelines for interpreting your self-puzzle picture. It can be valuable to repeat the self-puzzle on different occasions, to explore how your sense of self is affected by different contexts and life experiences. The idea of the self-puzzle has been adapted from Loo (1974).

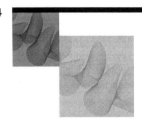

Thickening your autobiography: early memories

This exercise provides an opportunity to carry out some further exploration around the complexity and richness of your understanding of who you are – your autobiography. Many clients who seek therapy can be viewed as engaged in a struggle to achieve a coherent appreciation of many different, and often difficult, strands of their life experience. To be able to facilitate this kind of meaning-making it is invaluable to have undergone such a process yourself.

Early memories can often represent a highly significant source of meaning in a person's life. Take some time to identify, then write down, your earliest memories. Describe the memories in as much detail as possible. Begin by going back to your childhood and try to recall your *earliest* childhood memory. Try to recall a specific incident or event, not just a fragmentary impression. What are your impressions of yourself, and of each of the other people in the memory? Describe, also, the mood or feeling tone that goes with this memory.

Once you have written about your earliest memory you may find it useful to explore other early memories, for example, your first memory of your mother, father, siblings or other family members or memories of moments that were high points or formative turning points, in your life.

When reflecting on what you have written about your early memories, it is helpful to ask yourself whether the pattern of needs, relationships and emotions that are represented in these stories have persisted as themes in your life.

Suggested further reading

The importance of early memories was first recognized by Alfred Adler, one of Freud's inner circle. The specific early memory instructions used in this exercise are derived from research carried out by Martin Mayman and his colleagues. Further information on these studies can be found in:

Fowler, J.C., Hilsenroth, M.J. and Handler, L. (2000) Martin Mayman's early memories technique: bridging the gap between personality assessment and psychotherapy, *Journal of Personality Assessment*, 75, 18–32.

Many other researchers and therapists have explored the notion that early memories convey, in summary form, the key existential themes that influence the directions of a person's life.

Clark, A. (2002) *Early Recollections: Theory and Practice in Counseling and Psychotherapy*. New York: Brunner-Routledge.

Csikzentmihalyi, M. and Beattie, O. (1979) Life themes: a theoretical and empirical exploration of their origins and effects, Journal of Humanistic Psychology, 19, 45–63.

McAdams, D.P., Hoffman, B.J., Mansfield, E.D. and Day, R. (1996) Themes of agency and communion in significant autobiographical scenes, *Journal of Personality*, 64, 339–77.

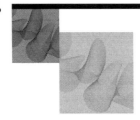

Giving and receiving feedback

Giving and receiving feedback represent basic building blocks of the process of personal development. The experience of using feedback to learn about how one is perceived by others consists of several discrete steps: that act of inviting or asking for feedback; receiving feedback in a non-defensive manner; reflecting on the meaning of the information that has been received and assimilating it into one's personal map of how one relates to others.

Offering feedback calls on a different set of skills: willingness to be responsive to the readiness of the other; communicating information that is specific, concrete and grounded in the personal experience of the other; receiving the reactions of the other in a non-defensive manner.

Instructions

- Identify one occasion within the past three months when you received feedback on your performance as a therapist.
- Identify one occasion within the past three months when you offered feedback to another person (for example, a client, a colleague), from your position as a therapist.
- For each event, take a few minutes to write about what happened, and what you felt, thought and did at each stage.
- How satisfied were you with the outcome of each of these feedback episodes?
- How have your understanding and skills around feedback developed since you entered training as a therapist?
- In what ways might your use of feedback be improved? Which elements of the feedback process are easier for you, and which bits are harder? How do you make sense of your strengths and difficulties around the feedback process – where do these qualities come from, in your life?

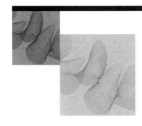

Exploring your relationship with your parents

It is clear in many cases that the difficulties that people have in their lives, and their whole way of being and relating with other people, is fundamentally shaped by their relationship with their parents in early life. Take some time to reflect on the questions listed below, and to write your responses in your personal learning journal. It may be that these questions stimulate other thoughts about the kind of relationship you had with your mother and father – write about these other aspects, as well. Note: This exercise refers to your relationship with the people who you regarded as your parents – not necessarily your biological parents.

- Describe your relationship with your parents, starting as far back as you can remember.
- Write down five adjectives or phrases to describe your relationship in childhood with your mother, and five adjectives or phrases to describe your relationship in childhood with your father.
- When you were upset as a child, what did you do, and what would happen?
- Describe your first separation from your parents. What happened? How did you react?
- Apart from your parents who else took care of you when you were little? Write down five adjectives or phrases to describe your relationship with each of these people.

As you are writing your responses to these questions, be aware of any feelings and emotions, or memories, that are triggered by this topic. Also, be aware of how easy or difficult it is for you to answer these questions. Make a note of these reactions.

Once you have mapped out the kind of relationship you had with your parents, it can be useful to try to make sense of these patterns in terms of *attachment* theory. How secure were your attachments in early life? To what extent did your mother and father provide you with an emotional 'secure base'? If there was a lack of security, then what form did this take? In what ways have these patterns of attachment persisted into your adult life? In what ways do they determine the kinds of relationships you have now with your partner/spouse, your own children and with friends and colleagues?

Finally – what are the implications of what you have learned about yourself through this exercise, for your work as a counsellor or psychotherapist and your capacity to offer a 'secure base' to clients who may have powerful unresolved attachment needs?

Suggested further reading

Further information on attachment theory can be found in:

McLeod, J. (2013) *An Introduction to Counselling*, 5th edn. Maidenhead: Open University Press (pp. 105–9).

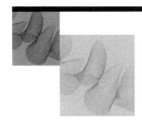

An inquiry into sexuality

The meaning and importance of sexuality is a topic that therapists need to be able to explore with clients. The aim of this activity is to provide a structure within which your experience of sexuality can be explored and the implications for your approach to counselling/psychotherapy can be identified.

Over the next two or three days, give yourself some time to engage in an inquiry into your sexuality. The following suggestions may help to get you started:

1 How has your sexuality developed? Draw a 'timeline', stretching from birth to the present, and enter the key events and stages/phases in the growth of your sexual awareness and behaviour.

2 Where does sexuality fit into your life? What part does it play? How do you use your sexual awareness and energy?

3 What are your attitudes and feelings in relation to people whose sexual orientation and behaviour differs from your own?

4 Describe how you have dealt with (or anticipate that you would deal with) a counselling relationship where:

   a you felt sexually attracted to the person you were helping

   b the person you were helping expressed sexual attraction toward you.

   How did you (or might you) respond in each case?

5 How would you react to a client who asked you to help them make sense of, and resolve, a sexual problem? Which sexual problems would you feel more/less confident in working with? What would you do if you did not feel confident or competent to work with the client in the way that they had requested?

6 How did you feel about reflecting on these questions, writing about them and perhaps discussing them in a group? What does this response tell you about your position in relation to sex and sexuality?

Once you have written and reflected around these questions (and possibly around other questions or themes that may have struck you as interesting in this area), then shift to consideration of the implications of what you have discovered for your sense of who you are as a therapist. For example, in what areas do you feel that you need to acquire more knowledge about sex and sexuality?

Suggested further reading

Denman, C. (2003) *Sexuality: a Biopsychosocial Approach*. London: Palgrave Macmillan.

Hudson-Allez, G. (2005) *Sex and Sexuality: Questions and Answers for Counsellors and Therapists*. Oxford: Wiley-Blackwell.

Your personal experience of therapy

One of the consistent themes in all approaches to counsellor and psycho-therapist training is that it is important for helpers to know what it is like to be the *recipient* of help. The aim of this activity is to encourage you to focus on your experience of being helped, and to reflect on the implications of that experience for your understanding of the helping process.

Instructions

What is your own personal experience of receiving therapy, either on a formal, contracted basis or informally from a friend, teacher or priest (or anyone else who is not a member of your immediate family)? Write a brief account of one useful or successful 'therapy' encounter that you have experienced. Make sure you write your story in a place that is private and confidential, so you can be as open and honest as possible.

You may find the following questions useful in terms of structuring your account,

- What was troubling you?
- At what stage of your life did this trouble emerge?
- What made you seek help, or be open to receiving help, at this particular point?
- How did you make contact with this 'helper'?
- What happened during the 'therapy' or 'helping' session or sessions?
- What were the most useful things your 'counsellor' did?
- Was there anything unhelpful that they did?
- How did this 'therapy' help you, what was the longer term impact on you?

Next, if possible, write a parallel account of a therapy/ helping episode (again, where you were the recipient of help) that was *not* helpful.

After you have written an account of your experience, take some further time to write about what you have learned about yourself, and about the process of therapy, from exploring these experiences.

Suggested further reading

Geller, J.D., Norcross, J.C. and Orlinsky, D.E. (eds) (2005) *The Psychotherapist's Own Psychotherapy: Patient and Clinician Perspectives*. New York: Oxford University Press. (This includes some fascinating accounts written by well-known therapists of their own personal experiences of being clients.)

McLeod, J. (2013) *An Introduction to Counselling*, 5th edn. Maidenhead: Open University Press (Chapter 24).

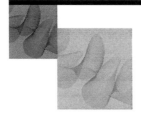

What you bring to therapy

For many people, the decision to become a counsellor or psychotherapist may follow a period of time studying and working in another profession or discipline, such as nursing, social work, teaching, the ministry or psychology. These early-career activities may shape the way that people are viewed, and 'helping' or 'therapy' are understood. Some trainees or students on therapy courses find that at the beginning of their training they have a tendency to look at issues through the lens or perspective of their primary profession. Others may be so highly motivated to leave their primary profession behind that they deny its relevance to their work as a counsellor.

This learning task invites you to reflect on *what you bring to therapy*, in terms of previous knowledge, skills and experience. The following questions are intended to focus your exploration of this issue.

1 Divide a page into two columns. In the left column, list all of the potential areas of your life experience that may be sources of knowledge, skills and experience that may be relevant to being a therapist. These could be jobs you have done (for example worked as an emergency room nurse for two years) or they could be linked to your family or personal life (for example my mother and father divorced when I was 10 years old).

2 In the right column, list the knowledge, skills and experience that you acquired as a result of the life experiences that you have identified. For example, working as an emergency room nurse may have helped you to 'understand how people behave in crisis' and to 'talk openly about death'. The divorce of your parents may have enabled you to 'be sensitive to the effect that loss of attachments in childhood can have on the rest of a person's life'.

3 What have you brought with you from your previous experience that might be a strength or asset in relation to your work as a therapist?

4 What have you brought with you that might be a hindrance or distraction? Examples: 'the "nurse" part of me wants to solve people's problems for them', 'studying academic psychology encouraged me to be objective and detached, rather than empathic'.

5 Some people find that therapy training seems to cut them off from what they already knew, in a practical sense, about helping others. Michael White (1997: 13) has described this process in these terms:

... entry into the culture of psychotherapy is associated with an induction in which the more local or folk knowledges that have been generated in a person's history are marginalised, often disqualified, and displaced by the formal and expert knowledges of the professional disciplines, and by a shift in what counts in regard to the significant memberships of a person's life. In this process the monoculture of psychotherapy is substituted for the diverse, historical and local associations of persons' lives.

To what extent have you been aware of this process taking place with respect to your own involvement in counselling training and practice? In what ways has therapy training moved you away from people and modes of helping within your family and community?

In order to make sense of the reflections and memories that have emerged during these activities, it may be valuable to consider that becoming a counsellor or psychotherapist can be viewed as a *journey*, which takes several years and on which many challenges must be faced. The questions above can help you to answer the question: what are the tools and skills that you take with you on this journey, and how best can you use them?

Suggested further reading

The experiences of counsellors and psychotherapists who have found ways to use their earlier work and study (in a wide range of professions and disciplines) to inform their therapy practice, are described in:

Thorne, B. and Dryden, W. (eds) (1993) *Counselling: Interdisciplinary Perspectives*. Buckingham: Open University Press.

The narrative therapist, Michael White, has argued forcefully that it is essential for therapists to remain in touch with the everyday life roots of their capacity to care for others:

White, M. (1997) *Narratives of Therapists' Lives*. Adelaide: Dulwich Centre Publications.

Exploring cultural identity

A sense of personal identity and belonging, of values and images of the 'good life', is rooted in the culture in which we live. When we meet someone else, we immediately begin to de-code all the cues relating to their cultural position – social class, gender, ethnicity, race, religion, sexual orientation, political affiliation, etc. At the same time, the other person is doing the same with us.

In therapy, it is necessary to be aware of the various strands of your cultural identity. This helps you to:

- be aware of the kind of impact you might be having on the other person;
- appreciate the cultural roots of the theory/model you are using;
- be sensitive to and curious about the other person's cultural identity;
- talk about cultural difference when this becomes relevant within the therapy relationship;
- appreciate the impact of social class, religion and other cultural factors in the life of the client;
- defuse your fear of the other.

The aim of this learning task is to help you to become aware of your cultural identity.

Instructions

1 Very quickly, without thinking too much about it, write down a list of your first 20 answers to the question 'Who am I?'. What does this list tell you about your cultural identity?

2 What are the different sources and strands of your cultural identity? Write out a genogram, or 'family tree', indicating beside each person (parents, grandparents, great grandparents) the information you have about their cultural and social position. What does this genogram tell you about your cultural identity: to what extent are these cultural themes influential in your life now?

3 What kind of cultural exploration have you carried out within your life? What new cultural influences have you been exposed to, or sought out? Draw a 'lifeline' from birth until now, and indicate on it the significant cultural shifts that you can recall. For example, have you moved away from, or towards, any of the cultural traditions represented by people depicted in your genogram? What new people or institutions have come into your life, bringing different cultural influences?

4 What is the meaning of 'home' for you? Where is the place you belong? (Home can be imaginary or real.)

Finally – reflect on, and write about, what you have learned about your cultural identity. How might you describe and sum up your cultural identity, if you were invited to work with a group of colleagues from another culture?

Suggested further reading

McLeod, J. (2013) *An Introduction to Counselling*, 5th edn. Maidenhead: Open University Press (Chapter 13).

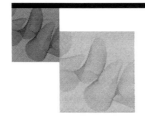

The Hofstede model of cultural dimensions

When offering a therapeutic relationship to a person from a different cultural background it is necessary to be able to take account of any differences in worldview that might arise. To be able to achieve such awareness, it is helpful to possess a framework for understanding cultural diversity. It is also necessary to be able to examine one's own position in relation to the factors specified in the framework. The Dutch social scientist Geert Hofstede has developed a model of the dimensions along which cultures differ, which has proved to be of value for counsellors and psychotherapists (Lago 2006). Through research in many countries, Hofstede (2003) has identified five key dimensions of cultural difference: power distance, individualism, masculinity, uncertainty avoidance, and long-term time orientation.

- *Power Distance* focuses on the degree of equality, or inequality, between people in a society. High power distance ranking indicates that inequalities of power and wealth have been allowed to grow within the society. Low power distance ranking indicates that the society de-emphasizes differences between power and wealth.

- *Individualism* reflects the degree to which a society reinforces individual or collective achievement and interpersonal relationships. High individualism indicates that individuality and individual rights are paramount within the society: individuals may tend to form a larger number of looser relationships. Low individualism indicates a more collectivist society with close ties between individuals, an emphasis on extended families, taking responsibility for fellow members of one's social group.

- *Masculinity* is the degree the society reinforces, or does not reinforce, the traditional masculine work role model of male achievement, control, and power. In high masculinity cultures, there is a high degree of gender differentiation and male domination. In low masculinity cultures, females are treated equally to males in all aspects of the society.

- *Uncertainty avoidance* focuses on the level of tolerance for uncertainty and ambiguity within the society. A high uncertainty avoidance culture is rule-oriented, with tight laws, rules, regulations and controls. Low uncertainty avoidance indicates more tolerance for a variety of opinions and greater acceptance of change.

- *Long-term orientation* is the extent to which a society exhibits a pragmatic future oriented perspective rather than a short-term point of view, reflected in a belief in investment in the future. Short-term orientation cultures live more for the moment.

Use your personal learning journal to reflect on where you stand in relation to these dimensions in terms of your own personal cultural values. Then, consider the following questions.

- Identify one or two people you know (friends or therapy clients) who are positioned differently in relation to the Hofstede dimensions. In what ways do these differences determine the type of relationship you have with these people?
- As a counsellor, which dimension positions would you find hardest to work with? How might you deal with the challenge of overcoming this cultural gulf between you and your client?

Suggested further reading

Hofstede, G. (2003) *Culture's Consequences, Comparing Values, Behaviors, Institutions, and Organizations Across Nations*, 2nd edn. Thousand Oaks, CA: Sage.

Lago, C. (2006) *Race, Culture and Counselling: the Ongoing Challenge*, 2nd edn. Maidenhead: Open University Press.

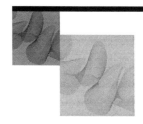

Feeling really understood

At the heart of counselling is the hope that someone else can accept and understand us for who we are, without judgement or analysis. The aim of this exercise is to encourage you to explore the significance, in your own life, of this type of moment.

Instructions

Part 1:
Sit quietly for a few seconds . . .
Think about the *last time you felt really accepted and understood by another person*. Once you have identified such an occasion, you should briefly describe (on a piece of paper):

- what the circumstances were;
- how you felt;
- what the consequences or effects of being accepted and understood were.

Following this piece of writing, take some time to reflect on the implications of the experience of being understood for your understanding of your relationships with other people.

Part 2:
Take another few moments to reflect on the people who have understood you, at various points in your life. Who were these people? How did they express their understanding? What impact did their understanding and acceptance have on your development as a person?

Part 3:
Allow yourself some further reflection on your experience of being with people who did not understand and accept you at different points in your life. What impact did their 'conditional' stance in relation to you have on the way that you felt about yourself?

Finally – write in your personal learning journal about these experiences, and their implications for your approach as a therapist. How important is it to you, to offer your clients an experience of being understood?

Suggested further reading

A research study that has analysed the experience of being understood is:

Bachelor, A. (1988) How clients perceive therapist empathy: a content analysis of 'received' empathy, *Psychotherapy*, 25, 227–40.

You may find it interesting to look at how your own experience compares with what was reported by participants in this investigation.

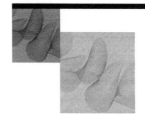

Mapping your relationship patterns

The aim of this activity is to give you an opportunity to explore the different types of relationships you have had with other people at various times in your life.

Take some pens and blank pieces of paper and make some simple diagrams that map out your relationships with the people who have been important to you at different stages in your life. It is best to draw each diagram on a separate piece of paper. In the middle of the page you should draw a circle to represent yourself. Write 'me' or your name inside this circle. Around yourself you should arrange the people who were important for you at that point in your life. The distance from you on the page should be used to represent their emotional, psychological or inner presence for you, rather than who was physically there, how far away they lived, or similar factors.

What you will end up with is like a map of the planets, with a set of circles around a central 'star'. Label each circle with the name of the person who belongs there.

There are two additional kinds of circles that you might find yourself wanting to draw. One is a 'dotted circle' to indicate someone who mattered a lot to you at that time of your life but who was not there at all as a physical presence. This might be someone whom you talked to in your head or thought about a lot even though you had no real connection with them at that time. Another kind of circle you might like to draw is a group circle. This you might draw to indicate people who were important as a group but didn't really matter as individuals. This might be important, for instance, if you wanted to indicate the importance of a sports team or Church group or something like that.

Draw these diagrams starting at age 5, then at 10-year intervals up to the present. Imagine yourself at age 5, try to fix yourself in time, and then pretend to interview yourself, asking about who is in your mind at that time. Then imagine yourself at age 15, 25, and so on up to your present age.

Once you have completed your diagrams, reflect on the following questions.

- Were there any moments of the interview when you had an emotional response? What do you think these feelings might mean?

- Were there any recurring themes or patterns that emerged around the types of relationships you have had over your life? What were these themes or patterns?

- What might be some of the implications of your relationship style for your work as a counsellor? How might the ways of relating that run through your life have an impact on your counselling? What kinds of relationships are you more likely to have with clients, colleagues, tutors/trainers and supervisors?

This activity is adapted from Josselson (1996). This book also provides a very useful framework for making sense of relationship patterns.

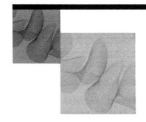

Engaging with difference

As a counsellor you may have little choice in relation to the characteristics of the people who use your service. Many people who seek your help will undoubtedly be easy to like, understandable, admirable. These are people with whom you may feel comfortable, and enjoy an easy rapport.

But there will be some service users who, for you, are difficult. These are people who make you feel far from comfortable, in whose presence you feel threatened, on edge, lost.

The purpose of this exercise is to explore the theme of *difference* in your life. Give yourself some time to reflect on, and write about, your responses to the following questions:

- which groups of people do you regard as being *most different* from you? Make a list;

- beside each group, write a set of adjectives that you might use to describe what they are like;

- generate another set of adjectives, to capture how you would imagine you might feel in the presence of a member of this group;

- what are the sources of your information about each of these groups of people? How much of your information is first hand, arising from personal contact, and how much from other sources? How much curiosity do you have about each of these groups?

Looking at what you have written, can you identify any themes in your responses? What lies at the heart of *difference*, for you? Is difference a matter of values, gender, social class, race, physical appearance . . .? What is it that makes someone different? Can you make connections between the meaning of difference, for you, and other aspects of your biography?

In relation to your work as a counsellor, imagine for a few moments who your least-preferred client might be. How would you react, and what would you do, if this client walked into your counselling room?

Finally: what is your personal experience of *being different*? What are the situations in your own life in which you have felt as though you did not 'fit in', were not accepted by others or did not 'know the rules'? What are your strategies for coping with such situations? How can you use your own experience of *being different* to inform your work as a counsellor?

Suggested further reading

The essential role of curiosity in dissolving difference is discussed in:

Dyche, L. and Zayas, L.H. (1995) The value of curiosity and naivete for the cross-cultural psychotherapist, *Family Process*, 34, 389–99.

A valuable collection of papers on the theme of identity and difference in therapy is:

McGoldrick, M. (ed.) (1998) *Re-visioning Family Therapy: Race, Culture and Gender in Clinical Practice*. New York: Guilford Press.

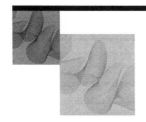

How do you cope with crisis in your own life?

The majority of people who use counselling do so in response to an immediate crisis. Even if a person has lived with difficulties for a considerable time, there is typically a particular event which triggers the decision to seek outside help. In order to appreciate what a person might be experiencing when they contact a counselling agency with a problem it is useful to reflect on your own personal experience of crisis.

Instructions

Write about your experience of a crisis in your own life, within the framework provided by the following questions.

- Briefly describe an episode in your life when you felt that you had reached a real crisis point as a result of a problem such as: work pressure; the demands on you as a carer; feeling depressed or hopeless; feeling really worried; feeling panic in particular situations; feeling traumatized after an accident or assault, etc.

- How was your capacity to cope affected during the worst points in this episode? Briefly describe the impact of the situation on your capacity to make decisions, take care of yourself, control your emotions, and 'think straight'.

- What helped you to get through this? Describe how you used both your own personal resources (such as humour, courage, spirituality) and other people, to help you to cope?

- How long did it take you to work through this crisis?

- What was the most difficult aspect of the crisis?

- What helped you most?

- What have you learned about yourself, and other people, as a result of this event? How have you changed?

- What have you learned, from your responses to these questions, that is relevant for your counselling practice?

Suggested further reading

James, R. and Gilliland, B. (2001) *Crisis Intervention Strategies*, 4th edn. Belmont, CA: Wadsworth.

Kanel, K. (1999) *A Guide to Crisis Intervention*. Belmont, CA: Wadsworth.

The experience of changing your own behaviour

Think of an occasion when you were able to change your own behaviour, in what you considered to be a positive direction. This should be an occasion when you intentionally planned to make a change in your behaviour and carried it through to completion. If it is not possible for you to identify a time when you were successful in changing your behaviour, then write about an episode in which you made an attempt to do so.

Instructions

Take a few moments to identify an unwanted habit or behaviour pattern that you have managed to eliminate or minimize in your life, or to establish a new pattern. The unwanted behaviour could be something like smoking, eating chocolate, arguing, being late . . . anything that you have wanted to change in yourself. A desired new behaviour could be something like taking more exercise, spending quality time with your family, or tidying up your room.

Describe what happened.

- What was the behaviour you decided to change?
- Why was this pattern of behaviour a problem for you?
- Had you tried – unsuccessfully – to change this habit before? Why had you been unsuccessful?
- What did you do to enable the change to take place this time?
- What helped you in making these changes?
- What hindered you?
- Did you experience any setbacks or relapses? How did you overcome them?
- What did you learn about yourself, and about how you would set about changing things in your life if you need to again in the future?

Have there been other change events in your life that have followed a different pattern, or is the event that you have described typical of how change happens in your life?

Finally: reflect on what you have written, in relation to the following questions:

- What are the implications of the episode you have described here for the way in which you understand change to take place in counselling/ psychotherapy?
- To what extent does your experience of changing your behaviour generalize to a counselling/psychotherapy situation?
- Which theories of therapy help you to make sense of the change process that you experienced?

The role of therapy in your life-story

People who seek counselling or psychotherapy are often stuck at a point of choice in their lives, faced with a dilemma over choices to make. To appreciate what this is like it is helpful to be able to draw upon an understanding of your own experience of making important life choices.

Instructions

Take a blank sheet of paper and a pen.

Starting with the year of your birth, draw a line to the first choice juncture that you can think of. Show that the path forks, giving you a number of alternatives. Which path did you take? Make sure to indicate the paths *not taken*, as well as the one that you did take. The choices should be ones that had an important effect on your life. When you have finished with one choice point, go on to the next one. Note your age at each choice point, and give each of the paths (taken and untaken) a brief label. Continue until you reach your present age.

The example below provides an illustration of the kind of choice map that you might generate (Figure 6.1).

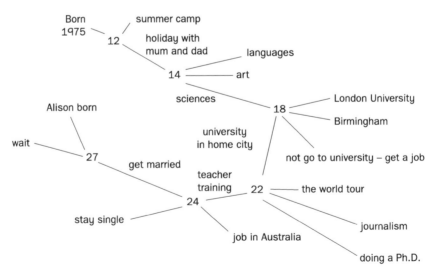

FIGURE 6.1 'My life choices', Andy Simpson, August 2013.

Reflecting on your choice map

Looking at your map as a whole, what patterns and themes do you see? Is there any consistency to the paths you have *not* chosen?

What has your involvement with therapy been around these choice points in your life? To what extent, and in what ways, has therapy facilitated your life decisions?

Suggested further reading

The choices in the life exercise have been adapted from the following paper:

Lewchanin, S. and Zubrod, L.A. (2001) Choices in life: a clinical tool for facilitating midlife review, *Journal of Adult Development*, 8, 193–6.

Reflecting on cycles of development in your life

Looking back over your own life try to identify cycles of change and development – periods of time during which an issue has emerged, became something pressing that needed to be dealt with, was addressed and then receded into the background.

Reflect on the following aspects of these cycles of change and development.

- How long did each cycle last?
- What were the triggers for the emergence of an issue: transition points in the course of our life (such as adolescence to adulthood)? External events? Being sufficiently stable and supported to have the resources to face a long-standing issue? Other triggers?
- To what extent did these cycles reflect separate and distinct areas of your life? Or does it make more sense to you to see them as all part of one core underlying issue?
- What did you do to enable each of these issues to be resolved? Can you see a recurring pattern around how you went about the task of dealing with each of these issues?
- How fully resolved were each of these cycles? Can you identify developmental cycles that opened up, but that you were not able to see through to a satisfactory conclusion?

What are the implications of what you have learned about yourself through this exercise?

- What are the implications in terms of your use of personal therapy, journaling and other personal development strategies?
- How can you make use of this knowledge to inform your work as a therapist? In what ways does your own experience sensitize you to the ways in which cycles of development occur in the lives of your clients?

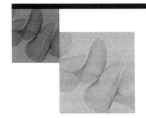

Knowing how your emotions are organized

The fundamental issue that drives most people to seek therapy is that they *feel bad* – there is some aspect of their emotional life that feels out of control, unmanageably painful or shameful. Often, when a person commences therapy, they may spend a lot of time rationalizing about what is the matter. Behind this talking and thinking there remains the same emotional struggle. All approaches to therapy, in their different styles, enjoin therapists to pay attention to the client's pattern of feeling and emotion, and to take these emotions seriously. In order to be able to do this with any degree of confidence and success it is necessary for anyone who practices counselling or psychotherapy to be aware, at a personal level, of how their own feelings and emotions are organized, and what they mean. This exercise is intended to facilitate self-exploration of personal emotional patterns.

Slowly read the following story to yourself: imagine that you are on your way to an important family occasion, a wedding that is being held in another country. In the run up to your trip to the wedding, you have been extremely busy. As a result, the other members of your family who are closest to you (for example your partner and/or children) have travelled in advance. You are booked on to the very last flight that will convey you to the city where the wedding is taking place, that will deliver you on time. It is a holiday weekend, and many people have decided to take flights to foreign destinations. You know that the road to the airport will be busy so you leave yourself plenty of time. However, there is an accident ahead of you on the road and you are completely stuck in a traffic jam for over an hour. By the time you have arrived at the airport, parked your car and run to the departure hall, it is too late to check in. Even though you have arrived at the check-in at least 30 minutes before the flight is due to board the staff absolutely will not let you go through. They insist that all passengers must check in 45 minutes before the boarding time. All of the other flights to your destination, or to cities that are near to your destination, are full. There is no way that you will be able to attend this important event that means so much to you.

As you realize what has happened, how do you feel? Give a name to that emotion. Reflect on the following questions.

- Is this feeling or emotion one that you typically experience in stressful situations?
- To what extent did this emotion or feeling make a contribution toward resolving your problem (at the check-in desk or in other situations in your life)? How functional is it?

- Is it a pattern of feeling or emotion that was particularly encouraged or rewarded in your family while you were growing up?

This exercise is adapted from Stewart and Joines (1987) and is linked to the transactional analysis model of emotional 'rackets'. However, it can also be used to explore other models of emotional functioning (see, for example, Greenberg 2002b).

What have you learned about yourself from this exercise? What are the implications of this learning, in relation to respond to your clients around emotional issues?

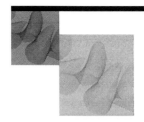

Becoming more emotionally available

An essential skill of being a therapist involves awareness of how you feel, and your emotional responses to another person, on a moment-by-moment basis. Emotional self-awareness is central to the process of developing a therapeutic relationship. The way you feel when you are with a client may be an indicator of how other people feel in the presence of that person. Alternatively, how you feel with a client may reflect how they feel, in themselves, at that moment – you may be resonating to their feelings. To be able to make use of these here-and-now emotional responses, you need to be able to differentiate between feelings that have been triggered by the client, and feelings that are concerned with your own life. In addition, clients may express, or be worried or ashamed about, a wide range of emotions. In order to make a connection with the client, a therapist needs to be open to all expressions of emotion. Being a 'sadness' specialist may be valuable with sad clients, but not so good for angry or fearful clients.

The two exercises below are intended to invite reflection on the development of emotional self-awareness.

Consider this list of emotion words: anger, anxiety, aversion, contempt, courage, dejection, desire, disgust, distress, fear, guilt, happiness, hate, hope, interest, joy, love, rage, sadness, shame, sorrow, surprise, terror, wonder.

- Which of these emotions do you feel most often in your own life? Least often?
- Which emotions to you overtly express most/least often?
- Which emotions are you most/least comfortable exploring with a client?
- What are the origins in your life of these patterns of emotional awareness and expressivity?
- What would your preferred pattern be?

Consider the following statements, which have been adapted from various widely used emotion self-awareness questionnaires:

1 I am clear about my feelings.

2 I pay attention to how I feel.

3 I often experience my emotions as overwhelming and out of control.

4 When I am upset, I can become angry with myself for feeling that way.

5 When I am upset, I become embarrassed for feeling that way.

6 I am often puzzled by sensations in my body.

7 I often don't know why I am angry.

8 It is difficult for me to reveal my innermost feelings, even to close friends.

- To what extent, and in what situations, do these statements describe your relationship with your own emotional life?

- In what ways would your answers have been different ten years ago?

- In what ways have the personal development activities you have undertaken as a therapist made a difference to these aspects of your emotional self-awareness?

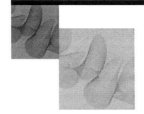

What are your defences?

A central theme in most approaches to therapy is the idea that the problems that a person has, are exacerbated and sustained by the fact that the person avoids them, rather than facing up to them and dealing with them in a direct manner.

Psychoanalytic theory makes sense of this process in terms of *mechanisms of defence*, for example:

- *repression* (motivated forgetting): the instant removal from awareness of any threatening impulse, idea or memory;
- *denial* (motivated negation): blocking of external events and information from awareness;
- *projection* (displacement outwards): attributing to another person one's own unacceptable desires or thoughts.

By contrast, behavioural theory tends to focus on patterns of behaviour that have the effect of avoiding painful emotions. For example:

- a person who experiences claustrophobia will not enter a lift or aeroplane;
- dealing with anxiety about an exam by eating chocolate;
- obliterating painful memories by getting drunk.

Learning task

Use your personal learning journal to reflect on, and write about, the following issues.

- What are the situations that are most likely to trigger your defences?
- What strategies do you use, in your own life, to avoid or defend yourself against situations, relationships, emotions or thoughts that are hard for you to face up to?
- What are the short-term and longer-term effects or consequences of using these defences? How effective are they, in keeping you safe?
- How conscious are you of implementing these avoidance strategies? Does it make sense for you, to regard them in psychoanalytic terms as processes that take place outside of your conscious awareness? Alternatively – to what extent do you make intentional plans to avoid certain situations and feeling states?

- What makes it possible for you to *stop* avoiding things (if you ever do)? For you, what have been the positive and negative consequences of ceasing to avoid things?
- The ideas of 'defence' is a metaphor, derived from warfare and sport. What are the implications of using this particular metaphor, to talk about the processes or activities that have been explored in this exercise? What other metaphors might be applicable? What are the pros and cons of these alternative metaphors?

Finally what are the implications for your work as a counsellor or psychotherapist of what you have learned from exploring this topic? How do your own defences or avoidance strategies impact on your work as a therapist? How are the defences or avoidance strategies of your clients expressed in their lives, and in the therapy room, and how do you work with these issues?

Suggested further reading

Clark, A.J. (2001) *Defense Mechanisms in the Counseling Process*. Thousand Oaks, CA: Sage.

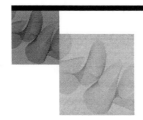

Identifying your 'signature theme'

Each of us can identify one or more issues that are struggles that are central to the way we live our lives. For example, one person may identify their core struggle as 'I can never really trust other people, and always have to be in control'. Another person may state that 'I can never accept that I am a worthwhile or loveable person – I always believe that other people know more than me, or are more interesting and likeable'.

Aponte and Kissil (2012) use the term 'signature themes' to describe these core struggles. They suggest that a major priority in therapist personal development is to become aware of one's signature theme or themes, make sense of how it has developed and appreciate how it shapes how one responds to clients.

- What is your own signature theme?
- Reflect on recent therapy sessions that you have facilitated. In what ways did your signature theme have an impact on the way you responded to your clients?
- In what ways might your signature theme represent a source of strength for you as a therapist? What does your personal experience of this issue open up for you, in terms of your understanding of your clients?

Suggested further reading

Further explanation and exploration of these ideas can be found in:

Aponte H.J. and Kissil, K. (2012) "If I can grapple with this I can truly be of use in the therapy room": using the therapist's own emotional struggles to facilitate effective therapy, *Journal of Marital and Family Therapy*, Dec 17 (epub ahead of print).

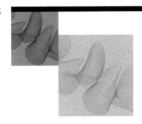

What is your psychopathology?

Everyone has a core issue, that they struggle with throughout their life. The psychoanalyst Michael Balint called this the 'basic fault'. For one person, the struggle may be around fighting off hopelessness, despair and depression. For another person, their life may be organized around controlling their fear of other people intruding on their boundaries. For a third person, the struggle may be around feeling loved and having a sense of being important to others.

The aim of this learning task is to give you an opportunity to reflect on your own enduring personal struggle. Take some time to reflect on, and write about, your responses to the following questions:

1 What is your own core issue or area of psychopathology? What is the pattern of thinking, feeling and action that gets you into trouble, or consistently undermines your life goals?

2 In terms of well-known models of psychopathology, would you describe yourself as schizoid, obsessional or personality disordered (or as having a tendency in any of these directions)?

3 Where does this pattern come from? How did this area of difficulty arise in your life?

4 What do you do to cope with this issue, or to manage it? Have you used different strategies at different points in your life? What strategies have been most and least effective?

5 Who knows about your 'basic fault'? How open or secretive are you, around this issue? What might it be like for you (or has it been like for you) to talk about this topic in your personal development group, or in other contexts?

6 How do you make sense of this key life dilemma or challenge? What models or theories have you found helpful (or unhelpful) in enabling you to understand, accept and resolve this issue?

7 What are the implications of your psychopathology, and your way of understanding it, for your work as a therapist?

Suggested further reading

An accessible introduction to the meaning of concepts such as 'schizoid' and 'obsessional' can be found in:

Joines, V. and Stewart, I. (2002) *Personality Adaptations*. Nottingham: Lifespace.

Essential reading on patterns of personality disorder is:

Benjamin, L.S. (2003) *Interpersonal Diagnosis and Treatment of Personality Disorders*, 2nd edn. New York: Guilford Press.

How relevant is spirituality?

The emergence of counselling and psychotherapy in the mid-twentieth century, as widely available forms of psychological care, was associated with an emphasis on a rational, scientific worldview that allowed little place for spirituality and religious experience.

However, more recently, influential figures in the therapy profession have called for a re-integration of spiritual experience into counselling theory and practice:

> Our experiences in therapy, and in groups, it is clear, involve the transcendent, the indescribable, the spiritual. I am compelled to believe that I, like many others, have under-estimated the importance of this mystical, spiritual realm.
>
> (Rogers 1980: 234)

> My own belief . . . is that anyone who wants to be a good psychotherapist has to have their own spiritual discipline which they follow.
>
> (Rowan 1993: 4)

What place does spirituality have within your approach as a counsellor? Consider the following questions:

1 What is your relationship with spirituality? What does spirituality mean for you?

2 In what ways do you (or might you wish to) draw upon spiritual practices (for example, prayer, meditation, yoga, reading, use of sacred objects) in preparing yourself for, or coping with the demands of, counselling work?

3 What types of spiritual experience have you encountered in your life? Have any of these experiences taken place during counselling, or similar work? What do you understand these experiences to signify?

4 How do you respond, when a counselling client, or a person during an everyday conversation, starts to talk about the importance of spirituality in their life?

5 Where do spiritual and religious factors fit into your theoretical approach as a therapist?

Suggested further reading

West, W. (2000) *Psychotherapy and Spirituality*. London: Sage (particularly Chapter 1).

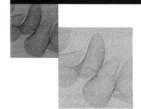

How do you cope under pressure?

Being a counsellor requires a capacity to be a companion to other people at their times of greatest anguish, despair or rage. In arguing for the importance of each counsellor developing an approach that is firmly based in their own personal way of being, Peter Lomas has argued that:

> . . . the business [of therapy] is to do with finding their own way, using their own intuition, learning to be themselves in the presence of someone who is asking for help, who is probably putting all kinds of pressures on them.
>
> (Lomas 1999: 25)

How have you responded in the past when someone with whom you have a relationship of care puts emotional pressure on you? Describe and explore the ways in which you have responded to the following life events:

- someone who is close to you is terminally ill;
- you are on your own looking after a baby or young child, who will not stop crying;
- you are with a child or teenager who has a tantrum because they cannot get what they want;
- someone you care about has received news of a loss;
- someone you care about is hurt;
- a person in your family has a 'breakdown', talks in ways that do not make sense, and declares that they are going away to end it all.

These are all very difficult situations, that can evoke a wide spectrum of feelings in a helper or companion. What has your emotional response been in these situations? What have you *done* – have you moved closer, retreated, withdrawn, displaced your concern into other behaviour . . .? How has the quality of your connection with the other person changed or shifted at these moments?

Once you have mapped out your way of reacting to these demanding situations in everyday life take some time to reflect on the potential implications of what you have learned for your work as a counsellor.

Do you have a preferred learning style?

Different people learn in different ways. For example, some people gain more from reading and individual reflection, whereas others learn better when actively doing things with others. The model of *experiential learning* developed by David Kolb (1984) suggests that the process of learning consists of four phases. For instance, if a person is interested in learning how to perform a task more effectively, the following processes can be observed.

- *Concrete Experience* occurs when the person is involved in carrying out a task.
- *Reflection* on that experience, on a personal basis – a process of individual sense-making.
- *Abstract conceptualization* is a phase that involves identifying general rules describing the experience, or the application of known theories to it, which leads to ideas about ways of modifying the next occurrence of the experience.
- *Active experimentation* represents the application of these new skills or ideas in practice, which in turn leads to a new set of concrete experiences, which are then in turn reflected on. . . . .

This sequence of learning steps may take place within a few minutes, or may extend over months, depending on the topic. Kolb, and other researchers, have noted that although any competent learner will have a capacity to function in each of these ways, individuals tend to grow up specializing in one or two 'preferred' learning processes. The theory of personal learning styles devised by Peter Honey is based on four primary learning styles, which correspond to the four phases of Kolb's cyclical model.

- Activists: involve themselves fully in doing things, enjoy team work, and eagerly embrace opportunities for practical, experiential activities. They are open to new learning experiences.
- Reflectors: prefer to stand back and look at experiences from many different perspectives. They collect data and prefer to think about it thoroughly before coming to any conclusions.
- Theorists: adapt and integrate observations into complex but logically sound theories. They are interested in concepts, and think problems through in a step-by-step, logical way.

- Pragmatists: keen to try out ideas, theories and techniques to see if they work in practice. They positively search out new ideas and take the first opportunity to experiment with applications.

A preference for any one of these learning styles is likely to mean that a person will be frustrated with learning experiences that are based in a different model. For example, activists may become impatient with theory and precise instructions, whereas theorists may be uncomfortable with the messiness and ambiguity of many practical situations.

What are the implications of your learning style for your personal approach as a counsellor? Consider the following questions.

- How do you define your learning style?

- In what ways does your preferred style of learning explain your level of interest and enthusiasm in different types of learning within your counsellor training (for example, reading about theory, participating in a personal development group, being an observer in skills practice sessions)?

- What are the links between your preferred learning style and the theoretical approach(es) with which you most identify?

- Could your way of working with clients, within an actual counselling session, be viewed as an expression of your learning style? Do you create certain kinds of learning opportunities for clients and not others?

- How sensitive are you to the learning styles of other people? How well do you respond to the learning process of clients who have learning styles different from your own?

- What are the implications of models of leaning styles for your capacity to empathically engage with the experiences of other people?

Suggested further reading

Honey, P. and Mumford, A. (1982) *Manual of Learning Styles.* London: Peter Honey Publications.
Kolb, D.A. (1984) *Experiential Learning: Experience as the Source of Learning and Development*. Englewood Cliffs, NJ: Prentice-Hall.

A number of self-test learning styles inventories are available on the internet.

What motivates you?

The list below includes some of the reasons that people give for wanting to be a counsellor or psychotherapist. How important are each of these sources of motivation for you in your counselling work? Place a '1' beside the most important, '2' for the second most important, etc. Add any additional sources of motivation that come to mind.

Contact with other people (clients) in a controlled situation   ___

Discovery – learning about human beings   ___

Social status and respect   ___

Payment, making a living   ___

Helping or healing others   ___

Being powerful and having an impact on clients   ___

Self-therapy, learning about myself through the work   ___

Vicarious experience, the interest of learning about other
people's lives   ___

Feeling wanted and needed   ___

Because I received therapy myself and want to 'give something back' ___

Doing a job that is intellectually challenging   ___

Other sources of motivation not included in the above list   ___

Once you have rank ordered these sources of motivation, consider the following questions.

- How open are you with other people, such as colleagues, about your motivation to do this work? There may be sources of motivation that you conceal from others – what difference would it make to own up to these factors?

- How do these sources of motivation/satisfaction influence and shape the way you work, for example the decisions you make about the kind of work that you do?

- How have you acquired these motives – where do they come from in your life? For example, are there experiences in childhood, or significant people you have met, that you can recognize as representing the origins of these motives?

- In what ways have the sources of motivation and satisfaction associated with your work as a therapist changed over the course of your training or career? What has triggered these shifts?

- How sustainable are these factors? Can you anticipate any of them becoming less motivating for you in the future? What would you do if this happened?

Suggested further reading

The issue of therapist motivation is discussed in:

Barnett, M. (2007) What brings you here? An exploration of the unconscious motivations of those who choose to train and work as psychotherapists and counselors, *Psychodynamic Practice*, 13, 257–74.

Farber, B.A., Manevich, I., Metzger, J. and Saypol, E. (2005) Choosing psychotherapy as a career: why did we cross that road? *Journal of Clinical Psychology*, 61, 1009–31.

Sussman, M. (2007) *A Curious Calling: Unconscious Motivation for Practicing Psychotherapy*, 2nd edn. New York: Jason Aronson.

Exploring the possibilities of reflective writing

Writing represents a tool for personal and professional development that many therapists have found to be valuable and meaningful. One of the factors that needs to be taken into account, when using this method for facilitating development, is that almost everyone needs to learn how to use writing as an aide to reflection. This is a genre of writing that is different from academic writing, keeping a diary or sending texts to friends. Some people feel self-conscious about reflective writing. Others may be more confident and open to the possibilities of writing, but unsure of how to proceed.

The books listed below provide a wealth of ideas, examples and exercises around the use of reflective writing for personal and professional development. Effective writing is a skill. To make best use of this skill it can be helpful to spend a bit of time learning from those with more experience of using it.

Suggested further reading

Adams, K. (1998) *The Way of the Journal: A Journal Therapy Workbook for Healing*. Baltimore, MA: Sidron Press.

Baldwin, C. (1992) *One to One: Self-Understanding Through Journal Writing*. London: Evans Publishing.

Bolton, G. (2013) *The Writer's Key: Creative Solutions for Life*. London: Jessica Kingsley.

Bolton, G., Howlett, S., Lago, C. and Wright, J.K. (eds) (2004) *Writing Cures: An Introductory Handbook of Writing in Counselling and Psychotherapy*. London: Brunner-Routledge.

Cameron, J. (1994) *The Artist's Way. A Course in Discovering and Recovering your Creative Self.* London: Souvenir Press.

DeSalvo, L.A. (2000) *Writing As a Way of Healing: How Telling Our Stories Transforms Our Lives*. Boston, MA: Beacon Press.

Fox, J. (1997) *Poetic Medicine: The Healing Art of Poem-Making*. New York: Tarcher Press.

Hunt, C. (2000) *Therapeutic Dimensions of Autobiography in Creative Writing*. London: Jessica Kingsley.

Hunt, C. and Sampson, F. (eds) (1998) *The Self on the Page. Theory and Practice of Creative Writing in Personal Development*. London: Jessica Kingsley.

Progoff, I. (1975) *At a Journal Workshop*. New York: Dialogue House.

Rainer, T. (1978) *The New Diary*. London: Angus and Robertson.

Rainer, T. (1997) *Your Life as Story: Writing the New Autobiography*. New York: G.P. Putnam.

Wright, J. and Bolton, G. (2012) *Reflective Writing in Counselling and Psychotherapy*. London: Sage.

Reflecting on the experience of writing about yourself

The activities in this chapter have invited you to write about many different aspects of your personal life. The technique of personal writing has been used by many therapists as a way of helping clients, for example in the work of the American psychologist James Pennebaker.

In reflecting on your experience of writing about yourself, consider the following questions.

- What impact has this experience had on you? Has it been helpful to write about yourself, or unhelpful?
- What are the ways in which writing has been useful or otherwise for you?
- What have you learned about what is the best time and place for you, in terms of productive personal writing?
- What have been the differences that you have noticed between talking about an issue or experience and writing about it?
- In what circumstances might you use writing activities with clients? How might you integrate writing tasks into your face-to-face conversations with clients?

In relation to the autobiographical dimension of these writing activities, it may be useful to reflect on questions such as the following.

- What effects have you noticed, in terms of your feelings about your life and your attitude towards yourself that have arisen from your autobiographical writing?
- Has your autobiographical writing helped you to identify episodes or events in your life that were previously out of your awareness? How useful (or otherwise) has it been for you to remember these instances?
- What are the distinctive personal strengths and accomplishments that you have uncovered, through exploration of your autobiography?
- How might a full and rich understanding of your own biography or life history help you in your work with clients?
- To what extent, and in what ways, do you encourage your clients to articulate and reflect on their life stories?

Suggested further reading

Bolton, G., Howlett, S., Lago, C. and Wright, J.K. (eds) (2004) *Writing Cures: An Introductory Handbook of Writing in Counselling and Psychotherapy*. London: Brunner-Routledge.

Hunt, C. (2000) *Therapeutic Dimensions of Autobiography in Creative Writing*. London: Jessica Kingsley.

McAdams, D.P. (1993) *The Stories We Live By: Personal Myths and the Making of the Self*. New York: William Murrow.

Pennebaker, J. (1997) *Opening Up: The Healing Power of Expressing Emotions*. New York: Guilford Press.

Pennebaker, J.W. (2004) *Writing to Heal: A Guided Journal for Recovering from Trauma and Emotional Upheaval*. Oakland, CA: New Harbinger Press.

Personal development through participation in a learning group

Introduction

There are several reasons why participating in a learning group can make an important contribution to the personal and professional development of counsellors, psychotherapists and mental health practitioners:

- the way that a person responds to being in a group typically recapitulates earlier experiences in family and friendship groups; the learning group provides a setting for learning about these areas of personal development;

- the group is a setting for giving and receiving support and challenge;

- responding to other members of the group provides ongoing practise in offering the qualities of empathy, congruence and acceptance in relationships;

- group members can give each other feedback, on their reactions to what a person has said or done in the group, thereby helping that person to become more aware of how they are viewed by others;

- group members can encourage each other to explore difficult topics in more depth;

- working in a group provides opportunities to learn how to engage constructively with people who may be experienced as threatening, hard to understand, or 'different';
- within a group it is possible to become more aware of the universality of human experience, and the interconnectedness of persons;
- counsellors are sometimes called upon to facilitate therapy groups – the experience of being a member of a learning group provides an appreciation of group dynamics and an introduction to what is involved in the role of group facilitator.

It is recommended that the learning tasks in this chapter should be explored not only individually, for example through the medium of a personal learning journal, but also collectively, in the context of a learning group. The group may be facilitated by a tutor or external consultant, or may be a peer group comprising only course members or co-learners. The group may be a formal element in a training course, or organized by course members within their own time. It is useful to complete the first two learning tasks in advance of the first meeting of the group. It is useful to try the *Making connections and being responsive to others* exercise near the beginning of the group – it is intended to function as a model or template for how a group might work together. Other exercises are intended to be completed as soon as possible after each meeting of the group. There are also some activities that can be used toward the end of the life of the group, to enable members of the group to reflect together on how the group has functioned, and what it has meant to them.

Exploring your feelings, fantasies and expectations about the group

Before the first meeting of your learning group, take some time to write freely about your feelings and fantasies about this group.

- What do you *hope* will happen in the group?
- What are your *fears*, in terms of awful things that might happen in the group, or that you might be called upon to do?
- Where do these reactions come from, in terms of your own life history?

Having explored your expectations for the group, what have you learned about how a counselling client might feel in making a first appointment and anticipating his or her first meeting with a therapist?

What are the group norms or rules that are particularly important to you? In relation to establishing 'groundrules' for the group, take a few minutes to note what **you** want to see happen, in relation to such factors as:

- starting and finishing on time;
- what happens if people do not turn up;
- talking outside the group about what has happened inside it;
- touching each other;
- what happens if someone walks out during a session;
- pressure to talk/freedom to remain silent;
- honesty;
- the role and responsibilities of the facilitator;
- the role and responsibilities of group members;
- how decisions are to be made about how the group uses its time.

Having explored some of your ideas about desirable and undesirable group norms, take some further time to reflect on the implications of what you have written, for your role as a counsellor, and your experience of being a client in therapy. To what extent, and in what ways, have you participated in discussing norms or groundrules for counselling and psychotherapy with your therapist or with your clients? How useful might it be to do more of this?

Finally, reflect on your reading of therapy theory so far, particularly the theory or theories of therapy around which your training course is built (or the theories that have most personal meaning and utility for you). What do these theories have to say about processes of therapeutic learning and change? What do you think should happen in the group if it is to become an environment within which these processes will occur to maximum effect? What does optimal (or non-optimal) group functioning look like, from the perspective of your preferred theories?

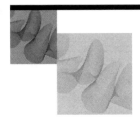

Using the group to experiment with new ways of relating to others

As we grow up, we tend to develop a specialized role in our family. For example, some people find themselves playing the role of 'peacemaker', whereas others will consistently be in the role of 'troublemaker', 'quiet one', 'joker', 'source of good ideas', 'dreamer', etc. Usually, people carry these roles into other groups in which they are involved. For example, someone who was a 'troublemaker' in their family might also ask awkward questions in staff meetings at work, or always be trying to bend the rules. The existence of these roles is inevitable, but also carries negative implications for the practice of counselling. Our clients require us to be able to respond to them in a wide range of ways, and not always to revert back to our preferred role position. The learning group provides an opportunity to experiment with your own role flexibility.

Instructions

- Identify the group role or roles that you have typically fulfilled in your family of origin or other groups.
- Identify a new and different role that you have seldom or never played in a group and which represents an aspect of yourself that you would like to make more available. For example, if you have tended to be the 'quiet one' in groups, you might choose to develop your capacity to be someone who is a 'constant source of ideas'.
- Plan and rehearse your strategies for acting this new role. For example, who are the models (people you know or people you have observed in movies or on TV) that you might base yourself on?
- Take every possible opportunity to play this new role in the group.
- Use your personal learning journal to reflect on the experience of this new role – what it felt like, how other people responded to you in a different way, what happened to the role that you previously fulfilled.

This exercise can include (optionally) disclosing to other group members what your 'experimental' role will be, and inviting them to give you feedback when they notice you performing both the new role and your older more familiar roles.

Toward the later stages of the life of the group reflect on the personal and professional implications of what you have learned through this activity. What are the implications for your own sense of self – the way that you understand yourself and describe yourself to others? What are the implications for your understanding of how people change in therapy through carrying out behaviour change 'experiments'?

Making connections and being responsive to others

The aim of this exercise is to explore the experience of being open to the experience of another person, and of letting that person know how their story has had meaning for you. These are processes that are essential aspects of the learning group, and are intrinsic to a narrative approach to working together in groups.

It is important to take responsibility for yourself – what you share is under your control. It is important to be respectful of others, by being supportive and honest, and holding confidentiality.

This learning task involves taking it in turns to carry out the activity described below.

1 *Telling the story of a development in your life*. Take a few moments to think about developments in your work or life that you are pleased with. Choose *one* such development to describe to the group. Tell a bit of the story of what happened. Say something about the beliefs, intentions and commitments that this development contributes to, in your life. Take time to get a rich description of the meaning of this development for you.

Once you have described this pleasing development in your life, reflect on these further questions.

Who is someone in your life who would be *least* surprised to hear you talking about these intentions or commitments – someone you know or once knew who would recognize and value the commitment you were talking about? It may be someone you actually know or knew, or it could be a character in a book or story. What is this person's name? What do they look like? When did you know them? Are there any special things about them?

What might this person have noticed you doing in the past that might have helped them to notice the commitment that you spoke of just now? What might it have meant to this person to have seen how this commitment was important to you, and the actions that you have taken to align yourself with it? What contribution do you imagine that this might have made to their life?

If you were to see yourself now through that person's eyes, what would you most appreciate about yourself?

What difference would it make to you, in your work and life, if you were to hold the presence of that person with you in what you do?

You will have about 10 minutes to tell this story in the group.

2 *The responses of those who witnessed the story.* The intention is not to praise/applaud or criticize the person who told the story, or to interpret their story in theoretical terms, or to offer a therapeutic response. The aim, when making a response to a story you have heard, is to use the experience to thicken your own story, and that of the teller, by making connections.

The following questions can be used to help you to shape your response.

What caught your interest? What touched or moved you in what you heard? As you listened which expressions caught your attention or captured your imagination?

What images of this person's life, of their identity, and of the world more generally, did these expressions evoke? What did these expressions suggest to you about the person's purposes, hopes, beliefs, values, dreams and commitments?

What did this have you thinking about, in relation to your own work and life? Which aspects of your own experiences of life resonated with the images and expressions of the teller? What is it about your own life that meant you were touched in this way?

Where does hearing this take you? How will it contribute to possibilities in your own life? Where have you moved to in your thinking or experience of life? How is your life different for having moved to this new place?

3 *The process of going round the group.* Each member of the group, in turn, shares his or her response to the 'story of a development . . .' that they have heard, until everyone has offered a response. Once this 'round' is complete, another member of the group tells his or her story of a 'pleasing development', followed by a further set of responses.

Leave 10 minutes at the end, after everyone has told their story and been responded to, to reflect together on the experience of doing the exercise. What did you learn about yourself and your relationships with others?

Suggested further reading

You can read more about this approach to working in groups (which derives from narrative therapy) in:

Morgan, A. (2000) *What is Narrative Therapy.* Adelaide: Dulwich Centre Publications (Chapter 14).
White, M. (1997) *Narratives of Therapists' Lives.* Adelaide: Dulwich Centre Publications (Chapter 10).

First impressions of group members

The first meetings of a learning group represent a situation in which it is possible to reflect on the significance of first impressions. The first encounter between people is one in which a great deal of information is processed very quickly. The process that takes place can be regarded as an example of *intuition*, where conclusions about a person are reached without being able to explain any logical grounds for them. This kind of intuitive competence is important for therapists, who need to be able to respond to clients on the basis of a holistic, immediate, 'felt' sense of what may be happening in the therapeutic relationship. As a relationship develops, a person is able to engage in 'impression management', to create a preferred image of who they are, in the minds of those with whom they interact. Being sensitive to first impressions opens up the possibility of being able to reflect on what it might mean that one's image of another person changes over time: 'when I first met them, I thought that they were . . . ., but as I got to know them, I realized that they were . . . .'

Make notes in relation to the following questions.

- What were your first impressions of other group members, and the group facilitator?
- For each person, who did they remind you of?
- Describe the physical presence of each person.
- Describe the voice quality of each person.
- Who did you feel close to from the start?
- Who did you want to move away from?
- Think of each group member as an animal – which animal would they be?
- What was it like for you, the first time you directly engaged in conversation with each member of the group?

Having recorded these first impressions, take some time to reflect on what they might mean.

- How do you make sense of these first impressions, in terms of the connections in your own mind between this group and other groups to which you have belonged? Are there the same set of 'characters' in this group as in other groups in which you have been a member? If so, what are the implications for your sense of the drama of your own life?

- How do you make theoretical sense of these first impressions? For example, if the members of your learning group trigger memories of people from your childhood, would this be a confirmation of the psychoanalytic theory of transference? In what other ways could you explain these first impressions?
- What are the implications of first impressions for the establishment of a collaborative relationship between a therapist and a client?

Suggested further reading

The topic of first impressions and intuitive decision-making is discussed in:

Gladwell, M. (2006) *Blink: the Power of Thinking without Thinking.* London: Penguin.

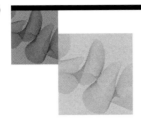

Talking about yourself in the group

At some point near the start of the learning group you will be expected to share aspects of your life-story with other members of the group. As the group moves on to other topics, you may be called on to disclose early memories, your feelings about your sexuality and other sensitive and personal topics.

Use your personal learning journal to reflect on your experience of talking about yourself:

- What was this like for you, to talk about yourself?
- How did you feel, when it was your turn? At what point did you volunteer – early or late?
- What did your way of dealing with disclosing sensitive personal stories tell you about yourself?
- What information about yourself did you hold back? To what extent was this a conscious choice, or did you just 'forget' to talk about certain areas?
- What held you back from telling your story (for example, lack of trust, a belief that other people would not be interested in you)?
- What made it easier for you to talk about yourself?
- What did you observe in other people, in terms of the ways in which they coped with these tasks?
- What was it like to listen to other stories? Did these personal stories help you feel closer to other group members, or otherwise? If it did help you to feel closer, then how and why is it that personal story-telling can have this kind of effect?

What are the implications for your practice of therapy, of what you have learned about the challenges involved in sharing personal stories, and the ways in which self-disclosure can be inhibited or facilitated?

How do you make sense of your own, and other people's performances, in terms of theories of personality and psychopathology? For example, to what extent does it make sense to interpret the ways in which people told their stories in the group, as examples of narcissism (listen to my story and you will realize how wonderful I am), early attachment difficulties (my story is not really very interesting – I do not expect anyone will want to hear it) or other patterns?

Suggested further reading

Farber, B.A. (2006) *Self Disclosure in Psychotherapy*. New York: Guilford Press.

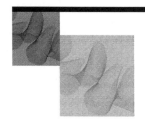

Reflecting on significant events in the group

After each session, take a few minutes to write a description of the most significant event that happened in the group that week. A significant event or moment can be anything that happened that is memorable and meaningful for you. Your account of the event should include:

- what led up to the event;
- what took place;
- what the consequences were (that is, whether and how the climate of the group shifted afterwards, and in what direction).

Describe your own involvement in the event (whether as an active participant or passive observer), including your thoughts, feelings and fantasies, and what you did and said (or wanted to do and say).

Creating a series of event descriptions of this kind can be invaluable in tracing the development of the group, and the changes taking place in your own role in the group. Yalom (2005a) suggests that there are different types of helpful factors in groups:

- group cohesiveness;
- instillation of hope;
- universality;
- catharsis;
- altruism;
- guidance;
- self-disclosure;
- feedback;
- self-understanding;
- identification;
- family re-enactment;
- existential awareness.

You can deepen your appreciation of group processes by looking at how the events you have described can be understood in terms of these categories, and reading Yalom's (2005a) discussion of the broader significance of these types of processes. It may also be of interest to reflect on the difference between significant events in which you were directly involved as a key actor and those where you were an observer. Finally, it can be illuminating to compare your ideas about significant events with the events identified by other members of the same group, and try to make sense of any differences in perception that emerge. Not everyone in the group will identify the same events as being significant.

If you have collected significant event descriptions over the life of the group, look at whether different types of event were observed in the later stages of the life of the group, compared with the early stages? If there are differences, what might this mean in terms of an understanding of group processes?

Finally – reflect on what you have learned from this exercise about the process of individual counselling and psychotherapy. Do different types of change events occur in individual therapy compared with group therapy? Or do the same kinds of things happen, but in a different form?

Suggested further reading

Bloch, S., Crouch, E. and Reibstein, J. (1981) Therapeutic factors in group psychotherapy, *Archives of General Psychiatry*, 38, 519–26.

Yalom, I.D. (2005a) *Theory and Practice of Group Psychotherapy*, 5th edn. New York: Basic Books.

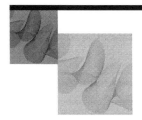

Endings: reflecting on the life of the group

In preparation for the ending of the learning group it can be useful for group members to reflect together on how they have worked together.

Exercise: being on a journey together

Take some time to draw a picture of the group and all its members as if it was a boat on some kind on a journey. What kind of a boat is it? What kind of a journey is it on? What roles have different members (and the facilitator) played – captain, crew, passengers, cargo, saboteurs, rescuers, etc.? What was the journey like – what were the most memorable episodes? Use your imagination, and imagery and colour, to create a picture that represents your own personal experience of the group over the past few months. Each person brings their picture into the group, shows it to their fellow group members and talks them through what it means. This exercise is intended to open up the process of reflecting on the group experience. The group journey metaphor allows members to sum up their feelings about the group as a whole.

Exercise: reflecting on key aspects of the group experience

There are many different processes that can take place in learning groups. In any particular group some of these processes may be more salient than others. Read through the list of questions below, and create a space to reflect and write on the ones that seem to you to be most significant in relation to your own learning group experience. If you have kept notes of what happened in the group week-by-week it will be easier to explore these issues in depth.

1 *The emotional climate of the group*. What were the main feelings and emotions that you experienced in the group? Did you have different feelings and emotions at different times? How did you express or act upon these emotions? How did you observe other people acting on their emotions?

2 *Leadership style*. What was facilitative, for you and other people, in the group? What kinds of processes made learning and change

possible? What was the facilitative style of the leader? What have been the advantages and disadvantages, or consequences, of that style for the group as a whole and for you as an individual?

3 *The development of group norms and culture.* Were there any phases or stages in the life of the group? How would you describe the different characteristics and 'feel' of each of these stages? What word or image would you use to describe each stage? Were there specific transition points or events that marked the shift from one stage to the next? What were they? How would you describe your own behaviour and activity at each stage or phase of the group? How did you behave or feel differently at each stage? At which stage did you feel most comfortable or 'at home'?

4 *Group roles.* In what ways did you act consistently in the group – for example, by saying the same kinds of things in different sessions, or responding to particular kinds of events in a certain manner? How would you describe your consistent way of being in the group? Did you have a specific role within the group? Did this role change over time? What roles did you observe other people playing? Did their roles change over time?

5 *Relationships between group members.* How was the issue of *intimacy* handled by the group? Getting close to others in a professional arena can be threatening and confusing. How did you cope with this. What did you feel? What did you do? Did you allow yourself to get close? When you observed intimacy between other group members how did you feel about this? What values, moral and ethical issues does the level of intimacy in the group raise for you?

6 *The group as an arena for family re-enactment.* What has being a member of this learning group evoked for you, in terms of your experience of being a member of a family? Did you enact roles and patterns of interaction that you learned in your family of origin?

7 *The group as a context for exhibiting therapist qualities and competencies.* Having spent all these hours in a learning group with a set of colleagues, who would you go to (or recommend a friend or family member to consult) as a therapist? Have you shared these views with colleagues in the group? Who do you intend to stay in contact with after the ending of the group?

Use these questions to reflect on the following.

- What you have learned about yourself as a person: the self-discoveries and insights that have been triggered by interacting with other members of the group on a shared learning task.

- What you have learned about the process of counselling and psycho-therapy: what did you experience and observe in the group that can be useful for your work as a therapist?
- What you have learned about how groups operate – for example group norms, stages in the life of a group, roles within groups.

Making sense: constructing a framework for understanding

Introduction

The work of a therapist inevitably involves listening to people talk in detail about complex situations in their lives. Often, the person's way of telling his or her life-story may be halting, incoherent or punctuated by strong emotion. Almost always, there will be gaps in the story – things not said, things that may be too embarrassing or shameful to share with another person. Listening to such stories in a context in which you are expected to do something to help can be a confusing and overwhelming experience. Where to start? What does all this information mean? What can I say or do to make things better? Theory provides a framework for understanding, a preliminary map of the territory that might be explored, a set of suggestions for possible directions of travel. It is one of the primary aims of therapist development to enable the practitioner to find a congenial theoretical 'home'.

The activities in this chapter invite you to build up a sense of your own personal framework for understanding. Many of the tasks ask you to iden-tify your own *position* in relation to the theoretical ideas that you are exploring. The rationale for this is that your own personal framework for understanding is always *more than* any single theory of therapy can provide. Responding to people in crisis always involves drawing upon your life experience and common sense, as well as your knowledge of therapy models. It is important, therefore, to know *where you stand* in relation to the theoretical traditions that inform your work.

The role of theory in counselling and psychotherapy practice is discussed in Chapter 4 of McLeod (2013).

What are the key theoretical ideas that you use?

If you read between the lines of most counselling, psychotherapy and personality textbooks, you will find that there is a set of core questions related to the basic processes of counselling that any theoretical model needs to be able to answer. These questions include:

- What are the causes of people's problems?

- What are the main mechanisms and processes of change? What changes? How?

- What is the role of the therapist? What is the optimal type of coun-sellor–client relationship? Why is the relationship important? Why is it necessary to have a strong 'therapeutic alliance'?

- What are the criteria for success and failure in counselling or psycho-therapy? What are the goals of therapy?

- What is the relative importance in terms of making sense of clients' problems and the process of therapy, of:
  - cultural factors (including social class, ethnicity and gender);
  - cognitive factors (the way the person thinks about things; the person's beliefs);
  - emotion (how the person feels about things);
  - biological/genetic factors?

Make brief notes in response to all of these questions. Just write down whatever answers come into your mind.

Which theoretical ideas and concepts appear in your answers to these questions? Do these concepts all derive from a single theoretical model or do your answers contain a mix of ideas?

You may find it helpful to use a large sheet or roll of paper to map out your thinking in relation to these key theoretical questions. What you produce will almost inevitably be complex and incomplete, and indicate potential areas for further reading and study.

What is your relationship with theory?

The social psychologist Kurt Lewin, once said: 'There is nothing as practical as a good theory'. Do you agree? How important is theory for you?
  As fully as possible, explore your responses to these questions:

- What are the theoretical ideas or concepts that you refer to most often in terms of your own personal thinking about counselling issues and your discussions with other people around these matters? How deeply have you studied these concepts? Have you mainly learned about these ideas or concepts from general reading, or listening to other people, or is your knowledge based on extensive reading?

- What are the theoretical tensions or dilemmas that you are aware of in your work as a counsellor (or in your reading as a trainee/student)? Are there times when you are caught between different ways of making sense of a client (or any person you are helping), or of your role in relation to a client? What do you do when you have this kind of experience?

- What is the direction of your theoretical development? Are there earlier theoretical ideas that you have 'grown out of'? Where do you feel that your theoretical interests are heading? What do you feel you want to (or *need* to) read next?

- For you, what is the ideal balance between making sense of the process of counselling in terms of an explicit theoretical formulation, and arriving at an intuitive, gut response to what is happening?

- On the whole, how satisfied are you with your current relationship with counselling/psychotherapy theory? Do you feel that you may sometimes overtheorize, and thus perhaps lose touch with what is taking place in the moment? Or do you struggle to detach yourself from the moment-by-moment complexity of counselling and perhaps lack an ability to develop a conceptual overview?

What are the implications of your responses to these questions, for:

1 Your practice as a therapist?

2 Your ongoing professional development – for example, in respect of further reading and study?

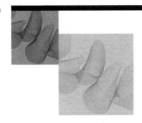

Meta-theories – how do they shape the way you think about therapy?

Mainstream approaches to counselling and psychotherapy – psychodynamic, person-centred and cognitive–behavioural – are based in competing psychological theories of personality. Making a choice between these alternative psychological models is no easy task. For the most part, the evidence from research does not make it possible to state with any confidence that one psychological model is correct or valid, and that another one is wrong. In practice, espousing a theoretical approach, or combination of approaches, tends to be influenced by other, broader sets of beliefs, values and ideas with which the counsellor identifies themselves. These ideas and beliefs can be described as *meta-theories*, because they can be viewed as overarching systems of thought within which psychological theories are embedded. The aim of this exercise is to identify the meta-theories that are significant for you, and to explore the ways in which these ideas shape your approach to counselling.

Instructions

On a piece of paper create a display of the ideas or systems of thought that are most significant in your life. Place the ideas that are most central for you in the middle of the page and the ones that are less important nearer to the edge.

These ideas can be drawn from a variety of domains.

1 Religious and spiritual beliefs that are important for you – for example, Christianity, Buddhism, Islam, atheism.

2 Philosophical ideas that are meaningful for you: for example, existentialism, phenomenology, empiricism, rationalism, postmodernism, constructivism.

3 Political ideologies that you support or oppose: for example socialism, capitalism, individualism, feminism, environmentalism, consumerism, trade unionism, gay rights.

4 Academic or scientific disciplines that have had a formative impact on the way you view the world: for example, mathematics, sociology, anthropology, economics, history.

5 Forms of artistic expression and creativity through which you find meaning: for example, poetry, drama, cinema, music.

Once you have drawn your personal 'meta-theory map', take some time to reflect on the implications of these ideas, beliefs and practices for your personal approach as a counsellor.

- Which sets of ideas are most relevant to your therapeutic theory and practice? Which ones are less relevant, or not at all relevant?
- In what ways might these ideas shape the way you are, and the choices you make, as a therapist?
- Which therapy theories and concepts are most (and least) compatible with your 'meta-theories'?

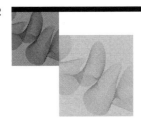

Applying theory: making sense of personal experience

Earlier, in Chapter 6, you were invited to write about a number of aspects of your own life that represented everyday therapeutic processes that you may have encountered either in the role of helper or as someone seeking help from another person. A valuable means of developing an awareness of your preferred position in relation to theories of counselling and psychotherapy is to reflect on what you have written about yourself, in theoretical terms.

1 Read through some of the autobiographical pieces that you have written, for example, *The story of a helping relationship, Thickening your autobiography: early memories* or *The experience of changing your own behaviour*. Identify any theoretical concepts that are implicit in what you have written. For example, you may have described your experience in terms of being *reinforced* by certain outcomes (a behavioural concept) or as involving the achievement of *insight* (a psychodynamic concept). Is there consistency in the constructs and terminology that you have used? If there is, what does this suggest to you about your preferred theoretical position?

2 Choose one specific theoretical orientation (for example, psychodynamic or person-centred). From this perspective, read and interpret a sample of the stories that you wrote in *Chapter 6: Reflecting on life experience*. Be rigorous in only applying ideas from that specific approach, and do your best to make use of a full range of concepts from the approach you have selected. Once you have done this, consider the following questions.

  a How satisfactory has this theoretical perspective been in accounting for all aspects of your experience? In what ways did using this perspective lead you to focus on some areas of experience at the expense of others?

  b In what ways, and to what extent, did the use of a specific framework enable you to develop a new or fresh understanding of the events and experiences you had written about?

  c What were the practical implications that were generated by the theoretical framework you applied? Did the theory you were applying stimulate further thinking and planning about how you might address issues in your life that were problematic to you?

d Reflecting on the 'experiment' of imaging yourself into a theoretical stance – in general terms how credible and convincing for you was the theoretical interpretation that you developed?

3 Apply different, alternative theoretical perspectives to your autobiographical writings, following the guidelines in the previous paragraph. Which of the perspectives seemed most useful to you? In what ways? Are there aspects of different theoretical models that you might wish to combine, to arrive at an ideal overall framework for understanding? If so, what are the principles or values that inform your choice?

Making sense of *self*

Self is a concept that occurs in most theories of therapy – for example self-concept (person-centred), self-object (object relations) and self-efficacy (CBT). The aim of this learning task is to help you to be clear about your own personal understanding of the idea of *self*.

1 Reflect on the words you use when talking about counselling. How often do you use the term 'self'? How often do you use other terms that are broadly equivalent, such as 'ego', 'identity' or 'personality'? Which of these terms sits most comfortably with your way of seeing relationships?

2 How important for you is the idea of *self*? Some philosophical approaches, such as Buddhism and postmodernism, take the view that 'self' is an illusion. Some cultures make little use of the idea of an individual self, preferring to talk in terms of 'we'.

3 How do you define 'self'? In Chapter 6, you may have completed an exercise titled *The self-puzzle*, in which you drew a picture of your 'self', with each of the 'parts' of the self labelled. Look again at that picture, and consider which of the following elements of different self-theories are expressed within it.

   a *Core and peripheral self*. Is there a central section of your puzzle or map, which contains qualities or values that are, in some way, essential to your sense of who you are? Are there sections toward the edge of your page that describe values and qualities that are somehow less essential?

   b *Internalized self-objects*. Object relations theory suggests that we include, within the self, images of significant others, or parts of these others (such as their words or voice) that are important to our emotional functioning. Are there any such figures in your puzzle?

   c *Relational self*. Have you portrayed a relational self (lots of links to other people) or a boundaried, autonomous self?

   d *Multiplicity or unity*. Does your picture convey a sense of a single entity, or are there separate parts (subselves) that are separated off from each other?

   e *Self-esteem and self-acceptance*. Person-centred theory assumes that the extent to which a person accepts or values all aspects of self is an indicator of well-being. To what extent is acceptance a theme in your picture?

    f *Self-efficacy.* Cognitive–behavioural theorists argue that the extent to which a person views themselves as being in control, and able to bring about change, is a key dimension of self. Does efficacy, or agency, appear as a theme in your drawing?

    g *Other dimensions of self.* There are other dimensions of self that may be relevant to you: conscious–unconscious, actualization and fulfilment, spirituality.

Once you have explored your self-puzzle in the light of these ideas, it may be useful to reflect on the degree to which your own personal 'theory of self' is consistent with the concept of self as articulated in the theoretical model(s) that inform your practice?

The balance between problems and solutions

Over the past decade, there has been a powerful movement within counselling and psychotherapy away from a preoccupation with helping people to analyse their *problems*, and towards the goal of building up the person's *strengths* and skills, and helping them to find practical *solutions*.

This trend is reflected in various approaches to counselling and psychotherapy, ranging from the emphasis on personal growth that is found in humanistic therapies, to the goal-oriented nature of behaviour therapy. However, it has found its clearest expression in *solution-focused therapy* and in *narrative therapy*.

This learning task gives you an opportunity to reflect on some of the implications of a strengths-based approach to therapy.

Think about some specific situations where you have been involved in a therapy relationship trying to help another person. Think also about occasions when you have been the recipient of therapy yourself.

In these situations:

- how much of the time was spent talking about 'problems' and how much time was devoted to 'strengths' and 'solutions'?

- in what ways was it helpful for you (or the person you were helping) to talk about the detail of their problems?

- in what ways was it helpful to talk about solutions (strengths, 'good news', achievements)?

- what is your sense of the right balance between a problem focus and a solution focus in the counselling episode(s) you have been looking at?

- what has made the difference for you, at times when you have struggled with an area of difficulty in your life: expressing and exploring your pain and distress, or expressing and exploring creative ways of resolving your difficulties?

More broadly:

- what does a person gain by becoming aware of, and taking note of, their solutions to problems?

- what can a person learn, or gain, from becoming aware of the possible causes of their problems?

In considering these questions, what have you learned about your own position as a therapist, in relation to the adoption of a solution-focused or problem-oriented approach to working with clients?

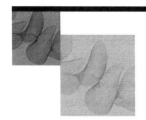

Positioning your practice in relation to social and political factors

Counselling and psychotherapy have evolved as forms of help that typically operate at an *individual* level. One of the most powerful critiques of contemporary counselling comes from those who argue that it functions within society to promote an over-individualized approach to problems that are in fact cultural, social and political in nature.

This critique has led in two directions:

- an argument that counselling/psychotherapy should be replaced by some form of social and political activism;
- attempts to make therapy more socially informed.

Take some time to reflect on, and write about, the following questions.

- Politics can be understood as referring to the way that different groups in society exert power, influence and control to advance their own interests and to ensure that their own vision of the 'good life' will prevail. In general terms, what is the role of therapy and therapists in this process? Is therapy (or should it be) an activity that stands outside the political arena? If it does not, then what is its role?
- What are the political factors that affect the lives of your clients and the therapeutic process that you engage in with them?
- What do you actually do yourself (if anything) to address political issues in your work with clients?
- What are your personal political beliefs and values? How do these beliefs and values influence your work as a counsellor?
- How seriously do you feel that the social critiques you have read threaten the basic mainstream approaches to counselling? Should these mainstream approaches be abandoned? If they should not be abandoned, do they need to be adapted or reconfigured to take better account of social factors? How could this happen? How might 'mainstream' approaches to counselling change in order to become more socially inclusive?
- What are the implications of these critiques for your own practice – for example in terms of your relationship with clients, the organizational setting in which you might wish to work and your theoretical model?

What brings about change? The relative importance of cognition and emotion

All theories of therapy acknowledge that the process of change involves an interplay of *cognitive* factors (changing the way that the person thinks about an issue) and *emotion* (for example, expressing repressed feelings). However, theoretical approaches differ significantly in the extent to which they emphasize one or the other of these key factors. For instance, the cognitive therapies of Beck and Ellis regard cognition as primary, with emotions being determined by the way that a person perceives or construes events. By contrast, both psychoanalysis and person-centred counselling regard the inner emotional life, or 'felt sense' of the person, as the main driver of therapeutic change and would view changes in the way a person thinks about an issue as following from changes in the way they feel.

What is your own position in relation to the relative importance of emotion and cognition? Your own personal experience and belief in relation to this issue will inevitably shape your choice of theoretical orientation.

Learning task

Read through the descriptions of personal learning and change that you created in response to some of the learning tasks in Chapter 6. Are there any recurrent themes in these descriptions concerning the relative importance of emotion and cognition. Do your descriptions include mainly examples of cognitive *insight* and *understanding*, or have you mainly written about moments of emotional release and catharsis?

When reflecting on what this learning activity has produced for you, it may be helpful to consider the following questions.

- What have you learned about the relative importance of cognitive and emotional processes in your own way of understanding change in therapy?

- How well does your own 'take' on cognition and emotion' correspond to the theoretical approaches that interest you, or with which you have identified yourself?

- What is your own personal model of the links between cognition and emotion? In your opinion, how do they link up – what causes what?

- How long have you held these ideas about cognition and emotion? Where and how did you learn them?
- What are the implications of your position on emotion–cognition for your *practice* as a counsellor?

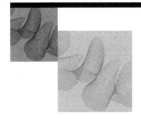

Behind the theory: the life of the theorist

Theories of counselling and psychotherapy have tended to be associated with the ideas of 'key figures', such as Sigmund Freud or Carl Rogers. These leading theorists are often revered as brilliant thinkers who transformed the field through their genius. However, it is possible to view the importance of these individuals in a different light. Any theory of therapy can be regarded as a set of ideas and assumptions that reflect the cultural milieu within which they were generated. In important ways, the theories of Freud and Rogers became influential because they somehow reflected and articulated aspects of human experience that were challenging and significant in pre-World War I Europe (for Freud) and in post World War II USA (for Rogers). The popularity of a theorist can be taken as indicating the extent to which his or her writings can operate as a channel for expressing the distinctive personal and interpersonal issues being faced by a particular group of people at a specific time in history. It is often pointed out that the childhood experiences of theorists such as Freud and Rogers play a large part in shaping their ideas. But, in important ways, these childhood experiences themselves may reflect broader aspects of the culture within which the person grew up.

In becoming a counsellor or psychotherapist, it is essential to develop a theoretical framework with which client issues, and the process of therapy, can be understood. Inevitably, this theoretical framework will largely draw upon the ideas of a small number of influential writers and theorists. In order to gain a full appreciation of these theories, it can be very useful to learn about the lives of the theoreticians themselves. To a large extent, their theories evolved to enable them to make sense of issues within their own lives, and in the lives of people they knew.

A useful learning activity is to make an effort to go beyond the kind of brief biographical snapshot that is provided in introductory textbooks, and read actual biographies of theorists who have had an influence on you. Although autobiographical writing may also be interesting and relevant, they are likely to be grounded in the worldview of the author – a good biographer should have the capacity to place the life and work of his or her subject in a wider cultural context.

Suggested further reading

Two books that explore the personal and cultural influences that have shaped the work of prominent theorists:

Atwood, G. and Stolorow, R. (1993) *Faces in a Cloud: Intersubjectivity in Personality Theory*, 2nd edn. Northvale, NJ: Jason Aronson.

Magai, C. and Haviland-Jones, J. (2002) *The Hidden Genius of Emotion: Lifespan Transformations of Personality*. Cambridge: Cambridge University Press.

The cultural context of understanding

How does your cultural identity influence your choice of counselling approach in relation to training and practice? The impact of the social, cultural and family environment on the ideas of mainstream therapy theorists has been widely documented. But what are the ways in which *your own* social, cultural and family environment has shaped your personal approach to counselling?

In the *Exploring cultural identity* activity that was introduced in Chapter 6 you were invited to examine various aspects of your cultural origins and experiences. Looking back at what you wrote in response to that activity, consider the following questions.

- What are some of the values and beliefs that you associate with your cultural background, which seem most relevant to your role as a therapist?

- Imagine explaining your work as a therapist, and the theories that you follow, to your grandmother. Would she be interested? Would she think that what you were doing was useful? What advice might she give you about how to be a better therapist?

- Are there areas of tensions in your cultural identity? For example, your mother and father may have grown up in quite different cultures. Or there may have been times in your life when you have deliberately attempted to distance yourself from your culture of origin? How has your awareness of these tensions informed your understanding of therapy?

- Are there any rituals within your 'home' culture that could be viewed as having a psychotherapeutic function (for example, confessionals in Church, family meetings, pilgrimages)? How might your engagement in such activities have informed your thinking about therapy?

- For you, is therapy a means of reinforcing and supporting the core values of your culture, or has it been a way of creating a new and different identity for yourself?

The underlying issue here is linked to the view of Lomas (1999: 25) that a person learning to become a counsellor needs to explore how best they can go about 'finding their own way, using their own intuition, learning to be themselves in the presence of someone who is asking for help'. Does your theoretical framework express who *you* are, including your sense of your own cultural identity?

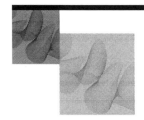

Dialogue between theorists

In the process of building a theoretical framework through which you can make sense of your work as a counsellor or psychotherapist you will almost certainly discover that you are drawn toward sets of ideas that are different from competing traditions or hard to integrate or reconcile with each other. It is valuable to regard such experiences as opportunities for learning. If you find meaning in different theories, then they are (by definition) meaningful for you. What may be lacking is a conceptual 'bridge' or idea that might enable you to see how the apparently conflicting ideas may be connected. This learning task provides a technique that you might like to use to make such connections.

Choose two theorists whose work is important to you, but who seem to be saying quite different things. (It is possible to carry out this exercise with more than two theorists, but it gets more complicated). Imagine that these theorists are in a room talking together, or are in email contact with each other. They are being stimulated and interviewed (by you) to engage in an exchange of views over some of their ideas. Write down this dialogue. Allow the dialogue to flow – the intention is not to come up with a version of each therapist's model that is necessarily factually accurate but to begin to explore what their ideas mean *to you*.

For example, you may be convinced by Carl Rogers' ideas about the therapeutic 'core conditions', and also interested in Erik Erikson's model of stages of psychosocial development, but be at a loss to understand how they might fit together. Your imaginary dialogue might look something like:

Interviewer: One of you has a very clearly worked out theory of development, but the other – Rogers – seems to talk only about 'conditions of worth'. How can these perspectives be reconciled?

Carl Rogers: I always knew about Erik's ideas, but I didn't want to go down that road. My fear was always that a too definite model of development would detract from the client's 'frame of reference' and impose a set of assumptions based on the therapist's theory, rather than the client's reality.

Erik Erikson: I share that fear. That's why I always argued that these themes (identity, trust and so on) were in a sense always present – even if they seemed to be most prominent at certain ages. I always thought there were big connections to be made between autonomy, initiative, trust and so on, and the way you talked about empathy . . .

Carl Rogers: Yes, in a sense accurate empathy involves trust, and being separate, and having a good sense of your own identity . . .

This is only a hypothetical example. Your own dialogue might take a very different direction. Your protagonists may find they have a lot in common . . . or they may end up shouting at each other!

When you read through the dialogue you have created, look for the connections that have been made, and also for the new concepts that may act as 'bridges' between the two sets of ideas.

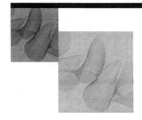

Letter to a theorist

One of the techniques that is used in both personal journal writing, and in some forms of narrative therapy, is to compose a letter to a person with whom one would like to have a discussion, but who is not actually available to talk with. In bereavement work, for example, a person may write a letter to the person who has died. The value of an unsent letter is that it can provide an opportunity to get thoughts and feelings out into the open and to begin, through a process of writing, to bring some order and structure to them.

This exercise invites you to make use of this technique to advance your understanding of theoretical issues in therapy.

Learning activity

Write a letter to a theorist who has some significance for you in terms of the way you make sense of therapy. Give yourself permission to write anything you wish to the person – what you like or do not like about his or her ideas, aspects of their thinking that make you angry or frustrated, questions that you have, counter-arguments, requests for help, compliments, invitations . . . .

It may be useful to consider different occasions that might call for such a letter:

- a theorist that you have just come across;
- a theorist who is a major influence on your thinking;
- a 'goodbye' letter to a theorist whose influence on your thinking you are trying to reduce or eliminate.

Once you have written the letter reflect on what you have learned about yourself, and your theoretical stance as a counsellor or psychotherapist.

Further related activities might include:

- writing letters to other theorists;
- writing a letter to yourself as a theorist;
- writing a letter from one of your clients to a theorist who has influenced and informed your work with that client;
- storing these letters and re-reading them at some time in the future as a means of tracking the development of your theoretical interests and concerns.

Building a relationship repertoire

9

Introduction

The task of evolving a personal approach as a therapist is not merely a matter of adopting a particular theoretical orientation, or assembling an integration of different theoretical ideas. For many counsellors, the process of discovering who they are as therapists only really hits them when they are faced with critical issues *in practice*. The aim of this chapter is to present a series of activities that evoke practical dilemmas that are associated with underlying questions such as 'what kind of a counsellor do I want to be?' and 'what is the personal style, or way of being with others, that suits me best?'

You may find that some of the scenarios and dilemmas described in these activities are already familiar to you from your work as a therapist. In these cases, your response to the learning task may help you to reflect more fully on your response to that situation or to begin to consider what your *preferred* response might be. Other scenarios and activities may be introducing situations that you may never have encountered in your actual work with clients. In these cases, you may be able to use the learning task to imagine, or rehearse, the ways in which you might approach such a situation when it does cross your path.

What kind of therapeutic relationship?

Therapy is a relationship between persons. There is a wealth of evidence, from carefully conducted research studies and practical experience that the quality of the therapeutic relationship has a huge impact on the amount that the client can gain from therapy.

However, relationships are difficult. We can all experience problems in making, keeping and ending relationships. The challenge in becoming a counsellor, of seeking to be some kind of 'relationship expert', is considerable. Clients may be seeking all sorts of different kinds of relationships with their counsellor and may create different kinds of barriers to forming a productive working 'alliance'. In turn, the needs and relationship patterns of the client may uncover gaps in the counsellor's capacity to relate.

These activities are intended to enable exploration of the relationship issues and challenges associated with counselling practice.

1 An experienced therapist, interviewed by Skovholt and Jennings (2004), described his way of seeing the relationship between counsellor and client in the following terms:

> One of the metaphors I often use with my clients is the metaphor of the 'Wilderness Guide', and the way I put that is they can hire me as a guide, because I know a lot about survival in the wilderness – my own, and I've travelled through a lot of wildernesses. I've got a compass, I can start a fire in the rain. I know how to make it through, but this is a new wilderness to me. I haven't been in this particular wilderness before, and so I can't quite predict what we're going to encounter. (p. 64)

Other metaphors of relationship can also be imagined:

- therapist as container;
- therapist as authentic presence;
- therapist as teacher, coach or scientist;
- the 'not-knowing' stance: therapist as editor.

Which of these images seem closest to the way that you experience yourself as being, or would aim to be, when in the role of counsellor or psychotherapist? What are the implications of each of these metaphors, both for you and for the client?

2 Petruska Clarkson (1994: 42) argued that effective counsellors should be able to relate to clients, if necessary, at a transpersonal level:

> the transpersonal relationship is . . . characterised . . . by a kind of intimacy and by an 'emptying of the ego' at the same time. It is rather as if the ego of even the personal unconscious of the psychotherapist is 'emptied out' of the therapeutic space, leaving space for something numinous to be created in the 'between' of the relationship. . . . It implies a letting-go of skills, of knowledge, of experience, of preconceptions, even of the desire to heal, to be present. It is essentially allowing 'passivity' and receptiveness for which preparation is always inadequate. . . . . It cannot be made to happen, it can only be encouraged in the same way that the inspirational muse of creativity cannot be forced, but needs to have the ground prepared or seized in the serendipitous moment of readiness.

To what extent is this form of therapeutic relationship meaningful for you? If it seems to you to represent an important dimension of therapy, how might you integrate this kind of possibility into your theoretical framework?

3 Return to the *Mapping your relationship patterns* exercise in Chapter 6. What did you write in response to that set of tasks? Looking now at what you wrote, what are the implications for your preferred ways of relating to clients? What are the implications in terms of difficulties that you might experience in relating fully to clients?

4 A wonderful book by Deborah Lott (1999) provides a rich account of women's experiences of their relationships with their therapists. The idea for this book arose from her involvement with a group of women friends who met regularly to 'share their therapy war stories':

> . . . it struck me that our exchanges resembled nothing so much as accounts of love affairs. We felt the same urgent need to get every detail straight, every word right . . . [. . .] We found the very structure of the therapeutic relationship problematic. It was inherently unequal: We needed our therapists more than they needed us, they were much more important to us than we were to them . . . To what extent was this even a *real* relationship, and if it wasn't real, *what* exactly was it? It wasn't friendship, and yet it was different from any other professional relationship we had ever had. (pp 1–2)

Is this an account of the therapeutic relationship that you recognize? If it is, what significance does this perspective account have for you, in terms of your work as a therapist?

In reflecting on these activities, it may be helpful to address the following questions.

- What is your preferred image, or model, of the client–therapist relationship?
- Which theories or concepts do you find useful in making sense of the therapeutic relationship?
- Are there aspects of the therapeutic relationship that, for you, seem to sit outside the established theories?
- How would you want a therapist to be with you?
- How do you want to be with clients?
- How have your ideas about relationships developed and changed, over the course of your life?

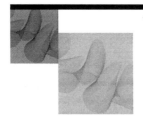

Exploring moral values

What are the moral values that are most important for you? Your practice as a therapist, and the way you relate to clients, is inevitably embedded in your sense of what it means to be a 'good' human being. The issues and choices that some clients make will undoubtedly challenge that sense of what is 'good' or 'right'. Your personal and professional development should incorporate an effort to develop a deeper appreciation of your own moral positions, as well as a capacity to respect the moral positions taken by others.

The three exercises described below are designed to enable you to begin to explore your personal moral values.

Instructions

Sources of moral influence in your life: take a piece of paper and draw a 'timeline', from your birth to present. Along this line, indicate the 'moral communities' that you have belonged to at various stages in your life. A moral community could be an organized religion, such as the Roman Catholic Church or the communist party, or it could be a less formal network, such as 'the rugby club', 'my friends' or 'the feminism seminar group'. A moral community is any grouping that sets standards for its members about 'correct' beliefs and the 'right' way to do things. For each of the moral communities, add a label listing the core moral rules or values for which it stood. You may find that at particular points in your life you may have been a member of more than one community. Once you have completed the timeline, reflect on what you have learned, in relation to the consistent moral themes in your life and the areas of moral tension or uncertainty.

Moral proverbs and sayings: a good way to begin to map out your personal moral beliefs is to think about the moral proverbs and sayings to which you make reference in everyday life. It is also of interest to identify, if you can, the person whom you heard saying these things to you in the first instance. For example, you may have heard your grandmother saying 'who does he think he is?', or 'men are only interested in one thing'. What do statements like these tell you about your moral values and beliefs?

Your vision of the good life: what would your ideal world be like? What would 'Utopia' be for you? Take a few minutes to write about the characteristics of the good life, from your own individual perspective.

Once you have completed these three exercises, bring together what you have learned about your moral values by drawing a list of the values or 'virtues' that are of central importance in your life.

The implications of your moral values for your approach as a therapist

The moral values and virtues that you espouse may help to shape the approach you take as a therapist in a variety of ways. For each of the dimensions of practice listed below write some notes on the possible implications that might arise from your moral position. For example, if aesthetic/artistic values are highly significant for you then this may imply developing a theoretical approach that makes space for creativity working in a setting that allows art therapy methods to be employed, etc. If socialist and egalitarian values are significant there may be quite different implications in terms of theoretical choice and work setting. It is likely that your individual style as a therapist arises from the ways that you have found in order to balance or reconcile different values in your own practice.

Theoretical orientation: different theoretical orientations tend to emphasize different values, such as rationality, individual autonomy, spirituality and so on. For you, what are the links between your values and moral position, and the theories of counselling that have meaning for you? It may be that certain theories allow you a vehicle fully to expressing your values. Alternatively, there may be areas of tension: a theoretical model may make a lot of sense to you in most respects but there can nevertheless be specific ways in which it is hard to align it with some of your moral beliefs.

Way of working as a therapist: there are many practical issues in therapy that reflect value choices. Some of these issues include: setting a limit to the number of sessions that a client can receive, charging fees, seeing a client individually or in a family context. Where do you stand on these matters?

Client groups: are there client groups that you are drawn towards, that you get satisfaction from? Are there groups of clients who are difficult for you to accept, or whose values are hard for you to appreciate and understand?

Practice setting: in what ways do your values influence the types of therapy settings within which you choose to work. For example, do you practice on a volunteer, unpaid basis, or in a paid job, or both? In what ways might the values of your colleagues matter to you? The values of organizational contexts may differ too – for example, some counselling agencies are grounded in religious commitment, whereas others embrace rational, 'evidence-based' practice. How much do these factors matter to you?

Once you have reflected on these practice domains and written some notes in response to the questions outlined above spend some time looking at the totality of your response: what have you learned about your own values and about the relationships between these values and your counselling practice?

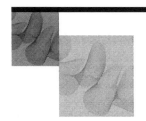

Creating and maintaining a therapeutic relationship with a client

The quality of the therapist–client relationship is considered within most schools of practice to represent a key factor in therapeutic success. It is important for any therapist to be aware of what they can do to promote a solid and reliable 'alliance' with clients.

The aim of this exercise is to give you an opportunity to reflect on what you do to create a therapeutic relationship with a client. When reflecting on the questions below, try to focus on the *relationship* dimension of your work with clients rather than on the therapeutic *process.*

Take a sheet of paper or page in your personal learning journal. Spend around 20 minutes writing about the following.

- What do I do in practice to create and maintain a relationship with my clients (this can include verbal and non-verbal behaviours, actions, strategies, etc)?
- What have I observed other therapists doing (for example in my own personal therapy, in videos, in case studies) around relationship building (both positive and negative)?
- What are the main cognitive resources (ideas, theories) that I use in making sense of how I create and maintain a therapeutic relationship?

Questions for further reflection

Take some further time to consider the following reflective prompts.

- What have I learned from this exercise, about the way I work with clients, and the theoretical basis of how I practice?
- What are my strengths and weaknesses around forming therapeutic relationships?

A study by Bedi *et al.* (2005) invited a sample of therapy clients to describe moments or incidents in their therapy that they believed had been important in terms of developing a relationship with their therapist. Compare the list of relationship-building strategies that you use in your own work, with the list of strategies that clients see as significant. Does this suggest any gaps in your 'relationship repertoire'?

Suggested further reading

Bedi, R.P., Davis, M.D. and Williams, M. (2005) Critical incidents in the formation of the therapeutic alliance from the client's perspective, *Psychotherapy: Theory, Research, Practice, Training*, 41, 311–23.

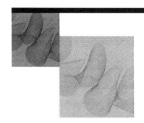

Expanding your relational responsiveness

The quality of the client–therapist relationship has emerged as possibly the single most significant factor in effective therapy. In the absence of a relationship of trust and a capacity to work together there is little hope that even the most well thought-out therapeutic activities will have much impact.

Different approaches to therapy are based on contrasting ideas about what might be the best kind of relationship to offer clients. For example, the psychodynamic approach advocates the establishment of a slightly distanced and highly consistent relationship that will function as a 'container' for painful or shameful emotional material. By contrast, CBT advocates a kind of athlete–coach, teacher–pupil relationship, where the therapist seeks to help the clients to acquire new skills.

Another way of looking at the therapeutic relationship is to take the view that different clients need different kinds of relationships at different times, and that the most effective therapists are those who have a broad enough 'relationship repertoire' to adapt to these needs.

What is you relationship repertoire? Howard *et al.* (1987) have identified four relationship modes that can be helpful for clients at different stages in therapy.

- *High direction/low support*. The therapist is in charge of what is happening. This style is appropriate when the client is unwilling or unable to move themselves towards the goals of therapy.

- *High direction/high support*. The therapist adopts a teaching/psycho-educational role, in relation to a client who has indicated a willingness to learn. This is relational style commonly found in CBT approaches.

- *Low direction/high support*. The therapist using this style is essentially accompanying a client who is engaged in a process of exploration and growth. This is the relational style associated with person-centred counselling.

- *Low direction/low support*. The therapist functions mainly as an observer of the client' progress. This relational style is characteristic of classical psychoanalysis.

Questions for reflection

- Which of these relationship styles do you use *most often* in your work with clients? Which style do you use *least often*?

- Which is your preferred style, the one that you are *most comfortable* with? Is there a relationship style that is *impossible* for you to exhibit?
- To what extent does this model help you to make sense of occasions when you have felt that you were not being helpful to a client? On these occasions was the client looking for a way of relating from you that you were unable or unwilling to fulfil?
- Identify one client with whom you have done good work. In what ways did your relationship with this person change over the course of therapy in response to the different learning needs of the client?

Suggested further reading

This includes a therapist relationship style questionnaire:

Howard, G.S., Nance, D.W. and Myers, P. (1987) *Adaptive Counseling and Therapy: a Systematic Approach to Selecting Effective Treatments*. San Francisco, CA: Jossey-Bass.

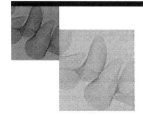

Touching and being touched

The question of whether it is valuable, or acceptable, to touch clients (or be touched by them) has been widely debated within the counselling and psychotherapy profession. The position that a practitioner takes in relation to touch can be highly significant in defining his or her personal approach. On the one hand, some therapists within the humanistic tradition would argue that touch is a basic and fundamental form of human relatedness and if clients are to 'come to their senses' touch will need to be involved at some point. On the other hand, some psychoanalytic and psychodynamic therapists would regard touching as deeply mistaken, reflecting a violation of the boundary between client and therapist. Some classical analysts sitting at the head of a couch situate themselves so that the patient cannot see them, never mind touch them.

The following questions are designed to allow you to begin to map out your position in relation to touch.

1 What are your own 'personal rules' about touching and being touched? Under what circumstances do you appreciate being physically 'in touch' with another person? What feelings do you associate with touch? What are the different meanings associated with touch around different parts of your body, or the other person's body?

2 There are several different types of physical contact that can take place between counsellor and client. Touch can be initiated either by the client or by the counsellor. Touch can take place at three times:

a before the sessions (for instance, on the way to the counselling room – shaking hands on arrival);

b during the session (for example, putting an arm round a client who is in distress);

c after the session (touching the client's shoulder on the way out of the room).

Which of these categories of touch do you engage in, or could imagine yourself engaging in? To what extent does this depend on the client? Are there categories of client who are, for you, 'touchable' or 'out of touch'?

3 What are the dilemmas that you have come across or can imagine coming across in respect of client–counsellor touch within your own practice?

Make some notes to record your reflections in response to these questions. Try to sum up your conclusions, in terms of your personal approach to touching in counselling. To what extent, and in what ways, might your personal position be in accordance with, or in conflict with, the 'rules for touching' implicitly or explicitly adopted by the theoretical model, workplace or training course within which you operate?

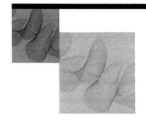

The meaning of boundary

The idea that relationships between people can be understood in terms of *boundaries* has had wide application within the domain of counselling and psychotherapy. The notion of boundary implies that there is a limit beyond which a person should not go in their relationship with the other. Venturing beyond that limit is a 'violation' or 'transgression' that may express something about the motivation of the violator.

There is much debate between therapists concerning the implications of the use of the idea of *boundary* in counselling practice. It is important to keep in mind that 'boundary' is a metaphor, which – like any metaphor – highlights some aspects of a phenomenon while concealing others.

This learning activity invites you to examine the meaning of the term 'boundary' in your own life, through the following questions.

- What are the boundaries that you draw in your own everyday life? What are the qualities or characteristics of these boundaries? How would anyone know that a boundary existed for you? How would they know when they had transgressed that boundary?

- A 'boundary' can be defined as the edge of a territory or space – where that territory meets another territory. What other words or images do you use to refer to this kind of phenomenon? (For example: wall, barrier, fence, interface, line . . .) How does the use of these alternative terms change the meaning of this phenomenon?

- When you meet another person for the first time what do you do to establish your mutual boundaries?

- With someone you have known for some time how do boundaries become re-negotiated or re-defined?

- What kind of boundary do you seem to need in different situations? (Boundaries can be strong or weak, flexible or rigid, permeable or impermeable.)

Once you have explored your personal experience of boundaries in your everyday life look at the implications of what you have learned for how you are (or how you would wish to be) as a counsellor or psychotherapist:

- What are the different kinds of boundaries that exist between you and your clients?

- How do you (and your clients) create and maintain these boundaries?

Indoors or outdoors? Using nature in therapy

Traditionally, influenced by the example of the doctor–patient consultation, counselling and psychotherapy sessions have taken place in offices. The content of therapy sessions has generally focused on either interpersonal problems that have been troubling the client, or difficulties the person has been having in regulating their thoughts and feelings.

In recent years, some practitioners have started to challenge these assumptions, in arguing that the relationship of a person with *nature* represents a crucial dimension of well-being, and that finding ways of bringing nature into the therapeutic process can be highly beneficial.

One approach to the use of nature is to hold therapy sessions out of doors, for example in a wilderness area. Another approach is to invite the client to consider their relationship with nature and to examine the link between that relationship and the problems they are experiencing in their life. Burns (1998) has devised a simple technique for facilitating this process, which he has called the *Sensory Awareness Inventory*. The client is given a piece of paper divided into six labelled columns: sight, sound, smell, taste, touch and activity. They are then instructed: 'under each heading, please list 10–20 items or activities from which you get pleasure, enjoyment or comfort'. What the client has written can be used in therapy in different ways. The client can be asked simply to consider what they have learned about themselves from completing the exercise. Typically, clients report that there are many sources of sensory pleasure, enjoyment and comfort that they have been neglecting in their life, and which would be valuable to restore or expand. Following further exploration, connections may often be made between personal problems and the absence of nature-based experience.

Questions for further reflection

How relevant is working in, and with nature, for your practice and your personal approach as a therapist? What are the advantages and disadvantages that you imagine might be associated with seeing clients out of doors? In what ways might working out of doors change your relationships with your clients?

Try the *Sensory Awareness Inventory* for yourself. What did you discover about yourself? Could these discoveries be of potential value in your therapy?

If you find, arising from these reflections, that nature-influenced work is attractive and meaningful for you, then also consider: what are the theoretical implications of working in this way, for the process of therapy and the client–therapist relationship?

Suggested further reading

Burns, G.A. (1998) *Nature-Guided Therapy: Brief Intervention Strategies for Health and Well-Being*. London: Taylor and Francis.

Developing a professional identity: putting it all together

Introduction

The aim of this chapter is to explore various aspects of your sense of identity as a counsellor, psychotherapist or mental health practitioner. The chapter also looks ahead at the future possibilities and next steps in your journey as a therapist in relation to the type of work you might do, and the further training and personal/professional development that might be helpful. Becoming a therapist is about more than learning theory and skills and acquiring practical experience. It is about evolving a professional identity, a sense of who you are in your work. Hopefully, by the end of this chapter, the outline of that professional identity, and its basis in who you are as a person, should be at least beginning to be more consistently visible.

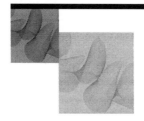

Reviewing your skills and qualities as a therapist

The aim of this exercise is to give you an opportunity to draw some conclusions from previous exercises you have completed in earlier chapters of this book.

Reflect on what you have learned in response to various learning tasks, and also on other sources of learning concerning yourself as a therapist (for instance, courses you have attended, work with clients).

Taking all this as a whole, how can you sum up your qualities as a therapist?

1 Make a list of your gifts, glittering qualities and strengths as a therapist.

2 Make a list of areas that might sometimes be personal limitations, gaps or 'blind spots' in your capacity to offer a therapeutic relationship.

3 Tell the story of at least one of the 'gifts' in a bit more detail: (a) what it was in your life that allowed you to develop this gift? (b) the effect this quality has on people you are helping?

4 Explore one of your limitations in a similar fashion: (a) what it was in your life that contributed to this limitation in your capacity to help? (b) the effect this limitation might have on people you are helping?

What are the implications, for you as a therapist, of what you have written in response to these questions? What do your responses say about who you are, and what you stand for, as a therapist?

Looking ahead: when you reflect on what you have learned from this exercise, what are the implications for:

- the type of work you do as a therapist (for example, long-term or short-term therapy with clients, specific client groups);
- your future learning needs, for instance through training, supervision or personal study;
- your role within the profession (as a supervisor, trainer, professional activist, writer, researcher).

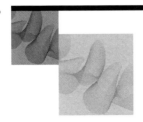

What are you aiming to achieve as a therapist? Selecting criteria for evaluating your effectiveness

One way of summing up your approach to counselling or psychotherapy is to be able to be clear about what it is you believe that therapy is trying to achieve. What are the desired outcomes of therapy? There are many competing ideas about the appropriate criteria for assessing the effectiveness of counselling and psychotherapy. Many research studies, and counselling organizations, use questionnaires that measure client change in terms of psychiatric categories such as depression and anxiety. Some practitioners view outcomes in terms of factors that are consistent with their theoretical approach. For example, person-centred counsellors look for change in self-esteem and self-acceptance, whereas cognitive–behaviour therapists seek change in observable behaviour and dysfunctional beliefs.

The CORE system is increasingly being used as an evaluation tool that provides an integrative focus, not rooted in any particular therapeutic model or ideology. The CORE questionnaire assesses client outcomes on four dimensions: subjective well-being, psychological symptoms, social and interpersonal functioning, and risk to self and others.

The *Just Therapy* centre in New Zealand, led by Charles Waldegrave, Kiwi Tamasese, Flora Tuhaka and Warihi Campbell, has developed an approach to therapy that draws on the traditions of the three main communities in their country: Maori, Samoan and Pakeha (European). Waldegrave identifies their criteria for effective work in the following way:

> . . . we have chosen three primary concepts that characterise our Just Therapy approach. When assessing the quality of our work, we measure it against the interrelationship of these three concepts. The first is belonging, which refers to the essence of identity, to who we are, our cultured and gendered histories, and our ancestry. The second is sacredness, which refers to the deepest respect for humanity, its qualities, and the environment. The third is liberation, which refers to freedom, wholeness and justice. We are interested in the inter-dependence of these concepts, not one without another. Not all stories of belonging are liberating, for example, and

some experiences of liberation are not sacred. We are interested in the harmony between all three concepts as an
expression of Just Therapy.

(Waldegrave 2003: 75)

Take a few moments to reflect on the outcome/effectiveness criteria that
you use in your work as a therapist. It may be helpful to think about clients
who you might consider to be 'good outcome' cases, and some who you
felt had 'poor outcomes'. What are the factors that made these cases
seem 'good' or 'not so good'?

Make a list of the outcome criteria that are important for you. What
does this list say about who you are as a therapist, and what you stand
for?

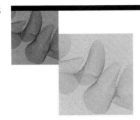

What's in your toolbox?

Therapists can be divided into those who have toolboxes and those who do not. A toolbox is a personal store of ideas, exercises, stories and strategies that the practitioner can draw upon to facilitate the therapeutic process or to move things on when the therapy seems to have reached an impasse.

An example of a therapist's toolbox can be found in a brilliant book by Susan Carrell, who describes more than 40 tools that she has acquired in over 20 years of practice. Some of these tools are tangible and take up space, for example a sand tray for adults. Others require only paper and pens, for instance a 'Life-Line' (timeline) exercise. Still others are virtual tools, stored in the counsellor's head. For instance:

> when your female client is agonizing over what to do about a difficult situation – her boyfriend is treating her poorly, a co-worker humiliated her, she suspects her husband is cheating her . . . . and she looks at you pleadingly seeking advice, ask her this question: What would you say to a girl-friend who came to you with this story? . . . . This question elicits responses that come from a deep place in a woman's psyche. It appeals to the sanctity of friendship between women and the long history of devotion that women friends have enjoyed . . . Women know that boyfriends come and go, husbands come and go, children come and go, but girlfriends are forever. She will give her girlfriend (and thus, herself) the best advice ever.
>
> (Carrell 2001: 184)

Some therapists might argue that such tools are inevitably superficial, and are no substitute, in the end, for the rigorous application of basic therapeutic principles, derived from a solid theory. But is this necessarily true? Maybe therapists who are grounded in a specific theory (unlike Susan Carrell, who could perhaps be described as a pragmatic eclectic) merely carry a kit of tools that are selected on the basis of theoretical consistency (as well as effectiveness).

Irvin Yalom is a leading figure in existential psychotherapy – perhaps one of the least 'toolbox-oriented' therapies that could be imagined. Yet he has published what he has described as a 'nuts-and-bolts collection of favourite interventions' (Yalom 2002: xiv). These include guidelines for challenging clients ('strike while the iron is cold'), strategies for checking into the here-and-now each hour, suggestions for making home visits and interviewing the client's significant other, and much else.

Instructions

Take a few minutes to list the items in your own therapeutic toolbox. Are there tools that you have once used, and have now discarded, or rarely employ? Are there tools that you would wish to include in your box, or that you have acquired and are uncertain about using?

Suggested further reading

Glimpses into the toolkits of some well-known therapists can be found in:

Carrell, S. (2001) *The Therapist's Toolbox: 26 tools and an Assortment of Implements for the Busy Therapist*. Thousand Oaks, CA: Sage.

Mahoney, M.J. (2003) *Constructive Psychotherapy: A Practical Guide*. New York: Guilford Press.

Seiser, L. and Wastell, C. (2002) *Interventions and Techniques*. Buckingham: Open University Press.

Yalom, I. (2002) *The Gift of Therapy: Reflections on Being a Therapist*. London: Piatkus.

Marketing yourself as a therapist: the one-minute intro

Developing a coherent and integrated sense of who you are as a therapist is not merely a personal development task. There are many situations where you may be called upon to explain or describe your approach to different audiences. This exercise invites you to write your response to the following scenarios.

1 *The one-minute intro.* You are in a group situation where you have been given one minute to introduce yourself and your therapy approach. Perhaps you have been invited to discuss your work with some trainees on a counselling course, or you are being interviewed for a job as a therapist, or you are joining a peer support group. What do you say about yourself?

2 *A leaflet.* You have been appointed as a therapist in a mental health clinic, student counselling service or some other setting. In order to help potential clients to access your service you need to design a leaflet that describes your therapy approach and explains what is involved in being a client. What do you write?

3 *A website.* As a means of promoting your private practice work you decide to develop your own website. How do you describe yourself within this medium?

4 *An activity.* Imagine that you have been asked to facilitate a two-hour workshop with a group of students of nursing or social work with the aim of helping them to learn about what your approach to therapy is about, at an experiential level. Is there *one* exercise or activity that might allow these students to go beyond a purely intellectual under-standing of your approach?

After you have completed these tasks, you may find it interesting to carry out a survey of leaflets and websites composed by other practitioners. Reflect on the different ways in which other colleagues have approached the task of depicting their approach.

Suggested further reading

Two writers who have explored their own struggle to characterize their approach, for external audiences, are:

Morgan, A. (1999) Practice notes: introducing narrative ways of working. In D. Denborough and C. White (eds) *Extending Narrative Therapy: A Collection of Narrative-Based Papers*. Adelaide: Dulwich Centre Publications.

Sween, E. (1999) The one-minute question: what is narrative therapy? In D. Denborough and C. White (eds) *Extending Narrative Therapy: A Collection of Narrative-based Papers*. Adelaide: Dulwich Centre Publications.

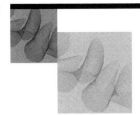

Your therapy room

The physical environment in which therapy takes place is an important, but seldom acknowledged, element of the therapy process. The furnishing and layout of a therapy room both raises expectations and sets limits regarding the ways in which clients can express themselves, how safe they feel, the extent to which movement is possible and much else. The location of the room – the building, how accessible it is, what the waiting area is like – also sets the scene for the type of therapeutic work that can occur.

Imagine your own *ideal* therapy room. In designing your therapeutic space, consider the following questions.

- What kind of building is the room in? Where is the building? What are the surroundings?
- How is the waiting area furnished and laid out? What does the client do while waiting?
- How is the therapy room furnished and laid out? What objects and images are in the room?
- What use is made of texture, colour, design, fragrance, sound . . .?

You may find it useful to make a sketch of this space. Once you have constructed your image of an ideal therapy environment, reflect on these further questions.

- What are the main differences between your ideal therapy room and counselling spaces that you have visited or worked in? What does this comparison tell you about possible goals for the future?
- What have you learned about yourself and your personal approach as a therapist from this exercise? To what extent could your ideal therapy room be understood as a projection of your core values as a therapist?
- In what ways does your design reflect the concepts and assumptions of your preferred theoretical approach(es)?

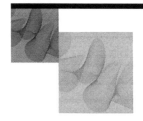

Building an effective support network

A critical aspect of developing a sense of professional identity as a therapist involves finding ways of dealing with the stress and pressure that can result from this kind of work. The construction of survival strategies depends to a large extent on the existence of a support network, comprising colleagues, therapists, supervisors and other people who can contribute to the maintenance of work–life balance.

The purpose of this learning task is to invite reflection on the elements of your own personal actual or intended support network and to consider the ways in which this network reflects or expresses your identity as a therapist.

Reflecting on your position in relation to supervision

- Write a character sketch of your ideal supervisor
- Write a character sketch of what would be, for you, the 'supervisor from hell'
- What do you need from supervision? What are you looking for?
- What would it take (has it taken) to make you change your supervisor?

Reflecting on your position in relation to personal therapy

- Write a character sketch of your ideal therapist.
- Write a character sketch of what would be, for you, the 'therapist from hell'.
- What do you need from your own therapy? What are you looking for?
- What would it take (has it taken) to make you enter therapy?

Stress and coping

- What do you find most stressful in your work?
- What activities do you find most satisfying and nurturing in your work?

- What strategies do you employ to cope with stressful aspects of your work?

- What would it take to make you review these strategies?

Make some notes in response to these questions. Once you have done some writing, consider the following additional issues:

- How well are you supporting yourself?

- What impact does the kind of support network you have constructed have on your work with clients?

- What impact does the kind of support network you have constructed have on your life outside your work?

- What does your support network say about who you are, and what you stand for, as a therapist?

Personal development within supervision

There is a lot that can be discussed within supervision. In the context of therapy with a specific client at various times it may be necessary and helpful to discuss the therapist's understanding or formulation of the case, ethical issues raised by the work, the use of different interventions, agency policies around length of therapy and referrals, and so on. Alongside these matters, therapy is also a matter of two (or more) people in a room, who are present to each other and affected by each other. Being a therapist is not merely a matter of how therapy works. It also allows a therapist to build up, case by case, a better understanding, a more differentiated and honest understanding, of who they are through reflecting on the facets of themselves that are revealed or hidden in the presence of that person. The issues that the client talks about also enable and invite the therapist to refine their own personal position in respect of these issues. For example, if a client struggles with the impossibility of making choices then it opens up a space where the therapist has the possibility of reflecting on their own process of making choices.

A question that encapsulates the personal development dimension of supervision on practice is: 'What did I learn about myself through my interaction with that client in that session?'

There are many ways in which the response to that question can be opened up and explored: in supervision, in therapy, through journal writing, within a peer group. It may also be valuable to reflect on the experience of arriving at an answer to that question: how open am I to my own learning? What is it like for me to follow through on the personal implications of this learning?

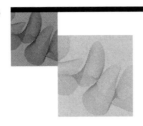

Your position in relation to research and inquiry

The primary focus of this book is to integrate the theory and practice of therapy within the narrative of your own personal life experience, with the goal of creating a 'knowledge base' that is firmly grounded in your everyday reality. However, it is important to acknowledge that there exists another knowledge base, which lies outside of personal experience – the knowledge that can be derived from systematic research.

In recent years, counselling and psychotherapy research has evolved in the direction of what is known as 'methodological pluralism'. In the past, research tended to mean statistics and experiments. Now, research and inquiry draw upon personal experience, interviews, action, stories and much else. Current research therefore represents a potentially rich source of knowledge for practitioners.

What is your relationship with the knowledge base represented by systematic research and inquiry? Take some time to write your responses to the following questions.

- In principle, how important do you think research is in relation to counselling and psychotherapy? What are the reasons for being interested in research at all?

- What are your criticisms of therapy research? What should or could researchers do in order to make research more relevant or useful?

- In what ways do you use research to inform your practice? List some research reports that you have recently read. How have these influenced how you think about your work as a counsellor? Do you use questionnaires to collect feedback from clients and monitor progress?

- How do you access research? How often do you read about research findings?

- If you were in a position to have some free time to do research, which questions or topics would interest you?

Once you have responded to these questions reflect on what you have discovered about who you are as a therapist, and also about future directions that your career or interests might take.

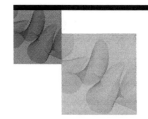

What kind of work suits you best? What is your niche within the profession?

Counselling, psychotherapy and mental health practice are fields that encompass a wide range of different work roles. Some of the key dimensions of therapeutic practice include:

- *length of context with client*: single-session drop-in work, brief therapy, long-term therapy;
- *model of delivery of therapy*: individual, couple, family, group, community;
- *medium of communication*: face to face, online, telephone, self-help books and manuals;
- *client characteristics*: age, gender, ethnicity, disability status, sexual orientation, social class, type of problem;
- *organizational context*: private practice, voluntary sector, health service, size of agency, political ideology of agency.

Further dimensions of a therapist's role include degree of collaborative working with other professional groups (such as doctors, teachers, social workers, complementary therapists) and degree of involvement in therapy-related roles such as being a teacher or trainer, supervisor, researcher, committee member and so on.

What are your own interests and gifts and limitations as a therapist? In what ways might these personal attributes lead you to be able to make a significant positive contribution within certain professional roles, or lead to dissatisfaction and limited effectiveness within other roles?

What have you learned from your experience so far about where talents are best channelled within the therapy world? What can you do to arrive at a clearer appreciation of what might be possible for you?

Keeping a personal and professional development portfolio

A personal and professional portfolio can serve a vital function as a means of documenting and reviewing personal learning over the course of a career. The following questions are intended to enable reflection on how this developmental tool can be used to best effect:

- What categories of information are most relevant for you, in terms of creating separate sections of a portfolio?

- What is the best way for you to store this information?

- What type of personal and professional development information are you expected to keep to meet the requirements of professional bodies or training courses?

- Would it be possible to interview more experienced colleagues around how they organize and use their record of personal and professional development activities?

- What would be most helpful for you, in relation to conducting a regular review of your personal and professional development record? How often might such a review take place? Who would be the best person or group to act as consultants to your portfolio? How frequently, and in what way, might you carry out a personal reflective review of your personal and professional development activities and goals?

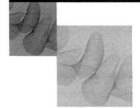

Ten years from now

Imagine that the date is ten years in the future. You have achieved all the main goals that you set yourself at the end of your period of training as a therapist. You are in a peer support group that has decided to devote a couple of sessions to giving each member time and space to review their career. You are being interviewed by these close colleagues and invited to explore the following questions.

- How do you sum up your work now – who you are in terms of your professional identity, where and how you work, and the approach you take?

- In what ways is this current situation different from your working life ten years ago?

- What have been the main challenges and choice points for you during the past ten years?

- What have been your main sources of support and assistance that have enabled you to achieve your aims?

- What are the most important things you have learned over this period of time?

- How have you changed, and how have you remained the same, as a person?

- What would you like to say to the 'you' of ten years ago?

Once you have responded to these questions, take some time to reflect on the implications of this piece of 'time travelling' for your professional identity now.

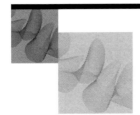

References

Addis, M.E. and Krasnow, A.D. (2000) A national survey of practicing psychologists' attitudes toward psychotherapy treatment manuals, *Journal of Consulting and Clinical Psychology*, 68, 331–9.

Addis, M.E., Wade, W.A. and Hatgis, C. (1999) Barriers to dissemination of evidence-based practices: Addressing practitioners' concerns about manual-based psychotherapies, *Clinical Psychology-Science and Practice*, 6, 430–41.

Alred, G., Davies, G., Hunt, K. and Davies, V.H. (eds) (2004) *Experiences of Counsellor Training: Challenge, Surprise and Change*. London: Palgrave.

Anderson, T., Ogles, B.M. and Weis, A. (1999) Creative use of interpersonal skills in building a therapeutic alliance, *Journal of Constructivist Psychology*, 12, 313–30.

Ankarberg, P. and Falkenstrom, F. (2008) Treatment of depression with antidepressants is primarily a psychological treatment, *Psychotherapy Theory, Research, Practice, Training*, 45, 329–39.

Anonymous (2011) Lessons learned from a long-term psychoanalysis on the telephone, *Journal of Clinical Psychology*, 67, 818–27.

Aponte, H.J. and Kissil, K. (2012) "If I can grapple with this I can truly be of use in the therapy room": using the therapist's own emotional struggles to facilitate effective therapy, *Journal of Marital and Family Therapy*, Dec 17 (epub ahead of print).

Back, K. (1972) *Beyond Words*. New York: Russell Sage.

Back, K. (1973) The experiential group and society, *Journal of Applied Behavioral Science*, 8, 7–20.

Bager-Charleson, S. (2012) *Personal Development in Counselling and Psychotherapy*. London: Sage.

Baldwin, M. (ed.) (2013) *The Use of Self in Therapy*, 3rd edn. New York: Routledge.

Barnett, J.E., Baker, E.K., Elman, N.S. and Schoener, G.R. (2007) In pursuit of wellness: the self-care imperative, *Professional Psychology: Research and Practice*, 38, 603–12.

Bassey, S. and Melluish, S. (2013) Cultural competency for mental health practitioners: a selective narrative review, *Counselling Psychology Quarterly*, 26, 151–73.

Bates, Y. (ed.) (2006) *Shouldn't I be Feeling Better by Now? Client Views of Therapy*. London: Palgrave.

Bedi, R.P., Davis, M.D. and Williams, M. (2005) Critical incidents in the formation of the therapeutic alliance from the client's perspective, *Psychotherapy: Theory, Research, Practice, Training*, 41, 311–23.

Bennis, W. and Shepard, H. (1956) A theory of group development, *Human Relations*, 9, 415–57.

Bike, D.H., Norcross, J.C. and Schatz, D.M. (2009) Processes and outcomes of psychotherapists' personal therapy: replication and extension 30 years later, *Psychotherapy Theory, Research, Practice, Training*, 46, 19–31.

Bloomgarden, A. and Mennuti, R.B. (eds) (2009) *Psychotherapist Revealed. Therapists speak about Self-Disclosure in Psychotherapy*. New York: Routledge.

Blow, A., Davis, S.D. and Sprenkle, D.H. (2012) Therapist-worldview matching: not as important as matching to clients, *Journal of Marital and Family Therapy*, 38, 13–17.

Bohart, A.C. (2006) The client as active self-healer. In G. Stricker and J. Gold (eds) *A Casebook of Psychotherapy Integration*. Washington, DC: American Psychological Association.

Bolton, G., Howlett, S., Lago, C. and Wright, J.K. (eds) (2004) *Writing Cures: An Introductory Handbook of Writing in Counselling and Psychotherapy*. London: Brunner-Routledge.

Brabender, V., Smolar, A. and Fallon, A. (2004) *Essentials of Group Therapy*. New York: Wiley.

Brightman, B.K. (1984) Narcissistic issues in the training experience of the psychotherapist, *International Journal of Psychoanalytic Psychotherapy*, 10, 293–371.

Buchanan, L. and Hughes, R. (2001) *Experiences of Person-centred Training: A Compendium of Case Studies to Assist Prospective Applicants*. Ross-on-Wye: PCCS Books.

Burns, G.A. (1998) *Nature-guided Therapy: Brief Intervention Strategies for Health and Well-Being*. London: Taylor and Francis.

Burns, L. and Dallos, R. (2008) A different world? Literary reading in family therapists' personal and professional development, *Journal of FamilyTherapy*, 30, 222–46.

Burton, M. and Topham, D. (1997) Early loss experiences in psychotherapists, Church of England clergy, patients assessed for psychotherapy, and scientists and engineers, *Psychotherapy Research*, 7, 275–300.

Caffrey, T.A. (2000) The whisper of death: psychotherapy with a dying Vietnam veteran, *American Journal of Psychotherapy*, 54, 519–30.

Cain, N.R. (2000) Psychotherapists with personal histories of psychiatric hospitalization: Countertransference in wounded healers, *Psychiatric Rehabilitation Journal*, 24, 22–8.

Callahan, J. L. and Ditloff, M. (2007) Through a glass darkly: reflections on therapist transformations, *Professional Psychology: Research and Practice*, 38, 547–53.

Carkhuff, R.R. (1969a) *Helping and Human Relations. Volume 1: Selection and Training*. New York: Holt, Rinehart and Winston.

Carkhuff, R.R. (1969b) *Helping and Human Relations. Volume 2: Practice and Research*. New York: Holt, Rinehart and Winston.

Carlsson, J. and Schubert, J. (2009) Professional values and their development among trainees in psychoanalytic psychotherapy, *European Journal of Psychotherapy and Counselling*, 11, 267–86.

Carlsson, J., Norberg, J., Sandell, R. and Schubert, J. (2011) Searching for recognition: the professional development of psychodynamic psychotherapists during training and the first few years after it, *Psychotherapy Research*, 21, 141–53.

Carrell, S. (2001) *The Therapist's Toolbox: 26 Tools and an Assortment of Implements for the Busy Therapist*. Thousand Oaks, CA: Sage.

Carroll, M. (2009) Supervision: critical reflection for transformational learning. Part 1, *The Clinical Supervisor*, 28, 210–20.

Carroll, M. (2010) Supervision: critical reflection for transformational learning. Part 2, *The Clinical Supervisor*, 29, 1–19.

Carroll, M. and Gilbert, M. (2011) *On Being a Supervisee: Creating Learning Partnerships*, 2nd edn. London: Vukani Publications.

Carroll, M. and Shaw, E. (2012) *Ethical Maturity in the Helping Professions. Making Difficult Life and Work Decisions*. Melbourne: PsychOz Publications.

Carson, D.K. and Becker, K. (2003) *Creativity in Psychotherapy: Reaching New Heights with Individuals, Couples, and Families*. New York: Routledge.

Centre for Outcomes Research and Effectiveness (2013) *Competence Frameworks for the Delivery and Supervision of Psychological Therapies*. London: Department of Psychology, University College London. Available at www.ucl.ac.uk/clinical-psychology/CORE/competence_frameworks.htm (accessed 11 November 2013).

Chang, J. (2011) An interpretive account of counsellor development, *Canadian Journal of Counselling and Psychotherapy*, 45, 406–28.

Charlés, L.L. (2007) Cultural competency as a relational process: scenes from a family therapy training context in the Philippines, *Qualitative Inquiry*, 13, 1160–76.

Clarkson, P. (1994) The psychotherapeutic relationship. In P. Clarkson and M. Pokorny (eds) *The Handbook of Psychotherapy*. London: Routledge.

Cleary, M., Horsfall, J., O'Hara-Aarons, M., Jackson, D. and Hunt, G.E. (2011) The views of mental health nurses on continuing professional development, *Journal of Clinical Nursing*, 20, 3561–6.

Comas-Dias, L. (2010) On being a Latina healer: voice, consciousness, and identity, *Psychotherapy Theory, Research, Practice, Training*, 47, 162–8.

Cook, J.M., Biyanova, T. and Coyne, J.C. (2009) Comparative case study of diffusion of eye movement desensitization and reprocessing in two clinical settings: empirically supported treatment status is not enough, *Professional Psychology: Research and Practice*, 40, 518–24.

Cooper, M. and McLeod, J. (2011) *Pluralistic Counselling and Psychotherapy*. London: Sage.

Corey, G. (2010) *Theory and Practice of Group Counseling*, 8th edn. San Francisco, CA: Broadman and Holman.

Costin, C. and Johnson, C.L. (2002) Been there, done that; clinicians' use of personal recovery in the treatment of eating disorders, *Eating Disorders*, 10, 293–303.

Crocket, K. (2004) Storying counselors: producing professional selves in supervision. In D. A. Pare and G. Lerner (eds) *Collaborative Practice in Psychology and Therapy*. New York: Haworth Press.

Curtis, R.C. (2011) Speaking freely: my experiences in individual psychotherapies, group therapies, and growth groups, *Journal of Clinical Psychology*, 67, 794–805.

Curtis, R.C. and Qaiser, M. (2005) Training analyses: historical considerations and empirical research. In J.D. Geller, J.C. Norcross and D. Orlinsky (eds) *The Psychotherapist's own Psychotherapy*. New York: Oxford.

Curtis, R.C., Field, C., Knaan-Kostman, K. and Mannix, K. (2004) What 75 psychoanalysts found helpful and hurtful in their own analyses, *Psychoanalytic Psychology*, 21, 183–220.

Davies, J. (2008) The transformative conditions of psychotherapeutic training: an anthropological perspective, *British Journal of Psychotherapy*, 24, 50–64.

Davis, J.D., Elliott, R., Davis, M.L., *et al.* (1987) Development of a taxonomy of therapists' difficulties: Initial report, *British Journal of Medical Psychology*, 60, 109–19.

DeLucia-Waack, J.L., Gerrity, D.A., Kalodner, C.R. and Riva, M. (eds) (2004) *Handbook of Group Counseling and Psychotherapy*. Thousand Oaks, CA: Sage.

Dirkx, J.M. (2000) Transformative Learning and the journey of individuation, *ERIC Digest*, 233, 1–2. Available at www.calpro-online.org/eric/docs/dig223.pdf (accessed 11 November 2013).

Donati, M. and Watts, M. (2005) Personal development in counsellor training: towards a clarification of inter-related concepts, *British Journal of Guidance and Counselling*, 33, 475–84.

Dryden, W. (ed.) (1987) *Key Cases in Psychotherapy*. London: Croom Helm.

Dryden, W. (2005) The personal therapy experience of a rational emotive therapist. In J.D. Geller, J.C. Norcross and D.E. Orlinsky (eds) *The Psychotherapist's own Psychotherapy: Patient and Clinician Perspectives*. New York: Oxford University Press.

Dryden, W. (ed.) (1994) *The Stress of Counselling in Action*. London: Sage.

Dryden, W. and Spurling, L. (eds) (1989) *On Becoming a Psychotherapist*. London: Tavistock/Routledge.

Duncan, B. (2005) When courage is enough. In J.A. Kottler and J. Carlson (eds) *The Client who Changed Me: Stories of Therapist Personal Transformation*. New York: Routledge.

Duncan, E.A.S., Nicol, M.M. and Ager, A. (2004) Factors that constitute a good cognitive behavioural treatment manual: a Delphi study, *Behavioural and Cognitive Psychotherapy*, 32, 199–213.

Dwyer, M.L., Deshields, T.L. and Nanna, S.K. (2012) Death is a part of life: considerations for the natural death of a therapy patient, *Professional Psychology: Research and Practice*, 43, 123–9.

Edwards, J. (2013) Examining the role and functions of self-development in healthcare therapy trainings. A review of the literature with a modest proposal for the use of learning agreements, *European Journal of Psychotherapy and Counselling*, 15, 214–32.

Eells, T. (2010) The unfolding case formulation: the interplay of description and inference, *Pragmatic Case Studies in Psychotherapy*, 6, 225–54.

Egan, G. (2004) *The Skilled Helper: A Problem Management and Opportunity Development Approach to Helping*, 8th edn. Belmont, CA: Wadsworth.

Elkin, I., Shea, M.T., Watkins, J.T., *et al.* (1989) National Institute of Mental Health Treatment of Depression Collaborative Research Program. General effectiveness of treatments, *Archives of General Psychiatry*, 46, 971–82.

Elman, N.S., Illfelder-Kaye, J. and Robiner, W.N. (2005) Professional development: training for professionalism as a foundation for competent practice in psychology, *Professional Psychology: Research and Practice*, 36, 367–75.

Erikson, E. (1950) *Childhood and Society*. New York: W. W. Norton.

Etherington, K. (2004) Heuristic research as a vehicle for personal and professional development, *Counselling and Psychotherapy Research*, 4, 48–63.

European Association of Psychotherapy (2013) *The Core Competencies of a European Psychotherapist*. Vienna: EAP. Available at www.psychotherapy-competency.eu/Documents/Revised_Core_Competencies_Feb_2013.pdf (accessed 11 November 2013).

Farber, B.A. (ed.) (1983) *Stress and Burnout in the Human Service Professions*. New York: Pergamon.

Farber, B.A. (2006) *Self Disclosure in Psychotherapy*. New York: Guilford Press.

Farber, B.A. and Heifetz, L.J. (1981) The satisfactions and stresses of psychotherapeutic work: a factor analytic study, *Professional Psychology*, 12, 621–30.

Farber, B.A. and Heifetz, L.J. (1982) The process and dimensions of burnout in psychotherapists, *Professional Psychology*, 13, 293–301.

Farber, B.A., Manevich, I., Metzger, J. and Saypol, E. (2005) Choosing psychotherapy as a career: why did we cross that road? *Journal of Clinical Psychology*, 61, 1009–31.

Fitzpatrick, M.R., Kovalak, A.L. and Weaver, A. (2010) How trainees develop an initial theory of practice: A process model of tentative identifications, *Counselling and Psychotherapy Research*, 10, 93–102.

Folkes-Skinner, J., Elliott, R. and Wheeler, S. (2010) 'A baptism of fire': a qualitative investigation of a trainee counsellor's experience at the start of training, *Counselling and Psychotherapy Research*, 10, 83–92.

Fordham, M. (1985) *Explorations into the Self*. London: Academic Press.

Forsyth, D.R. (2013) *Group Dynamics*, 6th edn. Pacific Grove, CA: Wadsworth.

Freeman, A. (2011) Manny's legacy: paying forward my personal therapy, *Journal of Clinical Psychology*, 67, 789–93.

Gabbay, J. and Le May, A. (2011) *Practice-Based Evidence for Healthcare. Clinical Mindlines*. London: Routledge.

Garrity, M.K. (2011) Counselling sexual-violence survivors: the evolution of female counsellors' critical political consciousness and the effects on their intimate relationships, *Canadian Journal of Counselling and Psychotherapy*, 45, 68–86.

Geller, J.S. (2011) The psychotherapy of psychotherapists, *Journal of Clinical Psychology*, 67, 759–65.

Gendlin, E.T. (2003) *Focusing: How to Open up your Deeper Feelings and Intuition*. New York: Rider.

Gilbert, P. and Stickley, T. (2012) "Wounded Healers": the role of lived-experience in mental health education and practice, *Journal of Mental Health Training, Education and Practice*, 7, 33–41.

Gilroy, P.J., Carroll, L. and Murra, J. (2001) Does depression affect clinical practice? A survey of women psychotherapists, *Women and Therapy*, 23, 13–30.

Glickauf-Hughes, C. and Mehlman, E. (1995) Narcissistic issues in therapists: diagnostic and treatment considerations. *Psychotherapy*, 32, 213–21.

Goldberg, C. (1988) *On Being a Psychotherapist: The Journey of the Healer*. New York: Gardner Press.

Goldfried, M.R. (2001) *How Therapists Change: Personal and Professional Reflections.* Washington DC: American Psychological Association.

Goleman, D. (2005) *Emotional Intelligence.* New York: Bantam Books.

Gratz, K. L. and Roemer, L. (2004) Multidimensional assessment of emotion regulation and dysregulation: development, factor structure, and initial validation of the Difficulties in Emotion Regulation Scale, *Journal of Psychopathology and Behavioral Assessment,* 26, 41–54.

Greenberg, L. (2002a) *Emotion-Focused Therapy: Coaching Clients to Work through their Feelings.* Washington DC: American Psychological Association.

Greenberg, L.S. (2002b) Integrating an emotion-focused approach to treatment into psychotherapy integration, *Journal of Psychotherapy Integration,* 12: 154–89.

Guggenbuhl-Craig, A. (1971) *Power in the Helping Professions.* Dallas, TX: Spring Publications.

Guy, J.D. (1987) The *Personal Life of the Psychotherapist.* New York: Wiley.

Haldeman, D.C. (2010) Reflections of a gay male psychotherapist, *Psychotherapy Theory, Research, Practice, Training,* 47, 177–85.

Halewood, A. and Tribe, R. (2003) What is the prevalence of narcissistic injury among trainee counselling psychologists? *Psychology and Psychotherapy: Theory, Research and Practice,* 76, 87–102.

Hansen, J.T. (2006) Counseling theories within a postmodernist epistemology: new roles for theories in counseling practice, *Journal of Counseling and Development,* 84, 291–7.

Hansen, J.T. (2009) Self-awareness revisited: reconsidering a core value of the counselling profession, *Journal of Counseling and Development,* 87, 186–93.

Hanson, J. (2005) Should your lips be zipped? How therapist self-disclosure and non-disclosure affects clients, *Counselling and Psychotherapy Research,* 5, 96–104.

Harding-Davies, V., Hunt, K., Alred, G. and Davies, G. (eds) (2004) *Experiences of Counsellor Training.* London: Palgrave Macmillan.

Harley, D.A., Jolivette, K., Collins, B. and Schuster, J.W. (2004) Professional portfolio development for rehabilitation counselors and human service providers: a tool for professional development and leadership, *Journal of Applied Rehabilitation Counseling,* 35, 3–8.

Hellman, I. D. and Morrison, T. L. (1987) Practice setting and type of caseload as factors in psychotherapist stress, *Psychotherapy,* 24, 427–33.

Hendin, H., Haas, A., Maltsberger, J., Szanto, K. and Rabinowicz, H. (2004) Factors contributing to therapist's distress after the suicide of a patient, *American Journal of Psychiatry,* 161, 1442–6.

Hendin, H., Lipschitz, A., Maltsberger, J., Haas, A. and Wynecoop, S. (2000) Therapists' reactions to patients' suicides, *American Journal of Psychiatry,* 157, 2022–7.

Henry, W.E. (1966) Some observations on the lives of healers, *Human Development,* 9, 47–56.

Henry, W.E. (1977) Personal and social identities of psychotherapists. In A.S. Gurman and A.M. Razin (eds) *Effective Psychotherapy: A Handbook of Research.* Oxford: Pergamon.

Henry, W.E., Sims, J.H. and Spray, S.L. (1971) *The Fifth Profession.* San Francisco, CA: Jossey-Bass.

Hill, A. (2002) Let's stay and hate: The role of community meetings on counsellor training courses, *Counselling and Psychotherapy Research,* 2, 215–21.

Hill. C.E. (2004) *Helping Skills: Facilitating Exploration, Insight and Action,* 2nd edn. Washington DC: American Psychological Association.

Hill, C.E. (2005) The role of individual and marital therapy in my development. In J.D. Geller, J.C Norcross and D.E. Orlinsky (eds) *The Psychotherapist's own Psychotherapy: Patient and Clinician Perspectives.* New York: Oxford University Press.

Hofstede, G. (2003) *Culture's Consequences, Comparing Values, Behaviors, Institutions, and Organizations Across Nations,* 2nd edn. Thousand Oaks, CA: Sage.

Honey, P. and Mumford, A. (1982) *Manual of Learning Styles.* London: Peter Honey Publications.

Honos-Webb, L. and Stiles, W.B. (1998) Reformulation of assimilation analysis in terms of voices, *Psychotherapy*, 35, 23–33.

Horton, I. (ed.) (1997) *The Needs of Counsellors and Psychotherapists: Emotional, Social, Physical, Professional*. London: Sage.

Howard, G.S., Nance, D.W. and Myers, P. (1987) *Adaptive Counseling and Therapy: A Systematic Approach to Selecting Effective Treatments*. San Francisco, CA: Jossey-Bass.

Hughes, J. and Youngson, S. (2009) *Personal Development and Clinical Psychology*. Chichester: Blackwell Scientific/Wiley.

Ieva, K.P., Ohrt, J.H., Swank, J.M. and Young, T. (2009) The impact of experiential groups on Masters students' counselor and personal development: a qualitative investigation, *Journal for Specialists in Group Work*, 34, 351–68.

Irving J. and Williams, D. (1999) Personal growth and personal development: concepts clarified, *British Journal of Guidance and Counselling*, 27, 517–26.

Jacobs, E.E., Masson, R.L. and Harvill, R.L. (eds) (2006) *Group Counseling: Strategies and Skills*, 5th edn. Belmont, CA: Wadsworth.

Jennings, L. and Skovholt, T. M. (1999) The cognitive, emotional and relational characteristics of master therapists, *Journal of Counseling Psychology*, 46, 3–11.

Johns, H. (ed.) (1998) *Balancing Acts: Studies in Counselling Training*. London: Routledge.

Johns, H. (2012a) Professional and personal development. In C. Feltham and I. Horton (eds) *The Sage Handbook of Counselling and Psychotherapy*, 3rd edn. London: Sage.

Johns, H. (2012b) *Personal Development in Counsellor Training*, 2nd edn. London: Sage.

Josselson, R. (1996) *The Space between Us: Exploring the Dimensions of Human Relationships*. Thousand Oaks, CA: Sage.

Kahn, S. and Fromm, E. (eds) (2000) *Changes in the Therapist*. Wokingham: Lea Publishing.

Kahn, W. L. and Harkavy-Friedman, J. M. (1997) Change in the therapist: the role of patient-induced inspiration. *American Journal of Psychotherapy*, 51, 403–14.

Kannan, D. and Levitt, H.M. (2009) Challenges facing the developing feminist psychotherapist in training, *Women and Therapy*, 32, 406–22.

Katz, R.S. and Johnson, T.A. (eds) (2006) *When Professionals Weep. Emotional and Countertransference Responses in End Of Life Care*. New York: Routledge.

Kirsch, T.B. (2005) The role of personal therapy in the formation of a Jungian analyst. In J.D. Geller, J.C Norcross and D.E.Orlinsky (eds) *The Psychotherapist's own Psychotherapy: Patient and Clinician Perspectives*. New York: Oxford University Press.

Knox, S. and Hill, C.E. (2003) Therapist self-disclosure: research-based suggestions for practitioners, *Journal of Clinical Psychology*, 59, 529–39.

Knox, S., Burkhard, A., Jackson, J., Schaack, A. and Hess, S. (2006) Therapists-in-training who experience a client suicide: implications for supervision, *Professional Psychology: Research and Practice*, 37, 547–57.

Kolb, D.A. 1984. *Experiential Learning: Experience as the Source of Learning and Development*. Englewood Cliffs, NJ: Prentice-Hall.

Kolb, D.A. and Fry, R. (1975) Toward an applied theory of experiential learning. In C. Cooper (ed.) *Theories of Group Process*. Chichester: Wiley.

Kottler, J. and Carlson, J. (2005) *The Client who Changed Me: Stories of Therapist Personal Transformation*. New York: Routledge.

Kottler, J.A. and Carlson, J. (2009) *Creative Breakthroughs in Therapy: Tales of Transformation and Astonishment*. New York: Wiley.

Kraus, D.R., Castonguay, L., Boswell, J.F., Nordberg, S.S. and Hayes, J.A. (2011) Therapist effectiveness: implications for accountability and patient care, *Psychotherapy Research*, 21, 267–76.

Lago, C. (2006) *Race, Culture and Counselling: the Ongoing Challenge*, 2nd edn. Maidenhead: Open University Press.

Lambers, E. (2006) Supervising the humanity of the therapist, *Person-centered and Experiential Psychotherapies*, 5, 266–76.

Lambers, E. (2013) Supervision. In M. Cooper, M. O'Hara, P.F. Schmid and A. Bohart (eds) *The Handbook of Person-Centred Psychotherapy and Counselling*, 2nd edn. New York: Palgrave Macmillan.

Lave, J. and Wenger, E. (1991) *Situated Learning: Legitimate Peripheral Participation*. Cambridge: Cambridge University Press.

Lawson, G. (2007) Counselor wellness and impairment: a national survey, *Journal of Humanistic Counseling*, 46, 20–34.

Lazarus, A.A. (1993) Tailoring the therapeutic relationship, or being an authentic chameleon, *Psychotherapy*, 30, 404–7.

Leiter, M. P. and Maslach, C. (2005) *Banishing Burnout: Six Strategies for Improving your Relationship with Work*. San Francisco, CA: Jossey-Bass.

Lemma, A. (1999) Starting from scratch: developing clinical psychology training and services in Bangladesh, *Psychodynamic Counselling*, 5, 193–204.

Lennie, C. (2007) The role of personal development groups in counsellor training: understanding factors contributing to self-awareness in the personal development group, *British Journal of Guidance and Counselling*, 35, 115–29.

Lepore, S.J. and Smyth, J.M. (eds) (2002) *The Writing Cure*. Washington DC: American Psychological Association.

Lewis, I. (2004) Gender and professional identity: a qualitative study of social workers practising as counsellors and psychotherapists, *Australian Social Work*, 57, 394–407.

Lieberman, M., Yalom, I. and Miles, M. (1973) *Encounter Groups: First Facts*. New York: Basic Books.

Lomas, P. (1981) *The Case for a Personal Psychotherapy*. Oxford: Oxford University Press.

Lomas, P. (1999) Interview with Peter Lomas (Sian Morgan). In L. King (ed.) *Committed Uncertainty: Essays in Honour of Peter Lomas*. London: Whurr.

Loo, C.M. (1974) The self-puzzle. A diagnostic and therapeutic tool, *Journal of Personality*, 42, 236–42.

Lott, D.A. (1999) *In Session: The Bond between Women and Their Therapists*. New York: W. H. Freeman.

MacKenzie, A. and Hamilton, R. (2007) More than expected? Psychological outcomes from first-stage training in counselling, *Counselling Psychology Quarterly*, 20, 229–45.

Magai, C. and Haviland-Jones, J. (2002) *The Hidden Genius of Emotion: Lifespan Transformations of Personality*. Cambridge: Cambridge University Press.

Mair, J.M.M. (1977) The community of self. In D. Bannister (ed.) *New Perspectives in Personal Construct Theory*. London: Academic Press.

Marmor, J. (1953) The feeling of superiority: an occupational hazard in the practice of psychotherapy, *American Journal of Psychiatry*, 110, 370–6.

Maroda, K.J. (2010) *Psychodynamic Techniques: Working with Emotion in the Therapeutic Relationship*. New York: Guildford Press.

Marrow, A. (1969) *The Practical Theorist: The Life and Work of Kurt Lewin*. New York: Basic Books.

Martin, J., Slemon, A.G., Hiebert, B., Hallberg, E.T. and Cummings, A.L. (1989) Conceptualizations of novice and experienced counselors, *Journal of Counseling Psychology*, 36, 395–400.

Martin, P. (2011) Celebrating the wounded healer, *Counselling Psychology Review*, 26, 10–19.

Marzillier, J. (2010) *The Gossamer Thread: My Life as a Psychotherapist*. London: Karnac.

Maslach, C. and Leiter, M.P. (1997) *The Truth about Burnout: How Organizations Cause Personal Stress and What to Do about It*. San Francisco, CA: Jossey-Bass.

Masson, J. (1991) *Final Analysis: The Making and Unmaking of a Psychoanalyst*. London: HarperCollins.

Mayfield, W.A., Kardash, C.A.M. and Kivlighan, D.M. Jr. (1999) Differences in experienced and novice counselors' knowledge structures about clients: implications for case conceptualization, *Journal of Counseling Psychology*, 46, 504–14.

McAdams, D.P. (1985) *Power, Intimacy, and the Life Story: Personological Inquiries into Identity*. New York: Guilford Press.

McAdams, D.P. (1993) *The Stories We Live By: Personal Myths and the Making of the Self*. New York: William Murrow.

McAdams, D.P. (2001) The psychology of life stories, *Review of General Psychology*, 5, 100–22.

McAdams, D.P. (2004) The redemptive self: Narrative identity in America today. In D.R. Beike, J.M. Lampien and D.A. Behrend (eds) *The Self and Memory*. New York: Psychology Press.

McAdams, D.P. (2006) *The Redemptive Self: Stories Americans Live By*. New York: Oxford University Press.

McAdams, D.P. (2009) *The Person: An Introduction to the Science of Personality Psychology*, 5th edn. New York: Wiley.

McAdams, D.P., Hoffman, B.J., Mansfield, E.D. and Day, R. (1996) Themes of agency and communion in significant autobiographical scenes, *Journal of Personality*, 64, 339–77.

McConnaughy, E.A. (1987) The person of the therapist in therapeutic practice, *Psychotherapy*, 24, 303–14.

McCullough, L. (2005) The lady cloaked in fog. In J.A. Kottler and J. Carlson (eds) *The Client Who Changed Me: Stories of Therapist Personal Transformation*. New York: Routledge.

McLeod, J. (2010) *The Counsellor's Workbook*. Maidenhead: Open University Press.

McLeod, J. (2013) *An Introduction to Counselling*, 5th edn. Maidenhead: Open University Press.

Mearns, D. and Cooper, M. (2005) *Working at Relational Depth in Counselling and Psychotherapy*. London: Sage.

Mearns, D. and Thorne, B. (2000) *Person-centred Therapy Today: New Frontiers in Theory and Practice*. London: Sage.

Mezirow, J. (1991) *Transformative Dimensions of Adult Learning*. San Francisco, CA: Jossey-Bass.

Miller, W.R. (2004) The phenomenon of quantum change, *Journal of Clinical Psychology*, 60, 453–60.

Mirsalimi, H. (2010) Perspectives of an Iranian psychologist practising in America, *Psychotherapy Theory, Research, Practice, Training*, 47, 151–61.

Morgan, A. (2000) *What is Narrative Therapy? An Easy-To-Read Introduction*. Adelaide: Dulwich Centre Publications.

Morrissette, P.J. (2004) *The Pain of Helping: Psychological Injury of Helping Professionals*. London: Routledge.

Najavits, L.M., Weis, R.D., Shaw, S.R. and Dierbeger, A.E. (2000) Psychotherapists' views of treatment manuals, *Professional Psychology – Research and Practice*, 31, 404–8.

Neimeyer, G.J., Taylor, J.M. and Cox, D.R. (2012a) On hope and possibility: does continuing professional development contribute to ongoing professional competence? *Professional Psychology: Research and Practice*, 43, 476–86.

Neimeyer, G.J., Taylor, J.M. and Rozensky, R.H. (2012b) The diminishing durability of knowledge in professional psychology: a Delphi poll of specialties and proficiencies, *Professional Psychology: Research and Practice*, 43, 364–71.

Norcross, J.C. and Prochaska, J.O. (1986a) Psychotherapist heal thyself – I. The psychological distress and self-change of psychologists, counselors, and laypersons, *Psychotherapy*, 23, 102–14.

Norcross, J.C. and Prochaska, J.O. (1986b) Psychotherapist heal thyself – II. The self-initiated and therapy-facilitated change of psychological distress, *Psychotherapy*, 23, 345–56.

Nouwen, H.J.M. (1979) *The Wounded Healer*. New York: Image.

O'Brien, J.M. (2011) Wounded healer: psychotherapist grief over a client's death, *Professional Psychology: Research and Practice*, 42, 36–243.

Okiishi, J., Lambert, M. J., Nielsen, S. L. and Ogles, B. M. (2003) Waiting for supershrink: an empirical analysis of therapist effects, *Clinical Psychology and Psychotherapy*, 10, 361–73.

O'Neill, L.K. (2010) Northern helping practitioners and the phenomenon of secondary trauma, *Canadian Journal of Counselling*, 44, 130–49.

Orlinsky, D.E. (1999) The master therapist: ideal character or clinical fiction? Comments and questions on Jennings and Skovholt's 'The cognitive, emotional and relational character-istics of master therapists', *Journal of Counseling Psychology*, 46, 12–15.

Orlinsky, D.E., Schofield, M.J., Schroder, T. and Kazantzis, N. (2011) Utilization of personal therapy by psychotherapists: a practice-friendly review and a new study, *Journal of Clinical Psychology*, 67, 828–42.

Pack, M. (2010) Transformation in progress: the effects of trauma on the significant others of sexual abuse therapists, *Qualitative Social Work*, 9, 249–65.

Paleg, K. and Jongsma, A.E. (2005) *The Group Therapy Treatment Planner*, 2nd edn. New York: Wiley.

Payne, H. (1999) Personal development groups in the training of counsellors and therapists: a review of the literature, *European Journal of Psychotherapy, Counselling and Health*, 2, 55–68.

Payne, H. (2010) Personal development groups in post graduate dance movement psycho-therapy training: A study examining their contribution to practice, *The Arts in Psychotherapy*, 37, 202–10.

Pearlman, L.A. and Mclan, P.S. (1995) Vicarious traumatisation: an empirical study of the effects of trauma work on trauma therapists, *Professional Psychology: Research and Practice*, 26, 558–65.

Pennebaker, J. (1997) *Opening Up: The Healing Power of Expressing Emotions*. New York: Guilford Press.

Pennebaker, J.W. (2004) *Writing to Heal: A Guided Journal for Recovering from Trauma and Emotional Upheaval*. Oakland, CA: New Harbinger Press.

Philipson, I.J. (1993) *On the Shoulders of Women: the Feminization of Psychotherapy*. New York: Guilford Press.

Pieterse, A.L., Lee, M., Ritmeester, A. and Collins, N.M. (2013) Towards a model of self-awareness development for counselling and psychotherapy training, *Counselling Psychology Quarterly*, 26, 190–207.

Pinsof, W.M. (2005) A Shamanic tapestry: my experiences with individual, marital and family therapy. In J.D. Geller, J.C Norcross and D.E.Orlinsky (eds) *The Psychotherapist's own Psychotherapy: Patient and Clinician Perspectives*. New York: Oxford University Press.

Polkinghorne, D.E. (1992) Postmodern epistemology of practice. In S. Kvale (ed.) *Psychology and Postmodernism*. London: Sage.

Poole, M.S. and Hollingshead, A.B. (eds) (2004) *Theories of Small Groups Interdisciplinary Perspectives*. Thousand Oaks, CA: Sage.

Prengel, S. and Somerstein, L. (eds) (2013) *Defining Moments For Therapists*. New York: LifeSherpa.

Prochaska, J.O. and Norcross, J.D. (1983) Psychotherapists' perspectives on treating them-selves and their clients for psychic distress, *Professional Psychology*, 14, 642–55.

Prochaska, J.O., Norcross, J.D. and DiClemente, C.C. (1986) Psychotherapists' self-change vs. laypersons' self-change: a comparative analysis of treatment strategies, *Journal of Clinical Psychology*, 42, 834–40.

Raskin, J.D. (1999) Metaphors and meaning: constructing the creative psychotherapy, *Journal of Constructivist Psychology*, 12, 331–47.

Rath, J. (2008) Training to be a volunteer Rape Crisis counsellor: a qualitative study of women's experience, *British Journal of Guidance and Counselling*, 36, 19–32.

Rippere, V. and Williams, R. (eds) (1985) *Wounded Healers: Mental Health Workers' Experiences of Depression.* New York: Wiley.

Rizq, R. (2009) Teaching and transformation: a psychoanalytic perspective on psychotherapeutic training, *British Journal of Psychotherapy*, 25, 363–80.

Robson, M. and Robson, J. (2008) Explorations of participants' experiences of a Personal Development Group held as part of a counselling psychology training group: is it safe in here? *Counselling Psychology Quarterly*, 21, 371–82.

Rogers, C.R. (1961) *On Becoming a Person.* London: Constable.

Rogers, C.R. (1980) *A Way of Being.* Boston, MA: Houghton Mifflin.

Ronnestad, M.H. and Skovholt, T.M. (2013) *The Developing Practitioner. Growth and Stagnation of Therapists and Counselors.* New York: Routledge.

Rowan, J. (1993) *The Transpersonal, Counselling and Psychotherapy.* London: Routledge.

Rowan, J. and Cooper, M. (eds) (1998) *The Plural Self: Multiplicity in Everyday Life.* London: Sage.

Rowan, J. and Jacobs, M. (2002) *The Therapist's Use of Self.* Buckingham: Open University Press.

Rowell, P.C. and Benshoff, J.M. (2008) Using personal growth groups in multicultural counseling courses to foster students' ethnic identity development, *Counselor Education and Supervision*, 48, 2–15.

Ryden, J. and Loewenthal, D. (2001) Psychotherapy for lesbians: the influence of therapist sexuality, *Counselling and Psychotherapy Research*, 1, 42–52.

Sammons, C.C. and Speight, S.L. (2008) A qualitative investigation of graduate-student changes associated with multicultural counseling courses, *The Counseling Psychologist*, 36, 814–38.

Satir, V. (1987) The therapist story. In M. Baldwin (ed.) *The Use of Self in Therapy.* New York: Haworth Press.

Saxon, D. and Barkham, M. (2012) Patterns of therapist variability: therapist effects and the contribution of patient severity and risk, *Journal of Consulting and Clinical Psychology*, 80, 535–46.

Schaub-de Jong, M., Cohen-Schotanus, A., Dekker, H. and Verkerk, M. (2009) The role of peer meetings for professional development in health science education: a qualitative analysis of reflective essays, *Advances in Health Science Education*, 14, 503–13.

Schaverian, J. (1999) The death of an analysand: transference, countertransference, and desire, *Journal of Analytical Psychology*, 44, 3–28.

Schroder, T. and Davis, J. (2004) Therapists' experiences of difficulty in practice, *Psychotherapy Research*, 14, 328–45.

Sexton, L. (1999) Vicarious traumatisation of counsellors and effects on their workplaces, *British Journal of Guidance and Counselling*, 27, 393–404.

Simon, G.M. (2003) *Beyond Technique in Family Therapy. Finding your Therapeutic Voice.* Boston, MA: Pearson.

Simon, G.M. (2006) The heart of the matter: a proposal for placing the self of the therapist at the center of family therapy research and training, *Family Process*, 45, 331–44.

Simon, G.M. (2012) The role of the therapist in common factors: continuing the dialogue, *Journal of Marital and Family Therapy*, 38, 1–7.

Skovholt, T.M. (2012) *Becoming a Therapist: On the Path to Mastery.* New York: Wiley.

Skovholt, T.M. and Jennings, L. (2004) *Master Therapists: Exploring Expertise in Therapy and Counseling.* New York: Allyn and Bacon.

Soldz, S. and McCullough, L. (eds) (2000) *Reconciling Empirical Knowledge and Clinical Experience. The Art and Science of Psychotherapy.* Washington DC: American Psychological Association.

Spencer, L. (2006) Tutors' stories of personal development training: attempting to maximize the learning potential, *Counselling and Psychotherapy Research*, 6, 108–14.

Spinelli, E. and Marshall, S. (eds) (2001) *Embodied Theories*. London: Continuum.

Steiner, C. (2003) *Emotional Literacy: Intelligence with a Heart*. San Francisco, CA: Personhood Press.

Stewart, I. and Joines, V. (1987) *TA Today*. Nottingham: Lifespace Publishing.

Strupp, H. (1978) The therapist's theoretical orientation: an overrated variable, *Psychotherapy*, 15, 314–17.

Theriault, A. and Gazzola, N. (2006) What are the sources of feelings of incompetence in experienced therapists? *Counselling Psychology Quarterly*, 19, 313–30.

Trotter-Mathison, M.J., Koch, J.M., Sanger, S. and Skovholt, T.M. (eds) (2010) *Voices from the Field: Defining Moments in Counselor and Therapist Development*. New York: Routledge.

Truell, R. (2001) The stresses of learning counselling: six recent graduates comment on their personal experience of learning counselling and what can be done to reduce associated harm, *Counselling Psychology Quarterly*, 14, 67–89.

Veilleux, J.C. (2011) Coping with client death: using a case study to discuss the effects of accidental, undetermined, and suicidal deaths on therapists, *Professional Psychology: Research and Practice*, 42, 222–8.

Waldegrave, C. (2003) 'Just Therapy' with families and communities. In C. Waldegrave, K. Tamasese, F. Tuhaka and W.Campbell (eds) *Just Therapy – A Journey*. Adelaide: Dulwich Centre.

Ward, E.C. (2005) Keeping it real: a grounded theory study of African American clients engaged in counseling at a community mental health agency, *Journal of Counseling Psychology*, 52, 471–81.

Waters, A. (2011) A letter to research, *Explorations: An E-Journal of Narrative Practice*, 1, 36–41.

Webb, K.B. (2011) Care of others and self: a suicidal patient's impact on the psychologist, *Professional Psychology: Research and Practice*, 42, 215–21.

Weingarten, K. (2010) Intersecting losses: working with the inevitable vicissitudes in therapist and client lives, *Psychotherapy Theory, Research, Practice, Training*, 47, 371–84.

Wenger, E. (1998) *Communities of Practice: Learning, Meaning, and Identity*, Cambridge: Cambridge University Press.

Wheeler, S., Goldie, J. and Hicks, C. (1998) Counsellor training: an evaluation of the effectiveness of a residential outdoor pursuits activity weekend on the personal development of trainee counsellors, *Couselling Psychology Quarterly*, 11, 391–405.

White, C. and Hales, J. (eds) (1997) *The Personal is the Professional: Therapists Reflect on their Families, Lives and Work*. Adelaide: Dulwich Centre Publications.

White, M. (1995) *Re-Authoring Lives: Interviews and Essays*. Adelaide: Dulwich Centre Publications.

White, M. (1997) *Narratives of Therapists' Lives*. Adelaide: Dulwich Centre Publications.

White, M. (2011) *Narrative Practice, Continuing the Conversations*. New York: Norton.

White, W.L. (2004) Transformational change: a historical review, *Journal of Clinical Psychology*, 60, 461–70.

Williams, D.C. and Levitt, H.M. (2007) A qualitative investigation of eminent therapists' values within psychotherapy: developing integrative principles for moment-to-moment psychotherapy practice, *Journal of Psychotherapy Integration*, 17, 159–84.

Wise, E.H. (2008) Competence and scope of practice: ethics and professional development, *Journal of Clinical Psychology*, 64, 626–37.

Wise, E.H., Hersh, M.A. and Gibson, C.M. (2012) Ethics, self-care and well-being for psychologists: reenvisioning the stress-distress continuum, *Professional Psychology: Research and Practice*, 43, 487–94.

Wood, J.K. (1984) Communities for learning: a person-centered approach. In R.F. Levant and J.S. Shlein (eds) *Client-Centered Therapy and the Person-Centered Approach. New Directions in Theory, Research and Practice*. New York: Praeger.

Wosket, V. (1999) *The Therapeutic Use of Self: Counselling Practice, Research and Supervision*. London: Routledge.

Yalom, I. (2002) *The Gift of Therapy: Reflections on Being a Therapist*. London: Piatkus.

Yalom, I. (2005a) *Theory and Practice of Group Psychotherapy*, 5th edn. New York: Basic Books.

Yalom, I. (2005b) *The Schopenhauer Cure*. New York: HarperCollins.

Zerubavel, N. and Wright, M.O. (2012) The dilemma of the wounded healer, *Psychotherapy*, 49, 482–91.

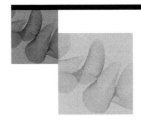

Index

Locators shown in *italics* refer to boxes, tables and figures.

COUNSELLING SKILLS
A Practical Guide for Counsellors and
Helping Professionals
Second Edition

John McLeod Julia McLeod

9780335244263 (Paperback)
2011

eBook also available

This bestselling book is designed to help counselling trainees acquire
and develop the skills and techniques needed to have therapeutic
impact with their clients. It also provides those in the helping professions with an easy-to-follow model of 'embedded counselling' that
provides tools and strategies for offering counselling relationships
within a diversity of work settings.

   This edition is thoroughly revised and features nine new chapters,
addressing such topics as: an A-Z of practical counselling skills, dealing with difficult relationships, issues caused by cultural diversity or
life transitions, and issues in loss and bereavement.

Key features:

- Key counselling skills such as caring, listening, questioning and
  reframing, reflection, attunement to a client, challenging and
  giving advice
- Building a counselling relationship
- Developing understanding of clients' issues

www.openup.co.uk

 OPEN UNIVERSITY PRESS
McGraw - Hill Education